By Christopher Cole

McCUDDEN, V.C.

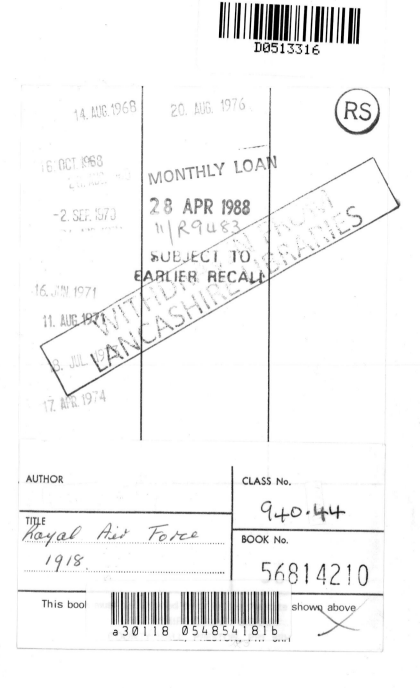

Ro

ROYAL
AIR FORCE
1918

Edited by
Christopher Cole

WILLIAM KIMBER
6 QUEEN ANNE'S GATE, S.W.1

PRINTED IN GREAT BRITAIN
BY W & J MACKAY & CO LTD, CHATHAM

Contents

Illustrations

Acknowledgements

The Royal Air Force Communiques are Crown Copyright, and thanks are due to the Controller of Her Britannic Majesty's Stationery Office for permission to publish extracts in this form.

Thanks are also due to Mr Leonard Bridgman for the line illustrations of R.A.F. aircraft, to Mr Charles King for the illustrations of German aircraft, and to Mr Peter Gray, Mr Ian Stair and Mr Ronald Moulton for the diagrams. For help in providing photographic material acknowledgement is gratefully made to The Ministry of Defence, Mr Frank Cheesman, The Imperial War Museum and the *Musée de l'Air*.

Introduction

The Royal Air Force was formed on April 1, 1918, by the amalgamation of the Royal Flying Corps and the Royal Naval Air Service. The R.F.C. had come into being on May 13, 1912, and the R.N.A.S. on June 23, 1914.

In the early part of the war, separate control of the air squadrons belonging to the two Services worked satisfactorily, but as the air war developed, and particularly during the temporary phases of enemy air superiority—such as the domination of the Fokkers in the winter of 1915–16, and the daylight raids on England in 1917—the shortcomings became apparent and there was prolonged public controversy about Britain's whole air organization. Some undoubted benefits had resulted from existence of the two Services. The excellent Sopwith fighters—the Pup, Triplane and Camel—had been initially ordered for the R.N.A.S.— but on balance the many problems created by the rapid growth of the air weapons clearly demanded some unified control.

In August, 1917, a Cabinet Committee formed after the Gotha raids on London and headed by General J. C. Smuts, recommended the formation of an Air Ministry to control and administer all aspects of the air war. Of the future Smuts wrote:

> . . . the day may not be far off when aerial operations with their devastation of enemy lands and destruction of industries and populous centres on a vast scale may become the principal operations of war, to which the older forms of military and naval operations may become secondary and subordinate.

This was followed in October by a further report proposing the amalgamation of the R.F.C. and R.N.A.S., and after the appropriate Parliamentary procedures, April 1, 1918 was chosen as the inaugural date for the new Royal Air Force.

From the earliest days of the R.F.C. there were some who appreciated the full military potential of the aeroplane, but initial progress was slow and the first few squadrons which went to war in 1914 were intended primarily for reconnaissance. None of the aircraft carried any regular armament and the squadrons simply improvised. The fastest reconnaissance aircraft, the small single-seat 'scouts', were fitted with mountings for rifles, then machine-guns, and early in 1916 the first full squadron of adequately armed 'fighting scouts' became operational. By the end of the war some 40 single-seat squadrons were deployed on the Western

Front for fighter and ground attack work, but the old designation of 'scout' remained in use.

Meanwhile other specialist aircraft had been developed and grouped in squadrons for particular roles, replacing the early system under which a unit was required to perform a variety of functions. Thus when the Royal Air Force came into being the main categories of aircraft were already well established—the single-seat fighters (scouts), two-seat fighter-reconnaissance, artillery observation (which ranged for the ground batteries and also flew bombing and reconnaissance sorties as required), day bombers and night bombers. There was a continual demand for better performance in all categories, and under development were more powerful engines and promising aircraft projects. But in the event only a few new aircraft types entered squadron service during the closing months of the war, and the Royal Air Force continued flying mainly the aircraft which had been used to good effect by the R.F.C. and the R.N.A.S.

The Sopwith Camel and the S.E.5a fighters, both introduced in mid-1917, had excellent qualities and remained effective to the end, though a well-handled German Fokker D.VII could probably outfight either. The more powerful Sopwith Snipe, which entered R.A.F. service during the last few weeks of the war, showed the capability of restoring technical ascendancy. In the fighter-reconnaissance role the famous Bristol Fighter, introduced in April 1917, was unequalled, and the type was used by the R.A.F. until 1931. The situation regarding day bombers was less satisfactory, since the D.H.9 which was selected for quantity production proved very prone to engine troubles, and only a few of the more powerful D.H.9As had been delivered by the end of the war.

There were two important developments during the period which followed the formation of the Royal Air Force. First was the introduction of a specialist night-fighter squadron on the Western Front. The interception of night raiders had presented many problems since the days of the Zeppelins, and the home defence fighter squadrons gradually improved their technique against the faster night bomber aircraft which had attacked England since 1917. The enemy night bombers were even more active against targets behind the lines, and it was to deal with these that a night-flying Camel squadron was deployed to France. It was particularly successful with intruder sorties against the enemy bomber airfields, destroying an impressive number of the raiders as they returned to base.

A major technical development during the last few months of the war was the introduction of parachutes for aircrews. Parachute jumping was a display spectacle before 1914, and balloon observers were provided with parachutes early in the war, but Germany was the first to develop a reasonably reliable chute which could be used from a fast-moving aircraft. The R.A.F. did not introduce the parachute for aircraft until some years after the war.

Apart from the re-numbering of the old Naval squadrons—No. 1 R.N.A.S. became No. 201 R.A.F., No. 2 R.N.A.S. became No. 202 R.A.F. and so on—and the adoption by R.N.A.S. officers of the military ranks used by the R.F.C., the inauguration of the new Service on April 1, 1918 made little immediate impact on the flying units at the Front. The air war continued as before, and within days of its formation the R.A.F. was bitterly engaged in the fierce fighting accompanying the German spring offensive, which inspired Haig's famous 'backs to the wall' message.

Regular communiques on air activities for circulation within the Royal Flying Corps had been issued since 1916, and these were continued after the Royal Air Force was formed. The R.A.F. Communiques Nos. 1 to 32 therefore describe British air operations on the Western Front up to the Armistice. Written by the Headquarters' staff from pilots' combat reports and other documents they tell a remarkable story of heroism and describe extraordinary exploits by the aircrews of the new Service, in machines which were primitive by present-day standards but had nevertheless progressed surprisingly in the mere six years which had elapsed since British military aviation was born. They cover the closing stages of the careers of outstanding fighter 'aces'—Bishop, Mannock and Collishaw—and describe the gallant single-handed combat against 40 enemy fighters for which Major W. G. Barker was awarded the V.C. They record the almost nonchalant way in which observers climbed out on to the wings of crippled aircraft to enable their pilots to regain control, and other almost forgotten episodes, reading more like extracts from a work of fiction—such as the aggressive manner in which airmen, lost in bad weather and about to land by mistake at enemy aerodromes, shot their way out of trouble.

The Communiques were not prepared by professional writers, but were a hastily-produced digest, primarily for internal consumption. They quoted extensively from the pilots' combat reports, where the enemy— with no particular feelings of malice—was often described as the 'Hun'.

Men of the fighting Services are traditionally modest and reticent about their wartime exploits, and those of the Royal Air Force in particular have always delighted in the under-statement. Some were embarrassed to see reports of their activities in general circulation, and the Communiques were irreverently known to all flying men as 'Comic Cuts'—a popular juvenile publication of the period.

In presenting for the first time the story of the day-to-day fighting as recorded by R.A.F. Headquarters from the facts available at the time, it should be noted that all claims for enemy aircraft driven down out of control could not be fully substantiated for many reasons, and should therefore be regarded as opinion rather than established fact.

This volume does not cover the activities of the R.A.F. squadrons with the Independent Force, formed in May 1918 to extend the bombing offensive against German industry, or the campaigns in other theatres. These formed the subject of separate communiques.

AIRCRAFT TYPES USED BY R.A.F. SQUADRONS

Squadrons listed in the R.A.F. Communiques used the following aircraft types:

S.E.5a FIGHTER
Nos. 1, 24, 29, 32, 40, 41, 56, 60, 64, 74, 84, 85, 92
No. 2 Australian Flying Corps

SOPWITH CAMEL FIGHTER
Nos. 3, 43, 46, 54, 65, 70, 73, 80, 151, 201, 203, 204, 208, 209, 210
No. 4 Australian Flying Corps
Nos. 17 and 148 United States Air Service

BRISTOL FIGHTER
Nos. 11, 20, 22, 48, 62, 88

SOPWITH DOLPHIN FIGHTER
Nos. 19, 23, 79, 87

SOPWITH SNIPE FIGHTER
No. 43 (from mid-Sept.), No. 4 Australian Flying Corps (from mid-Oct.)
No. 208 (late Oct.)

ARMSTRONG-WHITWORTH F.K.8 ARTILLERY OBSERVATION
Nos. 2, 8, 10, 35, 82

R.E.8 ARTILLERY OBSERVATION
Nos. 5, 7, 9, 12, 13, 15, 16, 21, 42, 52, 53, 59, 105, 3 Australian Flying Corps

D.H.4 DAY BOMBER
Nos. 18, 25, 27, 55, 57, 205

D.H.9 DAY BOMBER
Nos. 27 (from September), 49, 98, 103, 107, 108, 206, 211, 218

D.H.9A DAY BOMBER
Nos. 18 (from November), 205 (from August)

F.E.2b NIGHT BOMBER
Nos. 38, 58, 83, 100, 101, 102, 148

HANDLEY PAGE O/400 NIGHT BOMBER
Nos. 58 (from September), 100 (from August), 207, 214, 215, 216

LEADING PARTICULARS OF AIRCRAFT IN USE, APRIL—NOVEMBER, 1918

BRITISH

Type	Role	Entered service	Engine	Speed (max)
S.E.5a	single-seat fighter	Apr '17	200 hp Wolseley Viper	126 mph at 10,000 ft
Sopwith Camel	single-seat fighter	May '17	130 hp Clerget 150 hp B.R.1 etc	113 mph at 10,000 ft 121 mph at 10,000 ft
Sopwith Dolphin	single-seat fighter	Jan '18	200 hp Hispano	127 mph at 10,000 ft
Sopwith Snipe	single-seat fighter	Sep '18	230 hp B.R.2	121 mph at 10,000 ft
Bristol Fighter	two-seat fighter-recce	Apr '17	275 hp R. R. Falcon	113 mph at 10,000 ft
Armstrong Whitworth FK8	artillery observation	Jan '17	160 hp Beardmore	88 mph at 12,000 ft
R.E.8	artillery observation	Nov '16	150 hp RAF	92 mph at 10,000 ft
D.H.4	day bomber	May '17	275 hp R. R. Eagle	105 mph at 15,000 ft
D.H.9	day bomber	Apr '18	230 hp BHP	111 mph at 10,000 ft
D.H.9A	day bomber	Aug '18	400 hp Liberty	118 mph at 10,000 ft
F.E.2b	night bomber	Jan '16	160 hp Beardmore	90 mph at gd level
Handley Page o/400	night bomber	1917	2 × 250 hp R. R. Eagle	80 mph at 10,000 ft

GERMAN

Type	Role	Entered service	Engine	Speed (max)
Albatros D. VA	single-seat fighter	1917	170 hp Mercedes	96 mph at 13,000 ft
Fokker Dr I Triplane	single-seat fighter	Aug '17	110 hp Oberursel	103 mph at 13,000 ft
Fokker D. VII	single-seat fighter	May '18	180 hp Mercedes	103 mph at 13,000 ft
Fokker D. VIII	single-seat fighter	Aug '18	140 hp Oberursel	125 mph at gd level
Pfalz D. III	single-seat fighter	Sep '17	180 hp Mercedes	102 mph at 10,000 ft
Pfalz D. XII	single-seat fighter	1918	180 hp Mercedes	115 mph at 9,000 ft
Siemens D. IV	single-seat fighter	1918	200 hp Siemens	118 mph
Hannover CL IIIA	two-seat fighter-recce	1918	180 hp Argus	105 mph at gd level
Halberstadt C.V.	two-seat fighter-recce	1918	200 hp Benz	106 mph at gd level
L.V.G. C.V.	reconnaissance	1917	200 hp Benz	96 mph at 6,500 ft
Albatros C. XII	reconnaissance	1917	260 hp Mercedes	130 mph at gd level
Gotha G. IV	night bomber	1917	2 × 260 hp Mercedes	87 mph at 5,000 ft
Friedrichshafen	night bomber	1918	2 × 260 hp Mercedes	86 mph at 6,000 ft
Zeppelin-Staaken Giant	night bomber	1917	various	80 mph
A.E.G. G. IV	bomber	1917	2 × 260 hp Mercedes	90 mph at 5,000 ft

Editor's Note

The routine reports on artillery-ranging sorties and bombing raids which preceded the daily narrative in each communique, and some of the items under a 'miscellaneous' heading, have been excluded from this edited version. This has been done because without the contemporary official maps and other documents the information conveys little to the general reader.

The daily lists of successful pilots who gained victories in addition to those described in the extracts from combat reports have been consolidated into a weekly list at the end of each communique. Where a victory was credited to the crew of a two-seater aircraft the name of the pilot is given plus that of the observer, e.g. Lt A. B. Smith + Sgt C. D. Jones. Where a victory followed an action by several aircraft the names of the pilots or crews taking part are divided by a stroke, e.g. Lts A. B. Smith/ C. D. Jones/E. F. Robinson.

Abbreviations

E.A.	Enemy aircraft
A.W.	Armstrong Whitworth
S.E.5	Aircraft designed by the Royal Aircraft Factory, Farnborough, were known by initial letters denoting their class. S.E. signified Scouting Experimental. The version flown in 1918 was in fact the S.E.5a, though the loose designation S.E.5 was commonly used.
R.E.8	Reconnaissance Experimental
F.E.2b	Originally Farman Experimental, meaning a 'pusher' design similar to the Farman types.
(C)	shown after names in the later communiques indicates a Canadian officer.
Buckingham	was the standard British incendiary ammunition.

1 – 7 April

The bitter fighting which took place in the first week of the Royal Air Force's existence is indicated by the small difference between the number of enemy aircraft brought down and British machines missing. Aircraft claimed as 'driven down out of control' were normally claimed as victories, though it is accepted that a proportion of these, claimed in good faith, may have returned to base without major damage.

This communiqué recorded the names of several former R.N.A.S. and R.F.C pilots who became notable 'aces'—MacLaren (final score, 48 victories), Little (47), McElroy (46), Woollett (35), Kinkead (30), Gurdon (27), Staton (26), Bell (20) and Saunders (19). Saunders and Staton remained in the R.A.F. and later attained air rank.

COMMUNIQUÉ NO. 1

During the period under review we have claimed officially 57 E.A. brought down and 37 driven down out of control. In addition to this, seven E.A. were brought down by A.A. fire and by our infantry. Forty-three of our machines are missing. Approximately 85 tons of bombs were dropped, 380,173 rounds fired at ground targets and 3,301 photographs taken.

April 1st

The weather was fine and the visibility good ⌁ A total of 23 tons of bombs were dropped by night and 17 tons by day ⌁ Enemy aircraft were active south of the Somme, and enemy two-seaters were employed in low flying and firing at our troops. Several large formations of E.A. scouts were also encountered at a height ⌁ Two hostile balloons were shot down, and one hostile machine was brought down in our lines by infantry, in addition to those accounted for in aerial combat.

Capt G. E. H. McElroy, 24 Sqn, dived on three E.A. scouts; he reserved his fire until within 100 yards range and then fired a burst of 100 rounds from both guns into one E.A. which immediately went down in a slow spin and crashed north of Ignaucourt.

2 Lt W. A. Pell, 80 Sqn, fired about 200 rounds at close range into an E.A. two-seater which was seen to crash by other pilots of the patrol.

Lt Viscount Glentworth, 32 Sqn, observed four E.A. scouts attacking two S.E.5's. He immediately dived on one which went down to within 50 feet of the ground and then flattened out. Lt Viscount Glentworth kept on the E.A.'s. tail and fired 50 rounds at very close range into it; the E.A. crashed into the wood north of Beaucourt.

Lt W. J. A. Duncan, 60 Sqn, dived on an E.A., which was apparently firing at our troops; he followed the E.A., keeping on its tail, and it then landed in our lines in the vicinity of Gentelles. Lt Duncan also landed and found the German pilot wounded in the back.

Capt J. A. Slater, 64 Sqn, while leading his patrol, observed a formation of eight E.A. scouts; he manœuvred into a favourable position behind and then selected one E.A. scout upon which he dived, firing at about 200 feet range. After about 40 rounds the E.A. turned over on its back, emitting flames and smoke and fell vertically in this condition.

Capt F. McD. C. Turner and 2 Lt A. Leach, 57 Sqn, whilst on photography, were attacked by five E.A. triplanes; they fired a burst of 30 rounds into one at 100 yard range and the E.A. went down in flames. Ten other E.A. triplanes and scouts then joined the remaining four E.A. A drum was fired into one of these at a range of 150 yards and it was seen to turn over on its side and fall to pieces.

2 Lt W. L. Harrison, 40 Sqn, dived on the tail of an E.A. two-seater and fired 250 rounds into it. The E.A. stalled and went down in a slow spin, finally crashing just west of Izel.

Capt R. A. Little, 203 Sqn, engaged the rear machine of a formation of E.A. triplanes, firing about 200 rounds into it at close range. The enemy machine did a steep dive and the lower left-hand plane came off, the E.A. being seen to crash about three miles east of Oppy.

Capt D. J. Bell, 3 Sqn, fired a burst of about 80 rounds at close range into an E.A. triplane; the E.A. went down completely out of control and crashed.

2 Lt J. Jewkes, 65 Sqn, attacked a hostile balloon which he shot down in flames.

On the 27th ultimo, 2 Lt A. A. Macleod and Lt A. W. Hammond, 2 Sqn, were attacked by eight E.A. triplanes, three of which they drove down out of control. The A.W. then caught fire and dived steeply, being controlled from the side of the fuselage, and although wounded in six places, Lt Hammond continued to engage the E.A. while the machine was descending in flames. The machine eventually crashed in No Man's Land, and both 2 Lt Macleod and Lt Hammond, who had been wounded six times, were brought in to our trenches by infantry in spite of heavy machine-gun fire from the enemy's lines.

April 2nd

The weather was fine and the visibility good, but there were considerable banks of clouds over the lines at about 2,000 feet ⌒ A total of over 17 tons of bombs were dropped ⌒ Enemy aircraft were fairly active during the day between Lens and the River Scarpe, Albert and the Somme and south of the Somme.

2 Lt H. Luit, 65 Sqn, when flying at an height of 1,000 feet through the clouds, came out on top of three E.A. two-seaters escorted by one Albatross scout; he fired 200 rounds at point blank range at the nearest two-seater and the observer was seen to collapse into the cockpit. The E.A. pilot then put his machine into a steep glide and crashed into the ground about 1,000 yards north-west of Fresnoy.

Capt H. G. Forrest, 2 Sqn A.F.C.,* dived on an E.A. two-seater and fired about 100 rounds into it at moderate range; the observer in the E.A. was seen to collapse in his seat. The E.A. then dived and Lt R. L. Manuel, 2 Sqn A.F.C., continued to attack, firing about 200 rounds into it, the E.A. eventually crashing south-east of Demuin.

Capt S. T. Edwards, 209 Sqn, when leading a formation observed six E.A. immediately below him; he attacked and opened fire on the rear E.A. at 30 yards range. The E.A. stalled and dived vertically followed by Capt Edwards, who opened fire again at very close range. The E.A. then broke to pieces in the air.

Capt H. W. Woollett, 43 Sqn, attacked a hostile balloon and fired about 60 rounds into it; the two observers jumped out and the balloon fell in flames. He then attacked another hostile balloon which went down in flames; no one was seen to jump out of this balloon. A few minutes later Capt Woollett attacked a third balloon which was being pulled down, but after he had fired about 50 rounds into it the hostile balloon fell in flames.

2 Lt G. H. Blaxland, 2 Sqn A.F.C., attacked the rear machine of a formation of E.A. scouts; the same E.A. was also engaged by 2 Lt A. G. Clark, 2 Sqn A.F.C. Several bursts were fired into the E.A. by both pilots, who saw it crash near Corbie, apparently in flames.

Capt W. H. K. Copeland, 60 Sqn, engaged the leader of five E.A. scouts and one two-seater with indecisive result. Capt Copeland then attacked the rear machine, which he chased down to within 2,000 feet, firing 200 rounds at 80 yards range. The E.A. turned east, glided down and crashed south of Guillaucourt.

Capt F. G. C. Weare and 2 Lt G. S. L. Hayward, 22 Sqn, observed 10 E.A. scouts and led their formation round a cloud and then dived on one E.A. Fire was opened at an Albatross Scout which went down out of

* Australian Flying Corps.

control and was seen to crash. Two E.A. triplanes then got on the tail of Capt Weare's machine; 30 or 40 rounds were fired at the nearest triplane which glided down with smoke coming from it and when at a height of about 3,000 feet burst into flames.

2 Lt G. N. Traunweiser and Sgt S. Belding, 22 Sqn, fired a drum into an E.A. triplane, which crashed west of Vauvillers.

Capt R. S. C. McClintock, while leading a patrol of 64 Sqn, observed seven E.A. scouts against which he led his patrol; he engaged one E.A. diving at it and firing about 100 rounds at 40 yards range. The E.A. went into a flat spin and fell completely out of control and was observed to crash.

Capt E. R. Tempest, while leading a patrol of 64 Sqn, observed 11 E.A. below him; he dived into the rear of the enemy formation and fired about 90 rounds into one E.A. from 250 to 70 yards range. The E.A. dived underneath its own formation and Capt Tempest was then engaged by an E.A. two-seater. He did a climbing turn to the right and saw the first E.A. at which he had fired nose-diving to earth in flames and crash, still burning.

Lt Christie, 60 Sqn, brought down one E.A. scout which was seen burning on the ground.

April 3rd
Low cloud and rain interfered with flying ⌑ A total of 16 tons of bombs were dropped ⌑ Enemy aircraft activity was slight, with the exception of one large formation of E.A. scouts which were encountered by 27 machines of the 5th Brigade (65 and 84 Sqns), and successfully engaged.

Capt R. A. Grosvenor, 84 Sqn, dived on an E.A. scout, which went down and turned over in a ploughed field, crashing badly. Capt Grosvenor shortly afterwards attacked another E.A. scout, into which he fired a short burst, and the E.A. almost at once burst into flames.

Lt J. F. Larson, 84 Sqn, fired long bursts from both guns into an E.A. scout, which turned over on its back and was seen to crash into the ground about a mile east of Rosieres.

2 Lt H. W. L. Saunders, 84 Sqn, fired a good burst at point blank range into an E.A. scout, which immediately went down, followed by 2 Lt Saunders, who fired another burst into it. He broke off the combat at 3,000 feet and saw the E.A. crash into some trees south of Rosieres.

2 Lt R. T. Cuffe, 54 Sqn, was attacked by an E.A. scout; he turned and engaged it, and the E.A. was observed to crash near Rosieres. Six E.A. were still above 2 Lt Cuffe, but did not come down to attack him.

Maj J. A. Cunningham, 65 Sqn, attacked an E.A. scout which went down in a spin and Maj Cunningham lost sight of it; but Capt Grosvenor,

84 Sqn, confirms having seen the E.A. coming out of the spin and nose-dive vertically into the ground.

2 Lt D. R. MacLaren, 46 Sqn, fired about 100 rounds at 200 yards range into a hostile balloon. 2 Lt J. H. Smith, of the same squadron, also fired 100 rounds into this balloon. The observer jumped out and the balloon sagged badly, then crumpled up and fell.

During a fight between a patrol of 65 Sqn and a large number of E.A. scouts, 54 Sqn confirm two E.A. scouts having been crashed by Camels of 65 Sqn. As there were 28 indecisive combats reported during this fight, it is impossible to credit these machines to any particular pilots.

April 4th

In spite of low clouds and rain, machines of the 5th Brigade carried out 10 contact patrols, and a considerable amount of low-flying was done by our aeroplanes on the battle front ∽ A total of 1¾ tons of bombs were dropped ∽ There was no E.A. activity, except on the front of the 5th Brigade.

Capt T. Colvill-Jones and 2 Lt W. Hart, 48 Sqn, whilst on offensive patrol, engaged one E.A. scout and fired two long bursts into it. The E.A. went down in a steep dive with smoke coming from it and it was seen to crash by another pilot.

2 Lt J. G. Kennedy, 65 Sqn, engaged an E.A. two-seater, which he shot down in flames and was seen to crash near the Bois de Vaire.

Lt L. J. Primrose, 2 Sqn A.F.C., fired 200 rounds at close range into an E.A. scout which immediately burst into flames and was seen to crash just east of Villers Bretonneux.

2 Lt R. T. Mark, 24 Sqn, dived on an E.A. scout which immediately turned east and was then engaged by 2 Lt Farrell, of the same squadron. 2 Lt Mark dived on it again and fired 150 rounds and 2 Lt Farrell 40 rounds whereupon the E.A. crashed into a wood on our side of the lines and caught fire.

2 Lt H. B. Richardson, 24 Sqn, fired 30 rounds at close range into an E.A. two-seater. A Camel also engaged the E.A. which went down in flames, followed by the Camel, which also crashed in flames.

Capt G. E. H. McElroy, 24 Sqn, observed seven E.A. scouts flying east over the lines; he attacked one of the E.A., firing a burst into it from 50 yards range. The E.A. went down in a spin and crashed north of Warfusee.

Capt F. M. Kitto, 54 Sqn, engaged one of a formation of about eight E.A. scouts; after a short engagement the E.A. dived away east and was followed by Capt Kitto, firing the whole time. The E.A. kept on in a fairly steep dive and flew into the ground, crashing badly, the wreckage being seen later in flames on the ground.

Hannover CL IIIA

Charles King

April 5th

The weather was very bad, low clouds, mist and rain prevailing all day ⌒ Enemy aircraft activity was very slight ⌒ One enemy machine was brought down by infantry of the Third Army.

April 6th

In spite of low clouds and rain a considerable amount of flying took place, and many machines of the 3rd, 5th and 9th Brigades were out engaging with with their machine guns enemy troops which were massing north-east of La Motte ⌒ 2¾ tons of bombs were dropped ⌒ Enemy aircraft were active in the afternoon on the fronts of the 1st, 3rd and 5th Brigades.

2 Lt G. A. Lingham, 43 Sqn, was attacked by seven E.A.; he fired 60 rounds at close range into one E.A. which overshot him, whereupon the E.A. went down in a spin and was seen to crash.

2 Lt H. Daniel, 43 Sqn, while leading his patrol on a special mission, was attacked by seven E.A. (triplanes and scouts). He climbed above them and then dived on the nearest triplane, firing a short burst at point blank range. The E.A. burst into flames and went down in that condition.

Capt R. A. Little, 203 Sqn, attacked an E.A. two-seater from 200 yards, closing to 20 yards range, firing all the way. The E.A. observer was seen lying in the cockpit and the enemy machine dived into the clouds; on it coming out, Capt Little attacked it again, firing from about 20 yards. The E.A. stalled and went down emitting smoke, and was seen by other members of the patrol to fall in flames.

Lt W. L. Jordan, 208 Sqn, attacked one of two E.A., firing a burst of about 50 rounds into it. The E.A. immediately dived vertically and Lt Jordan attacked again, firing into it at very close range; the E.A. continued to dive, and when at 3,000 feet turned on its back, eventually crashing near Oppy.

Lt H. Carnegie, 40 Sqn, in a general engagement between S.E.'s and E.A. scouts, shot down one E.A. which fell completely out of control, and is confirmed by another pilot to have crashed north of Pont-à-Vendin.

Capt I. P. R. Napier, 40 Sqn, fired a burst at about 100 yards range into an E.A. two-seater; the E.A. did not return the fire but turned sharply and went down in a steep dive, followed by Capt Napier who fired long bursts from both guns into it from the rear. The E.A. flew straight on, losing height, and finally crashed into some houses near Brebieres.

A formation of 205 Sqn report that, while firing at hostile troops north-east of Villers Bretonneux, they were followed by five E.A. triplanes, one of which attacked Capt C. R. Lupton and A. M. Wood.

Tracers were seen to enter the E.A., and an S.E.5, attacking from above, sent the enemy machine down in flames.

Lt J. E. Drummond and 2 Lt H. F. Lumb, 48 Sqn, whilst engaged in low flying and attacking enemy infantry, were dived upon by three E.A. triplanes. Sixty rounds were fired into the leader of the E.A. formation, which immediately went into a vertical dive, and when about 600 feet from the ground burst into flames and was seen to crash.

Lt J. F. Larson, 84 Sqn, attacked an E.A. two-seater from very close range and shot the observer. 2 Lt H. W. L. Saunders, 2 Lt C. L. Stubbs, and 2 Lt H. O. MacDonald, of the same squadron, then dived down on the E.A., all firing, and tracers were seen going through it. The E.A. then started to go down in a spin. Lt Larson fired a further burst into it while it was still spinning, and the E.A. did a flat spin straight down from 11,000 feet, into the ground on our side of the lines north of Hangard.

2 Lt E. R. Maddox, 3 Sqn, attacked one E.A. at close range and fired a burst of about 50 rounds into it; the E.A. went down, crashed and burst into flames.

2 Lts E. K. Blenkinsop and C. F. G. Doran, 2 Sqn, were attacked by three E.A. triplanes and one enemy scout; 60 rounds were fired at close range into one of the triplanes, which was seen to go down in flames.

Lt C. Banks, 43 Sqn, attacked an E.A. scout and fired a short burst into it at 50 yards range and followed it down to 50 feet, firing several other bursts. The E.A. crashed into the ground and turned over. Lt Banks was heavily engaged from the ground and had both petrol tanks and elevator wire shot through, but managed to recross the line and land at Senlis, about two miles our side.

A patrol of 2 Sqn A.F.C. engaged one E.A. two-seater near La Motte; all members of the patrol dived on it and fired bursts at fairly close range. The E.A. turned over on its back and remained in this position until it hit the ground, when it burst into flames near La Motte. The following pilots took part in the combat:—Lt A. G. Clark, Lt L. J. Primrose, Lt G. H. Blaxland and 2 Lt A. L. Paxton.

Capt Rosevear, in a general engagement between a patrol of 211 Sqn and a number of E.A. triplanes, fired a burst at point blank range into one of the E.A. which fell completely out of control and was seen to crash in ploughed field. Lt Spence, of the same squadron, fired about 100 rounds at very close range into another of the enemy triplanes which came across the nose of his machine. The E.A. went down out of control and was seen to crash in a large field.

Lt T. Durrant, 56 Sqn, attacked an E.A. two-seater which he followed down until near the ground, when he was forced to leave the E.A. owing to the fact that four enemy triplanes were firing on him from long range. He evaded these and returned afterwards to find the enemy two-seater completely crashed on the ground. This machine was also seen on the ground by another pilot of 56 Sqn.

April 7th

The visibility was good, the sky for the most part being covered with clouds at a height ◇ A total of 13½ tons of bombs were dropped ◇ Enemy aircraft were not active except on the front of the 5th Brigade, where several large formations were encountered. During the day, two E.A. were brought down by A.A. in addition to those accounted for in combat.

2 Lt O. M. Baldwin, 73 Sqn, in a general engagement between his patrol and a formation of E.A. triplanes singled out one and opened fire at about 30 yards range. The E.A. turned over on its back and went down out of control followed by 2 Lt Baldwin, who saw it crash south of Cerisy.

A patrol of 203 Sqn, led by Capt R. A. Little, were attacked by 10 E.A. triplanes one of which Capt Little shot down completely out of control and it was lost to sight in the clouds, but at the end of the combat it was seen crashed on the ground about a mile south-west of Violaines.

Capt G. E. H. McElroy, 24 Sqn, dived on three E.A. two-seaters and reserved his fire until under the tail of the nearest into which he fired 70 rounds at 50 yards range. The E.A. fell in a nose-dive and crashed three miles east of Marcelcave. Shortly afterwards, while flying through the clouds at 3,000 feet, he saw three S.E.'s being attacked by five enemy triplanes. Capt McElroy got on the tail of one of the triplanes and fired 20 rounds at point blank range into it. The E.A. went down in a spin and crashed north of Moreuil Wood.

2 Lt W. A. Tyrrell, 32 Sqn, fired 150 rounds into an E.A. triplane which was attacking one of our machines; the E.A. went down in a fast spin, pulling out at 2,000 feet. 2 Lt Tyrrell, who followed the E.A. down, got on to its tail again and fired 100 rounds at close range; the E.A. then fell vertically and crashed into the ground north-east of La Motte.

Capt J. McDonald, 24 Sqn, attacked an E.A. two-seater which went down out of control. It was last seen crashed and smoking in a field in the vicinity of Moreuil.

Enemy machines were also driven down out of control during the period under review by:

Sqn 3 2 Lt N. R. Smuts, 2 Lt S. J. Squires. **5** 2 Lt R. S. Durno + Lt A. M. Morgan. **11** Lt H. W. Sellars + Lt C. C. Robson, Lt H. A. Hay + Sgt P. A. Sherlock. **22** 2 Lt B. C. Budd + 2 Lt H. J. Weaver, 2 Lt J. E. Gurdon + 2 Lt A. J. H. Thornton (2). **24** Capt G. E. H. McElroy (2), Lt M. C. Lambert. **32** 2 Lt A. L. Cuffe, 2 Lt C. J. Howson, 2 Lt H. F. Proctor, 2 Lt W. A. Tyrrell. **35** 2 Lt J. E. Phillips + 2 Lt M. Balston. **43** 2 Lt H. Daniel. **46** Capt C. J. Marchant/2 Lt M. M. Freehill, Capt S. P. Smith/Lt A. G. Vlasto/Lt H. G. W.

Debenham/2 Lt D. R. MacLaren/2 Lt R. K. McConnell. **48** 2 Lt C. L. Glover
+ Cpl W. Beales, 2 Lt V. Voss + Lt C. J. R. Gibson. **56** Lt K. W. Junor.
57 Capt F. McD. C. Turner + 2 Lt A. Leach, 2 Lts F. A. W. Mann + J. T.
White. **62** 2 Lts H. C. M. Nangle + T. C. Cooper, 2 Lt W. T. Staton + Lt
J. R. Gordon. **64** Lt P. S. Burge, Lt V. W. Thompson. **65** 2 Lt T. Williams.
70 Capt H. N. C. Robinson/2 Lt S. T. Liversedge. **73** Capt G. A. H. Pidcock,
2 Lt R. R. Rowe. **84** Lt J. F. Larson, 2 Lt W. H. Brown, 2 Lt W. E. Lunnon.
201 Lt Kinkead. **205** Capt A. Dixon + 2 Lt Scott. **208** Capt T. F. N. Gerrard/
Lt Cooper/Lt Sneath. **209** Lt O. D. Redgate.

HONOURS AND AWARDS

DSO Capt F. T. Digby, DSC. **DSC** Flt Cmdr L. H. Rochford, Flt Sub-Lt J.
M. Mason, Sub-Lt F. H. Stringer, Flt Cmdr C. B. Ridley, Flt Sub-Lt M. H.
Findlay, Flt Cmdr R. P. Minifie (2nd Bar), Flt Lt H. A. Millson, Flt Lt A. B.
Ellwood, Flt Cmdr C. H. Darley (Bar), Flt Lt V. E. Sieveking (Bar). **MC** Capt
J. B. Fox, Capt P. W. S. Bulman (Bar), Capt C. M. Leman, 2 Lt F. L. Herd,
2 Lt A. W. Franklin, 2 Lt D. R. MacLaren, Capt C. J. Marchant, Lt. H W.
Sellars, Capt H. W. Woollett (Bar), Capt J. A. Slater (Bar), Capt O. Horsley
(Bar), Capt R. C. Phillipps (Bar), Capt N. C. Millman, 2 Lt H. A. Cooper,
2 Lt E. R. Varley, Capt D. H. Oliver, Capt R. StC. McClintock, Lt E. D. G.
Galley, Lt J. E. Hanning, Lt E. G. Leake, Lt T. H. Upfill, Lt E. C. Batchelor,
Lt C. R. Cuthbert, 2 Lt J. L. S. Hanman, 2 Lt A. C. Atkey, Capt T. K. Twist,
2 Lt R. S. Durno, Capt J. P. Colin, Lt F. J. Scott, Capt G. F. Malley, Lt A. E.
Robertson, 2 Lt W. E. Warden, Lt J. R. Gordon, 2 Lt W. E. Staton, Capt T. L.
Purdon, Lt W. J. Harvey, 2 Lt J. Day. **DSM** Lt W. M. Naylor, PO A. Clarke,
1 AM R. J. Adkins (Bar). **MM** 1 AM W. C. Lindsay, 1 AM F. C. Mills, 1 AM
J. Ryder, 1 AM H. D. Tipler, 2 AM W. G. Worsdall, Sgt W. N. Holmes.

8 – 14 April

The outstanding day of this week was 12 April. First there was the brilliant feat of Capt H. W. Woollett, flying a Sopwith Camel, in shooting down six of the enemy in one day. (This had first been achieved a few weeks earlier by Capt J. L. Trollope, also of 43 Sqn.)

The other noteworthy event was the first successful action by the newly-formed 74 Sqn, which had arrived in France with its S.E.5a's on 31 March. The C.O., Maj K. L. Caldwell, survived the war, having gained 25 victories, and returned to New Zealand, where he became an air commodore in the R.N.Z.A.F. The 'A' Flight Commander, Capt Edward Mannock, was returning to operations after a successful 1917 duty tour in 40 Sqn.

Other 'ace' pilots referred to during the week include Gilmour (final victory score, 44), Beauchamp-Proctor (41), McCall (37), Quigley (34), Carter (31), Cobby (29), Leacroft (25), King (20) and I. D. R. Mac-Donald (20).

COMMUNIQUÉ NO. 2

During the period under review we have claimed officially 69 E.A. brought down and 35 driven out of control. In addition 6 E.A. have been brought down by A.A. or machine gun fire from the ground. Twenty-five of our machines are missing. Approximately 110 tons of bombs were dropped and 4,265 photographs taken.

April 8th
It rained most of the day and very little flying was possible ◇ *3 tons of bombs were dropped by day and 5½ tons by night* ◇ *Enemy aircraft activity was almost nil.*

Capt C. B. Ridley, 201 Sqn, fired 150 rounds at close range into an enemy kite balloon at 3,000 feet east of Boyelles. Capt D. J. Bell, 3 Sqn, also fired a burst of 150 rounds into the same balloon, which fell in flames.

April 9th
Very little flying was possible owing to thick mist and drizzling rain ◇ *Early in the morning the enemy launched an attack between Bois Grenier and the*

La Bassée Canal ∽ Machines of the 1st Brigade reconnoitred the front and attacked the enemy's troops with bombs and machine guns in spite of the unfavourable weather conditions ∽ A quarter of a ton of bombs were dropped during the day ∽ Enemy aircraft activity was nil, except on the front of the 1st Brigade between Armentières and La Bassée, where enemy low flying machines were active ∽ In addition to the E.A. brought down in combat, one was brought down in our lines by our infantry.

Capt R. A. Little and Lts J. A. Glen and A. B. Ellwood, 203 Sqn, attacked an E.A. two-seater doing contact patrol; the E.A. went down in a steep dive and crashed to the ground close to Givenchy.

Lt C. O. Rusden, 40 Sqn, was fired on from beneath; he turned, and observing an E.A. two-seater flying below him at a very low altitude, dived and fired about 50 rounds into it. The E.A. dived straight to earth and crashed near Rouge Croix.

Lt Mellings, 210 Sqn, attacked an E.A. two seater-which fired at him from about 150 yards and shot through his wind-screen. He fired 100 rounds into the E.A., the observer of which immediately disappeared into the cock-pit as though hit. The enemy pilot was also hit and the machine fell vertically into La Bassée and was seen to crash.

Lt Coombes, 210 Sqn, fired 150 rounds at 30 yards range into an E.A. scout. The back petrol tank of the E.A. burst into flames whereupon the enemy machine dived steeply in flames and crashed and continued to burn on the ground.

Capt A. W. Carter, 210 Sqn, while flying at 200 feet observed an E.A. two-seater slightly above him. He manœuvred for position and got within 100 yards of the E.A. which dived steeply and hit the ground near Neuf Berquin before he could flatten out. The E.A. was seen to burst into flames on the ground.

April 10th

The weather was again bad, but in spite of the mist machines of the 1st Brigade carried out several low-flying reconnaissances and 12 contact patrols, dropped many bombs and fired several thousand rounds at the enemy's attacking troops ∽ A number of machines of the 2nd Brigade were also employed in low-flying ∽ Thirteen reconnaissances were carried out ∽ 9½ tons of bombs were dropped during the day ∽ Low-flying E.A. were active on the battle front, but otherwise their activity was nil. Two enemy machines were brought down in our lines by infantry in addition to those accounted for in combat.

Lt A. H. Cobby, 4 Sqn A.F.C., observed an E.A. scout flying at a height of 200 feet just east of Estaires, so dived on it from 1,000 feet firing all the way, and the E.A. was lost sight of in the mist. Another

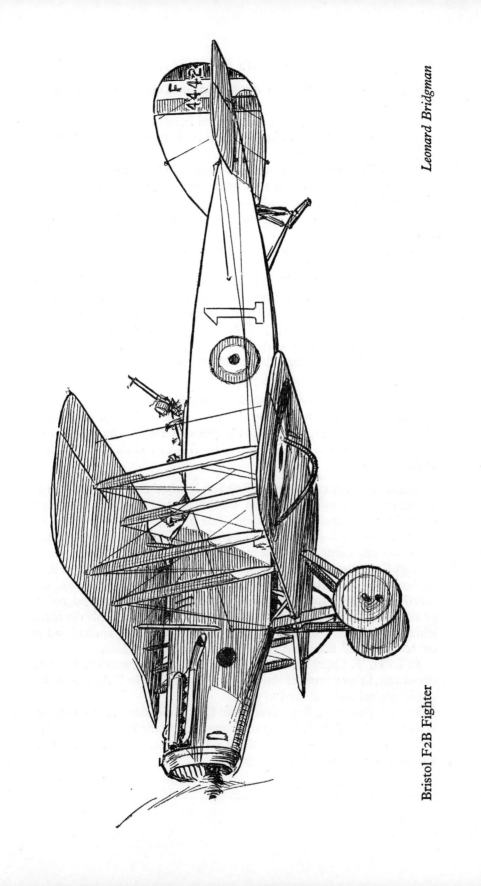

Leonard Bridgman

Bristol F2B Fighter

pilot of the same squadron saw this E.A. crashed on the ground between Estaires and La Gorgue.

Maj A. D. Carter, 19 Sqn, fired several bursts at close range into an E.A. two-seater from under its tail; the E.A. dived steeply from 800 feet and crashed into the ground.

Capt J. Gilmour, 65 Sqn, fired 50 rounds into an E.A. scout which went down vertically and was seen by another pilot of the patrol to crash about 1,000 yards east of Morcourt.

Capt R. A. Grosvenor, 84 Sqn, shot down one E.A. scout out of control.

Capt J. H. Tudhope, 40 Sqn, also shot down one E.A. scout out of control.

Lts H. L. Taylor and W. I. E. Lane, 52 Sqn, were attacked by nine E.A. triplanes, one of which they shot down out of control, and although wounded, Lt Lane continued to fire and succeeded in shooting down a second triplane in flames. This E.A. fell in our lines near the Bois de Gentelles. Lt Taylor was compelled to make a forced landing owing to serious damage by fire from the enemy triplanes.

April 11th

Low clouds and mist prevailed until 3 p.m., when the weather conditions improved ∽ 5 tons of bombs were dropped ∽ Enemy aircraft were active only on the battle front, but later in the afternoon when the weather cleared their activity increased on other parts of the front, particularly to the south of La Bassée.

During the day, 11 machines of 55 Sqn bombed the railway station at Luxembourg, dropping 22 112-lb. bombs. Several bursts were seen on the railway and around the station. Ten photographs were taken. All machines returned. A successful long distance photographic reconnaissance was also carried out by a machine of the same squadron.

Capt G. H. Lewis, 40 Sqn, whilst on patrol dived on one of seven E.A. triplanes but was forced to break off the combat owing to gun jams. He shortly afterwards found a solitary enemy triplane and dived on it, getting in long bursts from both guns whilst closing in towards the E.A., which turned over and went down in a slow spin out of control and is confirmed by 'C' Battery A.A. to have crashed east of Lens.

Lt L. H. T. Capel and Cpl E. Deighton, 20 Sqn, attacked an E.A. two-seater, firing a burst of about 25 rounds into it. The E.A. went down out of control and was seen to crash.

Lt C. S. Bowen, 54 Sqn, dived on an E.A. two-seater which was flying at a height of 2,000 feet. After a short engagement the E.A. went down in a spiral apparently out of control, hit a tree and crashed, bursting into flames as soon as it reached the ground.

Capt J. Gilmour, 65 Sqn, attacked the leader of 8 or 10 E.A. two-seaters presumably bombing Amiens. After about 300 rounds had been fired into it the E.A. went down in flames north-east of Moreuil Wood.

Maj R. S. Dallas, 40 Sqn, dived on an E.A. two-seater from behind, firing with both guns up to 30 yards range. The E.A. fell over on its left wing tip, dived to earth and was seen to crash.

Capt R. A. Little, 203 Sqn, observed three E.A. two-seaters which he attacked, assisted by other machines of his flight. They were then attacked by six E.A. scouts, one of which Capt Little engaged and the E.A. went down in a spin. Capt Little followed it down to 2,000 feet and saw it crash near Neuve Eglise.

Lt A. T. Whealy, 203 Sqn, dived on an E.A. two-seater and fired a burst of about 50 rounds from both guns at 100 yards range; the E.A. went into a vertical nose-dive and crashed close to the canal near Sailly-sur-Lys.

Lt Manuel, 210 Sqn, attacked an E.A. two-seater which was flying at a height of 800 feet; after he had fired a short burst into it the E.A. dived into the ground and crashed. Shortly afterwards Lt Manuel attacked one of three Pfalz Scouts at a height of 5,000 feet; he fired 200 rounds at the E.A. which side-slipped with engine on and was followed down to 300 feet by Lt. Manuel, who saw it crash

Lt J. A. Glen, 203 Sqn, engaged an E.A. two-seater, and after 300 rounds had been fired into it from close range the E.A. dived vertically and burst into flames. The E.A. was seen by the rest of the patrol to crash.

Capt J. H. Tudhope, 40 Sqn, dived on the rear machine of a formation of seven E.A. triplanes; he opened fire at very close range, getting in several good bursts from both guns. The E.A. stalled, commenced to spin and eventually crashed to earth near the Metallurgique Works.

Capt W. L. Harrison, 1 Sqn, met four Pfalz Scouts and with two other S.E.'s. attacked them. Almost immediately the original four E.A. scouts were reinforced by five others. Capt Harrison saw an enemy scout on the tail of an S.E. and fired about 75 rounds into the E.A. which turned over on its back, went down in a spin and crashed south of Armentières.

In the same engagement, Lt F. R. Knapp, 1 Sqn, attacked the leader of five E.A. scouts and fired two bursts into it, the first burst entering the centre section and the second entering the fuselage near the pilot's seat. Owing to the fact that Lt Knapp was attacked by four others E.A. scout, he was unable to see what happened to the enemy machine into which he had fired. Maj Maxwell, 54 Sqn, confirms a Pfalz scout going down apparently in flames after combat with an S.E.5.

2 Lt W. A. Tyrrell, 32 Sqn, attacked an E.A. two-seater and opened

fire at moderate range; the E.A. immediately turned and went east, and was followed by 2 Lt Tyrrell, who this time got to close range and fired 500 rounds into it in short bursts. The E.A. went down in flames and was last seen at 500 feet completely ablaze.

During a general engagement between a formation of 56 Sqn and 11 E.A. scouts, Capt L. W. Jarvis fired about 15 rounds into one of the E.A. A large volume of smoke immediately burst from the E.A. which went down and crashed. This was seen by several pilots of the patrol.

Lt T. Durrant, 56 Sqn, got on to the tail of an E.A. scout and opened fire at rather less than 100 yards range; the E.A. went down in a steep dive and a burst of flame appeared and the E.A. was lost to view in a cloud. This E.A. was seen in flames and crashed by three other pilots of the patrol.

Lt K. W. Junor, 56 Sqn, fired a burst from each gun into an E.A. scout, which was observed to emit puffs of white smoke and water and to go down in a steep dive. This E.A. is confirmed to have crashed west of Aveluy Village.

Capt D. J. Bell, 3 Sqn, fired on an L.V.G. two-seater at 60 yards range and the observer was seen to fall into the cock-pit. Lts Mayer, Franklyn and Hamilton, of the same squadron, also fired at the E.A. Capt Bell fired a further burst of 50 rounds into it at close range and the E.A. was seen by the whole formation to go down in flames.

2 Lts R. G. Hart and L. F. Handford, 15 Sqn, whilst on contact patrol, were attacked by four E.A. scouts and almost immediately the elevator and aileron controls of the R.E.8 were shot away. Twenty rounds were fired into the nearest E.A., both planes and the right-hand side of which broke off and the E.A. burst into flames, shortly before it crashed in our lines at Millencourt. 2 Lt Handford was then wounded in the knee but engaged the E.A., firing off the remainder of the drum before he lost consciousness. This enemy machine is confirmed by the 47th and 63rd Divisions to have fallen out of control in the enemy's lines. One E.A. followed down the R.E.8, which was almost out of control, until within 100 feet of the ground, and then left it.

April 12th

The weather was fine all day and the visibility exceptionally good ∽ A record number of hours flying was done, a record number of photographs taken, and a record number of bombs dropped for any 24 hours since the war started ∽ A total of 45 tons of bombs were dropped ∽ Enemy aircraft were active on the whole front, but particularly north of La Bassée Canal and in the neighbourhood of Hangard. Forty-nine machines were brought down and 25 driven out of control. Two hostile machines were also brought down by A.A. and six balloons were destroyed by our aeroplanes.

Capt W. L. Jordan, 208 Sqn, attacked a two-seater E.A. from above and behind and fired a burst of 100 rounds from a range of under 50 yards. The E.A. dived vertically and was seen to crash about one mile north-east of La Bassée.

Capt F. G. Weare and 2 Lt G. S. Hayward, 22 Sqn, brought down three Pfalz Scouts out of a formation of five. Two crashed in a field south-west of Sailly as the result of fire from the pilot's gun, and the third in a field north of this after the observer had engaged it.

Lt C. H. Marchant and 2 Lt E. F. Davis, 41 Sqn, attacked five Albatross Scouts, two of which were driven down out of control and were seen to crash.

Lt H. Daniel, 43 Sqn, dived on a formation of E.A., engaging one at close range, which went down and was seen to crash. On another patrol he dived with his formation on eight Albatross Scouts and fired a long burst into one at short range, which crashed near La Gorgue. He then attacked another which had shot down one of our machines. This went down out of control and was seen to crash.

Lt G. A. Lingham, 43 Sqn, fired 40 rounds into a hostile machine which went down in a series of stalls and crashed.

Lt G. G. Bailey, 43 Sqn, got on to the tail of an Albatross Scout and fired a burst at about 50 yards range. It turned over on its back, went down out of control and crashed near Cagnicourt.

Capt C. F. King, 43 Sqn, attacked one of eight Pfalz Scouts which, after several bursts had been fired into it, folded up in the air.

Lt C. C. Banks, 43 Sqn, got on to the tail of an Albatross Scout which went down vertically and crashed.

The following are the combat reports of Capt H. W. Woollett, 43 Sqn, who brought down six E.A. in one day, thus equalling the record made by Capt Trollope:—

10.30 a.m.—I led my patrol down on to eight E.A. just south-east of La Gorgue. I fired about 30 rounds into one single seater; machine spun down and crashed just west of La Gorgue. I then dived on to another E.A. (a two-seater); this I saw crash just north-east of La Gorgue.

I climbed up and got on the tail of an Albatross and after firing about 40 rounds it burst into flames, falling to pieces. I also saw another E.A. in flames, and also one crash which was shot down by Lt Daniel.

5 p.m.—I led patrol down on to 13 E.A. just north of La Gorgue. I fired about 30 rounds into one E.A. which was going east. This turned over on its back and fell to bits. I then climbed and got on to the tail of another Albatross; after firing several bursts into him, he spun down and crashed north-east of La Gorgue. On returning over lines I climbed up and found another E.A. at about 2,000 feet; this after about 20 rounds collapsed in the air and fell to bits. I saw two other E.A. crash, engaged by machines of my patrol.

Altogether, pilots of 43 Sqn brought down 13 machines.

Capt H. G. Forrest, 2 Sqn A.F.C., fired 150 rounds into a hostile two-seater which crashed at Vieille Chapelle.

Capt G. F. Hughes and H. Claye, 62 Sqn, encountered an E.A. two-seater and dived on it but mis-judged the dive. The observer then opened fire over the top plane and fired a double drum. The pilot then fired a burst of 50 rounds at close range, and the hostile machine burst into flames and crashed near Carvin.

Lt E. A. Clear, 84 Sqn, attacked a two-seater and followed it down, firing with both guns at about 30 yards range. The top right hand plane suddenly folded up and the machine fell into pieces. On another flight he was attacked by five E.A. He got on to the tail of one and fired a short burst. Both machines dived down almost to the ground. The hostile machine was seen to attempt to land, but hit a trench and turned on its nose.

Capt R. A. Grosvenor, 84 Sqn, whilst on patrol, was attacked from the rear by five Albatross scouts. One of the hostile machines overshot the formation and allowed him to dive and get within very close range. He fired a long burst from his Vickers gun. The hostile machine went down vertically and crashed into the wood east of Bois de Hangard. Another machine which he attacked burst into flames and fell north of Plessier.

2 Lt G. B. Foster, 24 Sqn, got on the tail of a Pfalz Scout, which was attacking a French Sopwith two-seater. The E.A. was taken by surprise, made no effort to get clear, and nose-dived into the ground just north of Moreuil Aerodrome.

2 Lt H. B. Redler, 24 Sqn, after firing a burst of 70 rounds into a Pfalz Scout at very close range, sent the hostile machine down out of control, and it was seen to crash by another pilot.

Capt I. D. R. MacDonald, 24 Sqn, got right up to an Albatross Scout and fired 80 rounds. The machine dived with its engine full on and crashed.

2 Lt E. W. Lindeberg, 24 Sqn, fired 200 rounds from a range of 20 yards into a blue and grey Pfalz Scout, which stalled on to its back and crashed close to a wood.

2 Lt J. J. Dawe, 24 Sqn, attacked a silver grey Pfalz Scout, firing 100 rounds at a range of 30 yards. The E.A. did half a roll, went down in a slow spin and crashed.

2 Lt R. G. Hammersley, 24 Sqn, attacked a violet and yellow Albatross Scout, which he sent down out of control and saw it crash.

2 Lt W. C. Lambert, 24 Sqn, fired 100 rounds into an Albatross Scout from a range of a few yards. The E.A. turned and opened fire, got into a vertical dive and crashed.

2 Lts F. C. Ransley and C. W. Davies, 48 Sqn, whilst photographing

the front line north of Moreuil, were attacked by six E.A., which drove them down to 6,000 feet. The observer opened fire at one of these, which went down in a spin and was seen to crash in Moreuil Woods.

Capt J. Gilmour, 65 Sqn, fired a burst at very close range at a two-seater E.A., which went down in flames, breaking up in the air.

Capt S. T. Edwards, 209 Sqn, whilst with his patrol, observed A.A. bursts over Amiens. He climbed in that direction and encountered a two-seater reconnaissance machine into which he fired a long burst. The hostile machine went down in a spin and crashed.

Sgts F. Johnson and W. N. Holmes, 62 Sqn, engaged 15 E.A. east of La Pensee. The observer fired a double drum into one of these which went down and stalled past the tail of his machine. It went down in a spin and crashed near Allennes. A few minutes afterwards they encountered an E.A. over Hantay. The pilot fired a long burst into this. Its left wing folded up, and the E.A. crashed just north of Chemy.

2 Lt O. M. Baldwin, 73 Sqn, was attacked by a formation of three Albatross Scouts. Into one of these he fired a burst at very close range. The E.A. burst into flames and disappeared from view.

Capt G. A. Pidcock, 73 Sqn, was attacked by five E.A. The right top plane of one of these, into which he fired a burst, folded back, and the machine fell in bits.

Capt A. R. Brown, 209 Sqn, brought down an enemy triplane after firing 100 rounds into it at close range.

Lt J. R. Moore, 54 Sqn, caused a Rumpler two seater-to dive into the ground one mile south of Armentieres.

Lt H. E. Dolan, 74 Sqn, fired two bursts from above into an Albatross Scout which turned over slowly, went down out of control and crashed.

Maj K. L. Caldwell, 74 Sqn, fired 15 rounds into the cock-pit of an Albatross Scout which crashed beside a balloon in a ploughed field.

Capt E. Mannock, 74 Sqn, after one or two pilots of his patrol had engaged a hostile machine without result, fired a burst into it. It then crashed east of Carvin. He fired a long burst with both guns at 30 yards into another E.A. which went down and crashed near the first machine.

Capt A. Waller, 18 Sqn, was attacked with his patrol by 20 E.A. A general engagement ensued in which one machine was brought down in flames and seen to crash.

Capt J. Leacroft, 19 Sqn, engaged 10 or 12 E.A. with his formation. He dived at one of these, firing several bursts, and the E.A. finally went down out of control and crashed.

Capt D. McGoun and 2 Lt F. H. Harrison, 22 Sqn, dived on a two-seater near Laventie. One hundred rounds were fired, after which the E.A. went down side-slipping and smoking, and crashed among the buildings of a small village.

Capt D. J. Bell, 3 Sqn, fired 100 rounds at a hostile machine whose wings fell off in the air.

2 Lt J. R. Riley, 3 Sqn, attacked an Albatross Scout, firing four bursts of 50 rounds at a range of between 20 and 50 yards. The E.A. fell on its back, spun, and crashed into the ground.

Lt A. M. Hamilton, 3 Sqn, followed a hostile machine down to about 4,000 feet, firing all the time, getting in about 250 rounds in all. He saw a burst of flame in the cockpit, which went out and began smoking. The machine, however, crashed and burst into flames.

During the whole of the day, pilots of the 1st and 2nd Brigades were employed bombing and machine-gunning from a low height, the enemy's attacking troops between Wytschaete and La Bassée Canal. Pilots flew from anything between 2,000 and 50 feet. At the same time, machines of the 9th Brigade flew at a height to fight hostile machines. Machines of the 1st Brigade dropped about 800 bombs and fired 61,000 rounds, while those of the 2nd Brigade dropped 500 bombs and fired 15,000 rounds. Very low reconnaissances were also carried out by machines of these Brigades, very useful information being brought in as to the position of our own and the enemy's troops. Especially useful reports as to the location in which hostile troops were massing were brought in, enabling our guns to engage them and our low-flying machines to go out and attack them with their machine guns and drop bombs on them.

April 13th

After 4 p.m. on the 12th, a great deal of work was carried out, but on the 13th, low clouds and mist prevented flying with the exception of low reconnaissances and contact patrols which were carried out by the 1st, 2nd, 3rd and 5th Brigades ◇ A total of 39 tons of bombs were dropped ◇ Enemy aircraft activity was very slight all day and practically no combats took place.

April 14th

Low clouds and mist prevailed on the whole front and very little flying was done except by the 1st Brigade, who, in spite of the weather, had machines out all day reconnoitring their Army front, bombing and machine-gunning the enemy's troops ◇ A total of 4½ tons of bombs were dropped during the day ◇ Enemy aircraft activity was nil and no combats took place.

Maj R. S. Dallas, 40 Sqn, though twice hit by machine gun fire from the ground, attacked 10 motor lorries south-west of Bailleul and one was seen to burst into flames.

Capts Stewart and Collins, 18 Sqn, with other machines of the same squadron, caused great damage with bombs and machine gun fire along the roads east and north-east of Merville. They returned for more bombs, taking out another machine, as owing to enemy machine gun fire their own machine was rendered unserviceable. On the second trip, their machine was again shot about, but they managed to land safely on our side of the lines.

Enemy machines were also driven down out of control during the period under review by:

Sqn 3 Capt D. J. Bell. **24** Lt G. Dawe, Capt I. D. R. MacDonald, Capt J. McDonald. **32** 2 Lt W. A. Tyrrell. **40** 2 Lt I. F. Hind, Capt G. H. Lewis, Capt J. L. Middleton, Capt I. P. R. Napier (2), 2 Lt C. W. Usher, 2 Lt J. W. Wallwork. **43** Lt G. G. Bailey. **62** 2 Lt C. H. Arnison + Lt S. Parry, 2 Lts L. Campbell + W. Hodgkinson, 2 Lts G. W. Hemsworth + A. J. Todd, Capts G. F. Hughes + H. Claye, Lt D. A. Savage + 2 Lt L. M. Thompson. **70** Lt E. H. Peverell. **73** 2 Lt R. N. Chandler, Capt W. H. Hubbard, 2 Lt G. Pilditch. **84** Lt L. de S. Duke, Lt G. O. Johnson, Lt W. E. Lunnon, Lt J. V. Sorsoleil, Capt E. H. Tatton (2). **201** Lt J. H. Forman. **209** Capt A. R. Brown/Lt Edwards, Lt O. M. Redgate, Lt Sidall. **210** Capt W. M. Alexander. **2 AFC** Capt A. G. Clark.

HONOURS AND AWARDS

DSO Capt G. E. Thomson, MC, Capt F. G. Quigley. **DSC** Flt Lt E. Dickson (Bar), Flt Cmdr S. W. Rosevear (Bar), Flt Lt A. T. Whealy. **MC** Capt J. Leacroft (Bar), Capt J. L. Trollope (Bar), 2 Lt W. Beaver, 2 Lt E. Lindup, Lt R. D. Leigh-Pemberton, Lt J. T. Richardson, Capt D. A. Stewart (Bar), Capt A. K. Cowper (Bar), Lt F. R. McCall (Bar), Lt F. H. Taylor, Lt J. M. Brisbane, Lt G. O. Johnson, 2 Lt P. K. Hobson, 2 Lt A. W. Beauchamp-Proctor, 2 Lt C. G. D. Napier, Capt A. J. Brown, 2 Lt P. J. Clayson, 2 Lt F. P. Magoun, Lt A. Rigby (Bar), Capt F. M. Kitto, Capt W. R. Fish, Capt E. Waterlow, 2 Lt G. Pilditch, 2 Lt W. S. Stephenson, Capt W. H. Park, Capt H. A. Hamersley, Lt H. R. Kincaid, Lt C. C. Robson, 2 Lt H. J. Greenwood, 2 Lt D. C. M. Brooks, Lt J. K. Hibbert (2nd Bar), Capt R. N. Walton (Bar), 2 Lt G. G. Walker, 2 Lt W. W. Jones, 2 Lt W. H. Brown, Capt R. E. Bryson, Capt W. Deane, Capt L. G. Paling, Capt H. F. S. Drewitt, Lt R. M. C. MacFarlane, 2 Lt A. E. Lancashire, Lt B. Head, 2 Lt L. F. Goodwin, 2 Lt H. P. Lloyd, Lt W. J. A. Duncan, 2 Lt E. R. Maddox, 2 Lt M. H. Picot, 2 Lt A. A. McD. Arnott, 2 Lt A. Leach, 2 Lt H. Wisnekonitz, 2 Lt L. C. Hooton, Capt A. K. Cowper (2nd Bar), Capt F. E. Brown (Bar), Capt K. M. StC. G. Leask (Bar), Capt J. F. Morris (Bar), Capt W. L. Wells (Bar), Capt W. R. Fish (Bar), Capt S. W. Vickers, 2 Lt E. I. Wells, 2 Lt H. B. Richardson, 2 Lt H. B. Redler, 2 Lt R. S. Herring, 2 Lt J. H. Reeves, 2 Lt W. H. G. Milnes, Lt J. E. Pugh, 2 Lt A. Koch, Lt G. H. H. Scutt, Lt R. St J. Dix, 2 Lt P. Hardy, 2 Lt E. A. Clear, 2 Lt W. G. MacKenzie, 2 Lt R. T. Mark, 2 Lt E. E. Stock, 2 Lt R. C. Crowdon, Lt A. P. Kelly, Capt F. G. C. Weare, 2 Lt H. F. Davison, Capt R. W. Chappell, Lt H. A. Chippendale, 2 Lt G. L. Hobbs, 2 Lt S. Adams, 2 Lt H. B. Pott, 2 Lt J. G. Burchett. **DCM** 1 AM M. H. Church, Cpl W. Beales. **MSM** Flt Sgt J. E. O'Shea.

15 – 21 April

The death of Manfred von Richthofen, top-scoring fighter pilot of the war, was the main event of the week. He had started flying as an observer in May 1915, and became a pilot in December of that year. Capt A. R. Brown, who shot him down, was flying a Bentley-engined Sopwith Camel.

COMMUNIQUÉ NO. 3

During the period under review we have claimed officially 20 E.A. brought down and 10 driven down out of control. In addition, 3 E.A. have been brought down by A.A. and machine-gun fire. Fourteen of our machines are missing. Approximately 93 tons of bombs were dropped and 3,515 photographs were taken.

April 15th

In spite of low clouds and mist, machines of the 1st Brigade again did a considerable amount of work during the day—all from a low altitude ◌ A total of 4¼ tons of bombs were dropped ◌ Enemy aircraft activity was practically nil, and no combats took place.

On the 1st instant, Lts R. G. D. Francis and R. Hainsworth, 3 Sqn, A.F.C., were attacked by an E.A. two-seater which dived past them. They immediately opened fire at the E.A. which turned into the clouds, pursued by the R.E.8, and the E.A. was intercepted each time it attempted to turn towards it own lines. When almost over the aerodrome at Abeele, several bursts were fired into the E.A. which went down and was seen to crash in our lines.

April 16th

The mist which had prevailed during the previous days turned to rain and very little flying was possible ◌ A total of 2¾ tons of bombs were dropped during the day ◌ Enemy aircraft activity was below normal. One hostile machine landed intact behind our lines.

Capt J. Gilmour, 65 Sqn, was attacked by an E.A. two-seater from above; he climbed up to the E.A. and fired a burst from both guns into it. The E.A. crashed in flames near the Bois de Hangard.

April 17th

Up to 11 a.m. the weather was clearer but after this low clouds and mist again set in ∽ A total of 10½ tons of bombs were dropped ∽ Enemy aircraft activity was slight and after 11 a.m. was practically nil.

Lt P. Dennett, 208 Sqn, dived on one of six E.A. scouts and fired a burst of 50 rounds into it at close range. The E.A. dived vertically followed by Lt Dennett, who fired another burst of 30 rounds into it and the E.A. eventually crashed just south of Merville.

Lt C. J. Mason, 54 Sqn, whilst on offensive patrol at a height of 1,000 feet, was attacked by five E.A. scouts; he fired a long burst into one E.A. which crashed north-east of Neuf Berquin.

April 18th

Low clouds and rain prevailed during the day ∽ A total of 2½ tons of bombs were dropped during the day ∽ Enemy aircraft activity was practically nil.

April 19th

There was a strong wind and snow and hail storms, with occasional bright intervals ∽ A total of 13¼ tons of bombs were dropped ∽ Enemy aircraft was slight, only a few combats taking place.

2 Lt Day, 101 Sqn, on a night bomb raid, in spite of a failing engine, crossed the line and bombed his objective. On the return journey his engine stopped twice, but by skilful piloting he succeeded in reaching the aerodrome despite the fact that he was losing height all the way.

April 20th

In the early morning the weather was fine, but during the day it became cloudy and very overcast and impeded flying at a height ∽ A total of 27½ tons of bombs were dropped ∽ Enemy aircraft were fairly active. One hostile machine was brought down by A.A. in addition to those brought down in combat.

Capt D. J. Bell, 3 Sqn, had an engagement with six E.A. triplanes and shot down one out of control which is confirmed by ground observers to have crashed.

Lt K. W. Junor, 56 Sqn, dived on an E.A. two-seater and fired 150 rounds into it from very close range. The top right wing of the E.A. came off, followed almost immediately by the other three wings, and the wreckage fell and burned up on the ground south-west of Puisieux.

Capt C. J. Marchant, 46 Sqn, whilst leading his patrol, observed two E.A. two-seaters. He dived on one of the E.A. from behind and fired a burst of 30 rounds into it. 2 Lt M. M. Freehill, of the same squadron, then dived on this E.A. firing 130 rounds into it. The E.A. dived steeply east, followed by Capt Marchant who fired another 100 rounds into it, whereupon the E.A. went down vertically emitting dense clouds of smoke and was seen to crash near Harnes.

Lt C. S. Bowen, 54 Sqn, with his patrol attacked 10 E.A. scouts at a height of 2,000 feet. Lt Bowen drove down one E.A. to 200 feet firing 10 to 12 bursts into it and he followed it down. The E.A. was observed to crash north of Neuf Berquin.

2 Lt G. B. Foster, 24 Sqn, fired 350 rounds into one E.A. scout which spun down and was followed to 700 feet by 2 Lt Foster, who saw it crash.

Capt I. D. R. MacDonald, 24 Sqn, led his patrol against a mixed formation of 13 E.A. He fired 30 rounds at close range into the leader before being observed. The E.A. turned over, making two very quick spins and dived vertically into the ground south of Marcourt.

101 Sqn carried out a very successful raid on Chalnes Railway Junction. At the commencement of the raid no searchlights or A.A. defences were encountered, but when the machines went out on the second trip five searchlights had been brought up, and many machine guns, A.A. Batteries and 'flaming onion' batteries came into action.

During the first raid E.A. showed a tendency for attacking, but these tactics were not pressed home to any great extent, and our machines were easily able to hold their own.

April 21st
The weather was fine and the visibility good ∽ 30 tons of bombs were dropped ∽ Enemy aircraft were active but by no means aggressive. Two hostile machines were brought down by anti-aircraft fire—one falling in our lines—in addition to those brought down in combat.

Capt M. von Richthofen, who is credited by the enemy as having brought down 80 Allied machines, was shot down and killed behind our lines near Corbie by Capt A. R. Brown, 209 Sqn.

Capt E. J. Jones and Lt A. L. D. Taylor, 3 Sqn, A.F.C., engaged one of two E.A. two-seaters which went down clearly out of control and was seen to crash and burst into flames on the ground.

Capt. R. McDonald, 208 Sqn, dived on an E.A. two-seater, firing 200 rounds from about 50 yards range and another 100 rounds at point blank range from below. The E.A. went down completely out of control and crashed beside a trench south-west of Henin-Liétard.

Lt G. O. Johnson, 24 Sqn, and 2 Lt W. C. Lambert, of the same squadron, both fired bursts into a hostile balloon which immediately went down and was seen smoking on the ground.

Capt A. R. Brown, 209 Sqn, dived on a red triplane which was attacking one of our machines. He fired a long burst into the E.A. which went down vertically and was seen to crash on our side of the lines by two other pilots of 209 Sqn.

2 Lt G. B. Irving, 19 Sqn, in an engagement between a formation of his squadron and 20 E.A. scouts, fired several long bursts at one E.A. at close range. The E.A. went down in a spin completely out of control and was seen by Maj Carter to burst into flames when near the ground.

Lt M. S. Taylor, 209 Sqn, fired about 300 rounds into an E.A. two-seater which went down emitting dense clouds of smoke and burst into flames before hitting the ground.

Lt F. J. W. Mellersh, 209 Sqn, in a general engagement between a formation of his squadron and a mixed formation of E.A. triplanes and scouts, fired about 50 rounds into one E.A. scout which went down in a vertical dive followed by Lt Mellersh, still firing, who saw the E.A. crash near Cerisy.

Lt P. K. Hobson, 84 Sqn, got on to the tail of an E.A. two-seater and fired a long burst from both guns into it; the E.A. went down in a steep dive which turned into a spin and finally broke to pieces, the wreckage falling south-west of Mezieres.

Lt D. A. Savage and 2 Lt L. M. Thompson, 62 Sqn, opened fire at one E.A. with the back gun and the E.A. crashed three miles west of Lille. Shortly afterwards they were attacked from behind by two E.A. scouts, and opened fire at one of these which fell vertically and broke to pieces in the air. The remaining E.A. broke off the combat.

Capt T. L. Purdon and 2 Lt P. V. G. Chambers, 62 Sqn, fired about 100 rounds into an E.A. triplane which went down and turned over in a spiral nose-dive. 2 Lt W. E. Staton of the same squadron fired about 150 rounds into this E.A. as it was going down, and it was seen to crash into the ground south-east of Estaires.

Capt C. C. Clark, 1 Sqn, together with Lt K. C. Mills, of the same squadron, dived on one E.A. scout and closed to within 50 yards firing all the time. They followed the E.A. down to 400 feet and saw it crash to the ground in the neighbourhood of Lompret.

Capt R. A. Little, 203 Sqn, attacked the rear machine of a formation of 12 E.A. and watched it fall to 1,000 feet near Vieux Berquin completely out of control. Capt Little was then attacked by six E.A. and was driven down through the formation below; he put his machine into a spin and his controls were shot away causing his machine to dive to within 100 feet of the ground when it flattened with a jerk, breaking the fuselage just under the pilot's seat. Capt Little undid the belt and was thrown clear when the machine struck the ground. The E.A. continued to fire at him, but he opened fire with his revolver at one E.A. which came down to about 30 feet; the E.A. were eventually driven off by our infantry with rifle and machine gun fire.

Enemy machines were also driven down out of control during the period under review by:

Sqn 4 2 Lts W. E. M. Whittaker + C. Sunderland. **18** 2 Lt A. C. Atkey + Lt P. Anderson. **19** Lt T. A. Aldridge, Maj A. D. Carter, Lt N. W. Hastings, 2 Lt J. D. de Pencier. **20** Capt D. G. Cooke + Lt H. G. Crowe. **24** 2 Lt H. D. Redler. **25** 2 Lts C. E. H. Allen + F. G. Wall, 2 Lts A. H. Herring + S. C. Eschmann, 2 Lt S. Jones + Cpl H. Edwards. **46** Capt D. R. MacLaren. **49** Lts G. A. Leckie + G. Cuttle. **62** 2 Lt C. H. Arnison + Lt S. Parry, 2 Lt G. M. Yuill + Lt E. W. Collis. **64** Lt A. A. Duffus, Capt J. A. Slater (2). **84** Lt P. K. Hobson. **98** Lts A. M. Phillips + C. P. Harrison. **3 AFC** Lts W. V. Hervert + A. Sewell. **4 AFC** Lt H. G. Watson.

HONOURS AND AWARDS

DSC Lt J. Gamon. **MC** Capt G. E. H. McElroy (2nd Bar), Capt E. R. H. Pollak (Bar), Lt A. W. Hammond (Bar), 2 Lt L. C. Hooton (Bar), 2 Lt J. P. Owen Holdsworth, Capt G. M. Cox, 2 Lt F. C. Farrington. **DSM** AG W. Naylor. **MM** 2 AM F. J. Knowles.

22 – 28 April

The restriction of flying activities, due to weather was reflected in the small number of aircraft losses on both sides.

Maj C. F. A. Portal, C.O. of 16 Sqn, whose artillery-spotting sortie was reported on 23 April, was Chief of the Air Staff for the greater part of World War II, and is now Marshal of the R.A.F. Viscount Portal of Hungerford.

Capt S. W. Rosevear, 201 Sqn, who gained a victory on 22 April, had a final victory score of 23 enemy aircraft destroyed.

COMMUNIQUÉ NO. 4

During the period under review we have claimed officially 34 E.A. brought down and 10 driven down out of control. In addition, 10 were brought down by A.A. and our Infantry's fire from the ground. Eight of our machines are missing. Approximately 87 tons of bombs were dropped, and 1,898 photographs were taken.

April 22nd
The weather was fine, though at times there were thick banks of clouds over the lines ◇ 26 tons of bombs were dropped ◇ Enemy aircraft were active on the First Army Front especially during the morning; on the remainder of the front the activity was normal. One E.A. was brought down in our lines by A.A. in addition to those brought down in combat.

2 Lt F. H. Baguley and Lt C.A. Horn, 2 Sqn, whilst on artillery observation, were attacked by eight E.A. scouts; the E.A. were driven away but returned shortly afterwards. Lt Horn engaged one E.A. and tracers were seen to enter the engine and the E.A. burst into flames, but owing to the presence of other E.A. it was not seen to crash. The remaining E.A. scouts were driven off and the work continued. Some time afterwards they were again attacked by E.A. scouts but succeeded in driving them away.

Capt A. T. Whealy, 203 Sqn, dived on one E.A. scout into which he fired a good burst at 50 yards range. The E.A. went down completely out of control and was confirmed to have crashed near Merville. Capt Whealy then dived on the tail of another E.A. scout which was attacking one of our machines. A long burst was fired into the E.A. which went into a spin and fell completely out of control into a cloud. This E.A. is confirmed to have crashed into a building on the Merville–Estaires road, near Merville.

Capt S. W. Rosevear, 201 Sqn, attacked one of seven E.A. scouts at point blank range, but the E.A. dived away. Capt Rosevear then got on to the tail of another E.A., firing at point blank range, and the E.A. flew along straight, seeming to partially stall, and then dived straight down. Capt Rosevear was then attacked by the remaining E.A. and dived through the clouds after the E.A. which he had previously attacked and saw it crash into the ground.

A patrol of 209 Sqn engaged one E.A. two-seater. All the pilots succeeded in getting off good bursts into it and the E.A. turned over on its wing and nose-dived, and when about 1,000 feet from the ground broke up, the wreckage falling on our side of the lines.

Capt H. W. Woollett, 43 Sqn, fired about 60 rounds into a balloon which fell in flames, the two observers jumping out. He then climbed through the clouds and flew north and dived on another balloon which he had previously seen. Forty-five rounds were fired into this balloon which fell in flames. No one was seen to jump out.

Capt C. Faber, 79 Sqn, shot down one E.A. in flames and got on to the tail of another E.A. which he saw crash. Shortly afterwards his engine cut out owing to a bullet going through the radiator: he came down to 1,000 feet and the engine picked up somewhat, but only ran intermittently. Capt Faber crossed the lines at 1,000 feet but was wounded by a machine-gun bullet from the ground and was admitted to hospital. Another pilot of the same patrol reports that he saw one E.A. going down out of control and Capt Faber close on the tail of another.

April 23rd
There were low clouds all day and the visibility was very bad ⌒ 10¾ tons of bombs were dropped ⌒ Enemy aircraft activity was slight until 5 p.m., after which hour there was a good deal of fighting. One hostile machine was brought down in our lines by A.A. in addition to those brought down in combat.

Capt C. C. Clark, 1 Sqn, dived on one of eight E.A. triplanes, firing a good burst into it at about 70 yards range. The E.A. burst into flames and went down over Aelbeke.

Capt E. Mannock, 74 Sqn, attacked the rear machine of a formation of E.A. scouts; an explosion was observed in the E.A. pilot's seat and the machine turned upside down and descended vertically, emitting volumes of smoke, and was seen to strike the ground east of Merville.

Capt E. R. Tempest, 64 Sqn, dived on a formation of eight E.A.

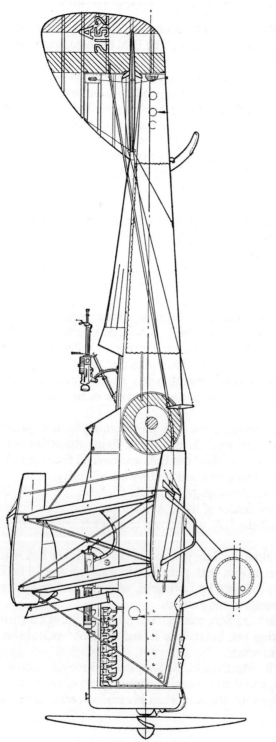

De Havilland D.H.4

scouts, firing about 60 rounds from his Vickers gun into one of them from about 200 to 60 yards range. The E.A. fell completely out of control and was seen to crash.

Lt T. Rose, 64 Sqn, dived twice on an E.A. two-seater, apparently without effect. He then got into a good position in front and above and fired about 100 rounds at close range into the E.A., which turned over on its back and got into a slow spin quite out of control, emitting clouds of blue smoke which gradually increased all the way down.

Maj A. D. Carter, 19 Sqn, got on to the tail of an E.A. scout and when about 25 yards from the E.A. fired a long burst into it, whereupon it stalled and dived from 1,000 feet into the centre of a field and was seen to break into pieces.

Capt J. Gilmour, 65 Sqn, attacked four triplanes; he fired a burst into one of these which did a steep turn and went down vertically, its wings falling off in the air.

2 Lt T. Williams, 65 Sqn, fired a burst of about 200 rounds into an E.A. scout at point blank range, and the E.A. dived down vertically in flames.

Capt Gamon and Lt Scott, 205 Sqn, after dropping their bombs were attacked by a large formation of E.A. scouts. Fire was opened on one of the enemy scouts, which was attempting to follow down one of our machines, and the E.A. went down in flames. An E.A. scout then got on the tail of Capt Gamon's machine and after 50 rounds had been fired into the E.A. it went down in a spin and one of its wings was seen to be folded back.

Lt F. J. W. Mellersh, 209 Sqn, on returning from a special mission, almost collided with an E.A. two-seater flying through the clouds. Lt Mellersh got on to the tail of the E.A. and opened fire; the E.A. fell over in a spin and was seen to crash south-west of Cerisy.

A patrol of 84 Sqn engaged 10 E.A. triplanes. Lt A. W. B. Proctor opened fire at the leader of the E.A. formation and after 200 rounds had been fired into it the E.A. went down completely out of control and was seen to crash.

Lt C. L. Stubbs, 84 Sqn, got on the tail of another E.A. triplane and fired a long burst from both guns into it at close range. The E.A. went down vertically followed by Lt Stubbs, who, from a height of 7,000 feet, saw the E.A. crash to the ground.

Lt R. T. Mark, 24 Sqn, attacked the rear machine of a formation of six E.A. scouts firing two bursts into it, and the E.A. went down in a spin and was seen to crash.

Capt I. D. R. MacDonald, 24 Sqn, dived three times on a formation of E.A. scouts, and then his engine choked. Two of the E.A. drove Capt MacDonald down to 200 feet when his engine picked up again and he

Bristol F2B Fighter

FIGHTING SCOUTS

Top: Sopwith Camel

Bottom: S.E.5a

was able to zoom above one of the E.A. and fire 50 rounds into it, the E.A. being seen to crash in the corner of a field.

Capt G. O. Johnson, 24 Sqn, fired 100 rounds into an E.A. scout which was of a silver colour; the E.A. went down in a spiral dive and was seen to crash.

Lts West and Haslam, 8 Sqn, whilst on early patrol, went over the lines a distance of 8,000 yards to attack enemy transport with bombs and machine gun fire as the transport was out of range for a zone call. Considerable damage was done to the transport and some of the personnel were killed and wounded. On the return journey they were met with considerable A.A. and machine gun fire, and the engine of their machine was hit and the aileron control shot away. Lt West, however, managed to land the machine 100 yards this side of the trenches and both he and Lt Haslam got away safely.

Maj Portal, 16 Sqn, carried out two successful shoots between 3.45 p.m. and 7.45 p.m. with the 2nd and 10th Canadian Siege Batteries.

April 24th

There were low clouds and mist all day and very little flying was possible ⌒ 26¾ tons of bombs were dropped ⌒ Enemy aircraft activity was very slight and no combats took place except on the front of the 5th Brigade, where a few low-flying E.A. were encountered. One E.A. was brought down in our lines by infantry, in addition to those brought down in combat.

Lt C. G. Edwards, 209 Sqn, while dropping bombs near Warfusee-Abancourt, was attacked from behind by a Pfalz Scout. Lt Edwards did a climbing turn to the right and the E.A. turned to the left and dived. Lt Edwards then fired a short burst of 20 rounds at the E.A. which went down and crashed on the ground.

Although a large amount of night bombing took place, the weather conditions were most indifferent; considerable mist prevailed, especially in the south, and later clouds began to drift across the sky.

2 Lts Brook and Chantrill, 101 Sqn, obtained three direct hits with 112-lb. bombs on the railway junction at Chaulnes. 2 Lts Preston and McConville succeeded in hitting an ammunition dump on the south side of the railway near Rosieres. A great explosion took place immediately, followed by a tremendous blaze and further explosions. The fire and explosion were seen by several other pilots, who reported the matter on their return. When the second raid took place the fire was again observed by all pilots, who reported that it had increased enormously and was rapidly spreading; at one place it had crossed the railway line and was burning on the north side as well as on the south, and explosions were still taking place. The fire served as a useful landmark for pilots, as it could be easily distinguished from Amiens.

April 25th

There were low clouds and mist with occasional bright intervals ⌒ 15 tons of bombs were dropped ⌒ In the early morning low-flying E.A. were active on the 2nd Brigade front; during the remainder of the day there was practically no activity until after 5 p.m., when the weather cleared considerably and several combats took place. Four hostile machines were brought down by A.A. and two by infantry, in addition to those brought down in combat.

Lt W. Beaver and Cpl M. Mather, 20 Sqn, whilst on a long-distance reconnaissance, attacked five E.A. scouts which turned and flew east. Getting to within 200 yards of the nearest E.A., Lt Beaver fired a burst of 100 rounds into it and the E.A. went down out of control and burst into flames on the ground just north of Ploegsteert Wood.

Lt K. C. Mills, 1 Sqn, with the rest of his patrol dived on a formation of E.A. scouts, but owing to engine trouble he was cut off from his patrol. He was then attacked by two triplanes and two E.A. scouts; after manœuvring for some time, he fired a good burst with both guns at close range into one of the triplanes which went down vertically with black smoke coming out and was seen to crash between Becelaere and Dadizeele.

Capt J. Gilmour, 65 Sqn, dived on a formation of seven E.A. scouts and attacked the rear machine. After firing a short burst into it the E.A. went down in flames.

Lt R. H. Little and Sgt W. Beales, 48 Sqn, attacked one E.A. two-seater and fired a drum of Buckingham into it from a range of 300 yards. The E.A. put its nose down and flew into the ground, crashing one mile east of Harbonnieres.

Lt E. A. Clear, 84 Sqn, fired a good burst with both guns into one E.A. scout: he then dived at it and the E.A. went down in a very steep dive and crashed near the railway east of Wiencourt. Lt Clear, whilst returning home, saw an E.A. two-seater flying around Hangard. He dived on it and fired a good burst from long range, the E.A. turning east and shortly afterwards coming back. Lt Clear dived again without any apparent result and the E.A. again turned east. Lt Clear then flew into the clouds for a short time, and finally made another attack on the E.A. which went down out of control and crashed south of Hangard Wood, bursting into flames upon hitting the ground.

Lt R. Manser, 84 Sqn, in a general engagement between his patrol and a formation of E.A. scouts, observed one E.A. on the tail of one of our machines. Lt Manser fired at it from both guns from a range of about 50 yards and continued his bursts until within about 30 yards of the E.A., which stalled and fell in a vertical dive, followed for a short

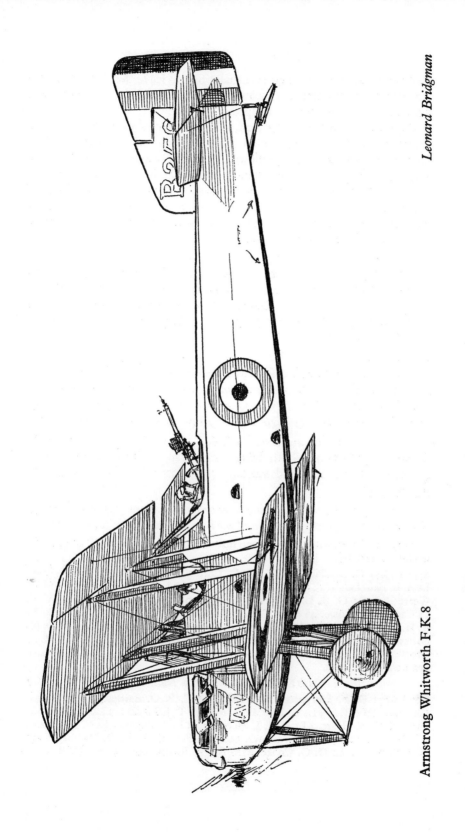

Leonard Bridgman

Armstrong Whitworth F.K.8

distance by Lt Manser, who eventually had to leave the E.A. as he was attacked by three other E.A. scouts. The E.A. which he had shot down out of control, was seen to collapse in the air.

Capt R. A. Grosvenor, 84 Sqn, whilst on patrol observed five E.A. scouts upon which his formation dived; he engaged one E.A. at close range and it started to dive, followed by Capt Grosvenor down to about 4,000 feet when the top right-hand plane of the E.A. crumpled up.

Capt J. V. Sorsoleil, 84 Sqn, in the same engagement observed one of our machines fighting two E.A. scouts; he dived on one and fired a long burst from both guns into it. The E.A. went down vertically, emitting smoke, and finally burst into flames.

April 26th

There was a thick mist all day, but in spite of this 14 reconnaissances were carried out ∽ 5½ tons of bombs were dropped ∽ A few low-flying E.A. were seen in the vicinities of Kemmel and Villers-Bretonneux; two of these were brought down by machine gun fire from the ground—one falling in our lines. No combats took place.

April 27th

Flying was rendered almost impossible owing to a thick mist; but the 5th Brigade carried out 11 reconnaissances and five contact patrols, and neutralized one hostile battery ∽ One ton of bombs was dropped ∽ Enemy aircraft activity was very slight and only two combats took place.

A patrol of 209 Sqn attacked five E.A. Lt O. M. Redgate and Lt N. S. Taylor singled out one, both firing at close range. The E.A. was seen to go down out of control and was later seen crashed on the ground.

April 28th

Low clouds, mist and rain almost entirely prevented flying ∽ Enemy aircraft activity was very slight, and one indecisive combat only took place.

Enemy machines were also driven down out of control during the period under review by:

Sqn 1 Capt C. C. Clark. **19** Maj A. D. Carter/Lt G. B. Irving/Lt C. S. Hall, Lt A. B. Fairclough (2). **22** Lt S. F. Thompson + 2 Lt C. G. Gass, Capt F. G. C. Weare + 2 Lt G. S. L. Hayward (2). **23** Capt E. M. Mansbridge, Lt Way. **24** Capt C. N. Lowe. **48** Capt T. Colvill-Jones + 2 Lt J. M. J. Moore. **49** Lt A. H. Curtis + 2 Lt P. T. Holligan. **54** Capt G. H. Hackwill. **56** Capt E. D. G. Galley. **62** Capts G. F. Hughes + H. Claye (2). **84** Lt L. de S. Duke, Capt R. A. Grosvenor (3), Lt P. K. Hobson, Lt H. W. L. Saunders, Capt J. V. Sorsoleil. **210** Lt E. L. Nelson.

HONOURS AND AWARDS

DSO Capt D. F. Stevenson, MC. **DSC** Lt C. P. O. Bartlett, Flt Lt S. M. Kinkead, RN & RAF, Lt G. B. S. Bain. **MC** Lt T. J. Findley, 2 Lt L. T. Handford, 2 Lt R. G. Hart, 2 Lt J. M. J. Moore, 2 Lt L. A. Payne, 2 Lt E. H. Stanes, 2 Lt W. I. E. Lane, Lt H. G. Crowe, Lt E. M. Forsyth, Lt L. W. Mawbey, Capt H. J. Hamilton, Lt D. G. Cooke. **MM** Sgt A. Remington, Sgt A. S. Allan.

29 April – 5 May

Maj R. S. Dallas, C.O. of 40 Sqn, whose novel method of provoking the enemy was reported on 2 May, had been flying in the R.N.A.S. since December 1915. and had commanded 1 Naval Sqn in 1917. He took over 40 Sqn on 1 April 1918, and had gained 40 combat victories when he was killed in action on 19 June 1918.

COMMUNIQUÉ NO. 5

During the period under review we have claimed officially 51 E.A. brought down and 13 E.A. driven out of control. In addition, four E.A. have been brought down by A.A. and our infantry's fire from the ground. Sixteen of our machines are missing. Approximately 63 tons of bombs were dropped and 7,024 photographs taken.

April 29th
Despite low clouds and bad visibility, a certain amount of flying was carried out ⌒ 3¼ tons of bombs were dropped ⌒ Enemy aircraft activity was slight, but a few enemy two-seaters were seen attempting to do low work and reconnaissance. One E.A. was brought down by our infantry in addition to those brought down in combat.

Capt H. A. Rigby, 1 Sqn, dived on one of three E.A. two-seaters, started firing at about 200 yards and by the time he had fired 150 rounds into the E.A., he almost collided with it. The lower plane of the E.A. crumpled up near the fuselage and it went down in a spin.

Capt I. P. R. Napier, 40 Sqn, together with 2 Lt P. D. Learoyd and 2 Lt L. H. Sutton, of the same squadron, observed an E.A. two-seater near Bruay. They flew towards the E.A. keeping between it and the lines. Capt Napier obtained a good position behind and below the E.A. and fired a drum of Lewis from close range; he zoomed above the E.A. and the hostile observer was not to be seen. He then changed drums and fired a further burst into the E.A. from above and behind. 2 Lt Sutton fired two bursts of about 100 rounds each from both guns from above the E.A. 2 Lt Learoyd then attacked and fired a long burst of Lewis and continued to fire short bursts from his Vickers until the E.A. was forced to land under control on our side of the lines. The E.A. was found to be riddled with bullet holes and the observer hit in two places.

Capt C. B. Glynn, 74 Sqn, observed an E.A. triplane approaching from behind trying to get above him. Capt Glynn zoomed upwards and turned towards the E.A., firing long bursts from the Vickers gun and a short burst from the Lewis gun. The E.A. triplane was seen a few seconds afterwards by Capt Mannock and Lt Dolan to dive vertically into the ground just south of the scene of the engagement.

Lt H. E. Dolan, 74 Sqn, engaged one E.A. scout and fired about 50 rounds into it from a range of about 20 yards. The E.A. was seen to break to pieces and fall to earth.

Capt E. Mannock, 74 Sqn, fired about 40 rounds at close range into an E.A. scout which immediately burst into flames and was observed to fall in pieces.

Capt J. G. Manuel, 210 Sqn, with his patrol, attacked nine E.A., the majority of which spun down under control. Capt Mannock got on to the tail of one as it came out of a spin and fired a burst at close range. The E.A. went down out of control and crashed north-east of Hollebeke.

Capt J. Gilmour, 65 Sqn, whilst on offensive patrol with his formation, encountered 15 E.A. (scouts and two-seaters). He attacked one E.A. scout from slightly behind and fired 250 rounds into it. The E.A. dived vertically into the clouds and was lost to sight. 15 Observation Company confirm an E.A. scout falling out of control in this vicinity and smoke rising from the ground immediately afterwards.

Whilst on a practice formation, Lt J. Todd, 70 Sqn, and Lt V. C. Chapman, of the same squadron, observed an E.A. two-seater being engaged by our A.A. guns over Villers-Bretonneux. They manœuvred to the east of the E.A. and both dived together, intercepting the E.A. as it turned east and firing 400 rounds into it. This E.A. was then attacked by Lt H. W. L. Saunders, 84 Sqn, and Lt C. F. Falkenberg, 84 Sqn, who both fired bursts into the E.A. at very close range, and by continuous firing, prevented the E.A. from turning east and forced it down to the ground on our side of the lines.

Enemy machines were driven down out of control by Capt C. C. Clark, 1 Sqn, and 2 Lt T. Rose, 64 Sqn.

April 30th
The weather was again bad, there being low clouds, mist and rain ⌒ Nearly 4 tons of bombs were dropped ⌒ Enemy aircraft activity was very slight all day.

Lt M. H. Dolan, 74 Sqn, attacked an E.A. two-seater, which he forced to land in our lines near Dickebusch.

May 1st
Low clouds and mist again prevailed ⌒ 3 tons of bombs were dropped ⌒ Enemy aircraft activity was practically nil all day.

May 2nd

The weather was fine but the visibility very bad ◇ Over 3½ tons of bombs were dropped ◇ Enemy aircraft were not very active considering the fine weather, although a number of enemy machines were encountered on the 5th Brigade front about noon.

Lt A. W. Blake, 19 Sqn, during a big fight got on to the tail of an E.A. scout and fired several bursts at it from close range, whereupon the E.A. turned in front of him and he followed it, firing the whole time. Lt A. B. Fairclough, 19 Sqn, then attacked the E.A. from the side, and it eventually burst into flames and broke up into many pieces.

Lt E. R. Jeffree, 4 Sqn, A.F.C., observing an E.A. scout below him, left his patrol and dived on the E.A., opening fire from close range. After diving twice and firing two bursts into the E.A., Lt Jeffree saw it put its nose down and dive steeply towards the ground and eventually crash. This is confirmed by another member of the patrol.

2 Lt T. Williams, 65 Sqn, fired a burst of about 100 rounds into one E.A. two-seater which was seen to crash in flames.

Lt W. F. Scott-Kerr, 65 Sqn, fired about 250 rounds into one E.A. two-seater which went down vertically through the clouds emitting a stream of smoke, and was confirmed by the Australian Corps to have fallen in Monument Wood.

Capt J. Gilmour, 65 Sqn, with his flight attacked a formation of eight E.A. two-seaters, one of which he shot down in flames almost at once. He then engaged another enemy two-seater, which was separated from the rest; this E.A. went down and crashed in flames near the south-east edge of Bois l'Abbe.

Lt M. S. Taylor, 209 Sqn, with his patrol dived on eight E.A. triplanes and fired a burst at about 20 yards range into one E.A. which went down on its back out of control and was seen to crash by another pilot of the patrol and also by 65 Sqn.

Maj R. S. Dallas, 40 Sqn, encountered two E.A. scouts slightly below and ahead of him; he fired a burst of 50 rounds into the nearest E.A. which fell out of control and crashed near Brebieres.

Capt H. A. Rigby, 1 Sqn, fired a burst from both guns into an E.A. scout which fell to pieces in the air.

Capt L. W. Jarvis, 56 Sqn, led his patrol against seven E.A. scouts and three triplanes. Capt Jarvis engaged a triplane, and after firing 50 rounds into it at close range the E.A. turned on its back and was seen to crash.

Capt D. V. D. Marshall and Lt H.A. Lamb, 98 Sqn, while returning from a bomb raid encountered six E.A. scouts. Capt Marshall dived on the leading E.A. firing a burst of 130 rounds into it from 100 yards range. The E.A. did a steep turn to the left then nose-dived vertically emitting a cloud of black smoke, and was observed by another pilot to go down in flames.

Capt S. T. Edwards, 209 Sqn, fired 100 rounds at close range into the rear machine of a formation of E.A. scouts which went down in a turning vertical dive and was seen to crash.

Maj R. S. Dallas, 40 Sqn, flew over La Brayelle Aerodrome at a low height and fired on the hangars to attract attention. He then dropped a parcel with the following message inside: 'If you won't come up here and fight, herewith one pair of boots for work on the ground. Pilots— for the use of.' Getting into the mist, he waited until a party of men had collected to examine the parcel, when two bombs were dropped, one burst being observed near the target. He also fired 100 rounds into the troops, scattering them and causing a general panic. On the return journey he shot down an E.A. scout.

May 3rd

The weather was fine and enabled a great deal of work to be done ⌒ 25½ tons of bombs were dropped ⌒ Enemy aircraft were active, especially about noon and after 4 p.m., when large formations were encountered in the neighbour- hood of Armentières and south of Arras. Three E.A. were brought down by A.A. in our lines, in addition to those brought down in combat.

On the night of the 2nd–3rd instant, 18 machines of 100 Sqn left the ground at 9.45, but 11 machines were forced to return owing to weather conditions. The remaining seven machines dropped 18 112-lb. bombs on the railways at Amagny-Lucquy, Juniville and Warneville. The visi- bility was bad, but several good bursts were observed, including two O.K.'s on the railway at Amagny-Lucquy.

Capt W. Beaver and Capt N. W. Taylor, 20 Sqn, whilst on offensive patrol with 10 other Bristol Fighters, dived on 12 E.A. scouts. They opened fire at one from about 200 yards range, and after 200 rounds had been fired into it the E.A. went down completely out of control and was seen to crash near Gheluvelt.

Capt T. P. Middleton and Capt F. Godfrey, 20 Sqn, dived on one E.A. scout and followed it down to 2,000 feet, opening fire from 100 feet range. About 200 rounds were fired into the E.A., which turned over on its back and crashed south of Ploegsteert Wood.

Capt D. G. Cooke and Lt H. G. Crowe, 20 Sqn, were attacked by an E.A. triplane into which they fired 50 rounds. The E.A. went down in a steep dive with bursts of flame coming from it at intervals. Shortly after- wards the E.A. burst completely into flames and crashed, still burning, south-east of Hollebeke.

Capt I. D. R. Macdonald, 24 Sqn, attacked an E.A. scout which had been driven down by two other S.E.'s and fired 200 rounds at close range as the E.A. dived. At 3,000 feet the E.A. went into a spin and crashed near a Red Cross Hospital.

Lt W. A. Tyrrell, 32 Sqn, was attacked by two E.A. two-seaters. He manœuvred on to the tail of one E.A. and fired 50 rounds into it at point blank range. The E.A. turned west, followed by Lt Tyrrell, who prevented it from turning east again by firing short bursts, and the E.A. was finally forced to land in our lines about a mile W.S.W. of Poperinghe.

Capt I. P. R. Napier, 40 Sqn, observed an E.A. two-seater being fired at by our A.A. guns; he attacked the E.A. and wounded the observer in the first few minutes of the fight. The E.A. then turned and attempted to attack Capt Napier, who managed to keep behind the E.A. and fire further bursts into it. The E.A. immediately put its nose down, followed by Capt Napier, who fired another burst from both guns into it, whereupon it went down in a spin and crashed.

Capt D. R. MacLaren, 46 Sqn, dived on an E.A. two-seater and fired 75 rounds into it from 50 yards range. The E.A. fell into a spin and then burst into flames. Later Capt MacLaren engaged two more E.A. two-seaters, diving on one from the rear and firing 50 rounds into it from 50 yards range. 2 Lt V. M. Yeates, of the same squadron, also fired 50 rounds into this E.A. Capt MacLaren then dived on the E.A. again, firing another 50 rounds into it. The right-hand wings came off and the E.A. was seen to crash.

Lt T. Durrant, 56 Sqn, fired two bursts of about 40 rounds into an E.A. two-seater which went down out of control and crashed just south of Pozieres. Shortly afterwards Lt Durrant attacked another two-seater, firing a short burst from both guns. He was then compelled to break off the combat owing to jams. The E.A. observer was seen hanging over the side of the cockpit. The E.A. dived steeply, followed by Capt E. D. Atkinson and Lt W. R. Irwin, 56 Sqn, who both fired at it. Lt Irwin continued firing at the E.A. and saw it crash at Montauban.

Capt H. Rees-Jones and 2 Lt J. Bruce-Norton, 62 Sqn, whilst on offensive patrol were attacked by three E.A. scouts; they fired at one of the E.A. which went down in a nose dive and was seen to crash and burst into flames south of Armentières.

Lts W. E. Staton and J. R. Gordon, 62 Sqn, in a general engagement attacked one E.A. scout and fired 50 rounds into it at close range. The E.A. turned over on its back, then dived vertically and started to spin, and was seen to crash and burst into flames about two miles south of Armentières. Later, when Lts Staton and Gordon were rejoining their formation, they encountered an E.A. two-seater which was flying just behind and below the formation. They turned and fired a burst of 50 rounds at close range into the E.A. which went down out of control.

Another burst was fired into the E.A. and it was seen to crash about a mile south-east of Ploegsteert Wood.

Capt T. L. Purdom and Lt P. V. G. Chambers, 62 Sqn, attacked an E.A. two-seater and fired two bursts into it, whereupon the E.A. went down in a fast spin and crashed north of Merville.

Lts E. T. Morrow and H. E. Merritt, 62 Sqn, were attacked by eight E.A. scouts which dived on them from above. 50 rounds were fired at one E.A. which went down in a spin. They then dived on to the E.A. formation and turned and fired at the nearest E.A. from 100 yards range; after firing about 150 rounds the left-hand top plane of the E.A. crumpled up and the enemy machine went down in a spin and was seen to crash.

Lts C. H. Arnison and S. Parry, 62 Sqn, while rejoining their formation were attacked by an E.A. scout from underneath. A long burst was fired at the E.A. which went down and burst into flames.

Capt G. E. Gibbons and Lt S. A. W. Knights, 62 Sqn, dived on three E.A. scouts and then climbed to regain their formation; they then dived again and found there were about 24 E.A. scouts coming up from below. They fired about 100 rounds into one E.A. which went down in flames. Afterwards they dived on another E.A. and fired about 70 rounds into it, passing over the top of the E.A. to avoid collision. Two drums from a double gun were then fired into the E.A. which went down in a slow spin and crashed on the Lille–Carvin road.

Capt P. S. Burge, 64 Sqn, attacked an E.A. two-seater underneath its tail. Lts W. C. Daniels and B. A. Walkerdine, of the same squadron, dived on either side of the E.A. firing about 30 rounds from close range. Lt Daniels then fired a burst of about 100 rounds into the E.A.'s fuselage at point blank range and Lt Walkerdine also fired about 50 rounds. The E.A. fell in flames after Lt Daniels had fired, the tail falling off before the enemy machine reached the ground.

Capt E. R. Tempest, 64 Sqn, dived on an E.A. scout and fired about 170 rounds into it from 150 to 70 yards range. The E.A. fell in a vertical nose dive for about 5,000 feet, appeared to come out of the nose dive for a few seconds and then fell again and was observed to crash. (Confirmed by 56 Sqn.)

Capt L. E. Whitehead, 65 Sqn, dived on one of two E.A. two-seaters, and coming up under the tail of the E.A. fired a long burst from both guns, whereupon the E.A. went down under control and landed on our side of the lines near Heilly.

Lt W. Stephenson, 73 Sqn, in a general engagement between his patrol and a formation of E.A. triplanes and scouts, singled out one E.A. scout and fired about 250 rounds into it. The E.A. went down and was followed for a short distance by Lt Stephenson who watched it going down and eventually nose dive into Ploegsteert Wood.

Zeppelin-Staaken Giant

Charles King

A patrol of 74 Sqn engaged an E.A. two-seater and all fired at it from close range, whereupon the E.A. went down in a spin and was seen to crash. The following officers took part in the combat: Capt E. Mannock, Lt H. E. Dolan, Lt A. C. Kiddie and Lt H. G. Clements.

Capt A. T. Whealy, 203 Sqn, attacked an E.A. two-seater and opened fire at it from a range of about 150 yards. The E.A. commenced to go down in a long dive, followed by Capt Whealy who got to within about 100 yards and then fired a long burst. The E.A. immediately went down in a vertical dive and is confirmed to have crashed into a house about one mile north-east of Lens.

Lt L. R. Warren and Aerial Gunner O'Brien, 206 Sqn, whilst returning from a bomb raid, were attacked by seven E.A. scouts. They fired 170 rounds into the foremost E.A., which went down in a nose dive and was seen to crash.

Lt E. D. Cummings, 2 Sqn, A.F.C., attacked an E.A. triplane and fired a burst from both guns into it. The E.A. immediately went down in a spin followed by Lt Cummings, still firing. The E.A. then turned on its back and finally crashed north-east of Meteren. At this point Lt Cummings was attacked by four E.A. triplanes, who shot away his elevator controls, instrument board, petrol and oil; his machine went down almost out of control but he managed to keep it out of a spin until it reached the ground in our front line, where it crashed. His safety belt broke and he was thrown clear of the machine into a shell-hole, where he remained until he was able to get shelter in one of our trenches. Our infantry confirm that the E.A. attacked by Lt Cummings crashed and burst into flames on reaching the ground.

Lt E. R. Jeffree, 4 Sqn, A.F.C., dived on to an E.A. scout and opened fire from close range, following the E.A. down to about 500 feet when it side-slipped to the ground and was seen to crash.

Capt Batchelor and Sgt Badger, 214 Sqn, bombed Zeebrugge Lock Gates. Three 550-lb. bombs were dropped from 200 feet and fell in close proximity but west of the objective. Considerable anti-aircraft and machine gun fire was experienced over Zeebrugge Mole, and location of the objective was difficult owing to the number of searchlights which were concentrated on the machine.

May 4th
There was a thick mist and rain ⌒ Over 12 tons of bombs were dropped.

Lt H. A. Hay and Sgt P. A. Sherlock, 11 Sqn, whilst on reconnaissance were attacked by six E.A. scouts; they opened fire on the leading E.A. which dived steeply after a burst of 50 rounds had been fired into it and was later observed to burst into flames.

May 5th

Low clouds, mist and rain greatly interfered with flying ∽ 11¼ tons of bombs were dropped ∽ Enemy aircraft activity was very slight; no combats took place.

Enemy machines were also driven down out of control during the period under review by:

Sqn 1 Lt P. J. Clayson. **3** Lt W. Hubbard/Lt W. D. Tipton. **19** Maj A. D. Carter, Lt L. W. Hustings, Capt J. Leacroft. **32** Lt W. A. Tyrrell (2). **41** Capt H. T. Fox-Russell. **43** Lt G. G. Bailey, Lt G. A. Lingham. **46** Capt D. R. MacLaren/ 2 Lt R. K. McConnell/Lt H. L. M. Dobson, Capt C. J. Marchant/2 Lt J. H. Smith, Lt A. G. Vlasto. **56** Lt H. J. Burden, Lt T. Durrant, Lt T. Durrant/Lt R. W. Irwin, Capt L. W. Jarvis/2 Lt C. Parry. **62** Lts C. H. Arnison + S. Parry (2), Lt H. C. M. Nangle + 2 Lt T. C. Cooper, Capt T. L. Purdom + Lt P. V. G. Chambers, Capt H. Rees-Jones + 2 Lt J. Bruce-Norton. **73** Lt G. L. Graham, Capt G. A. H. Pidcock. **84** Lt W. A. Southey. **98** Capt D. V. D. Marshall + Lt H. A. Lamb. **201** Lt H. P. Guard, Capt S. M. Kinkead/Lt H. L. Wallace/Lt R. E. Bright/Lt H. Riddell/Lt G. C. Brading/Lt A. G. A. Spence, Capt C. B. Ridley. **203** Capt H. F. Beamish, Lt E. T. Hayme. **208** Capt W. L. Jordan. **209** Capt S. T. Edwards.

HONOURS AND AWARDS

DSO Maj C. F. A. Portal (Bar), MC, Lt J. E. G. Mosby. **DSC** Capt D. R. Lupton (Bar). **MC** Capt J. Gilmour (Bar), Lt J. L. Morgan, Capt D. McK. McGoun, Capt the Hon R. A. Grosvenor, Lt D. M. Dening, 2 Lt W. E. MacLean, 2 Lt H. W. Collier, 2 Lt J. W. Wallwork, Capt A. W. F. Glenny (Bar), 2 Lt J. J. Quinn, Lt J. J. Sweeney, Lt A. Lomax, 2 Lt A. G. Wilson, Lt L. H. Short, Capt T. Owen, Lt J. E. M. Middleton, Lt J. A. G. Haslam, Lt F. M. F. West, Lt D. A. Savage. **DCM** Cpl P. A. Ovenden, Sgt F. Johnson (Bar).

6 – 12 May

The V.C. awarded to Lt A. A. McLeod, 2 Sqn, was for an action on 27 March 1918, before the formation of the R.A.F.

Lt R. G. Landis, 40 Sqn, credited with a victory on 8 May, was one of the small group of Americans sent to train with the R.F.C. in 1917. Later he was given command of an American squadron.

Lt J. I. T. Jones, who gained a victory on 8 May, ended the war with a score of 40.

COMMUNIQUÉ NO. 6

During the period under review we have claimed officially 84 E.A. brought down and 24 E.A. driven down out of control. In addition, one E.A. has been brought down by A.A. Twenty-eight of our machines are missing. Approximately 84 tons of bombs were dropped and 7,349 photographs taken.

May 6th

The weather was again bad, with low clouds, mist and rain ∽ 1½ tons of bombs were dropped ∽ Enemy aircraft activity was practically nil until the evening when a certain amount of fighting took place.

A patrol of 46 Sqn attacked an E.A. two-seater, which they shot down on our side of the lines. The following officers took part in the combat: Capt D. R. MacLaren, Capt C. J. Marchant, 2 Lt J. H. Smith, 2 Lt V. M. Yeates and 2 Lt H. T. W. Manwaring.

2 Lts W. S. Hill-Tout and A. G. H. Williamson, 22 Sqn, dived on one E.A. scout, which they shot down out of control. Another pilot of 22 Sqn confirms this E.A. as having crashed near Fresnoy.

Lt H. E. Dolan, 74 Sqn, fired about 130 rounds at close range into an E.A. triplane, which was seen to crash near the east corner of Zillebeke Lake.

Capt E. Mannock, 74 Sqn, engaged one E.A. triplane and forced it into a spin. He followed the E.A. down, firing short bursts and the E.A. finally turned on its back and crashed.

2 Lt F. H. Baguley and Lt C. A. Horn, 2 Sqn, whilst on artillery patrol were attacked by an E.A. scout. Fire was opened on the E.A. at a range of about 200 yards; the E.A. dived to within 20 yards and then

zoomed up. Immediately afterwards it dived down steeply and when about 100 feet from the ground burst into flames and finally crashed on our side of the lines.

Lt H. A. R. Biziou, 87 Sqn, dived on an E.A. two-seater and followed it down to 3,000 feet. The E.A. then emitted clouds of black smoke and was seen to crash.

Lt W. J. Duncan, 60 Sqn, together with 2 Lt J. S. Griffith, of the same squadron, engaged an E.A. scout which they followed down to within 200 feet of the ground, firing continuously at it. The E.A. appeared to be very well-handled, but it suddenly dived vertically and crashed just behind a line of trenches.

Lt R. Roxburgh-Smith, 74 Sqn, shot down an E.A. triplane, which is confirmed by an A.A. battery as having crashed.

May 7th

Rain impeded flying ∽ 6¾ tons of bombs were dropped ∽ There was practically no enemy aircraft activity until the evening when a large enemy formation was encountered by 22 Sqn in the vicinity of Douai.

102 Sqn dropped 111 25-lb. bombs on Warlencourt–Ervillers–St. Leger Road, Bapaume and neighbourhood, during the night 6th–7th.

2 Lts A. C. Atkey and C. G. Gass, 22 Sqn, encountered seven E.A. in the vicinity of Henin-Liétard. These E.A. were also attacked by 2 Lts J. E. Gurdon and A. J. H. Thornton, 22 Sqn, and a general engagement ensued during which the E.A. were reinforced by two other formations which made their total up to twenty. During the fierce fight, which lasted half-an-hour, several E.A. were seen to spin away. Eight E.A. were accounted for as follows: 2 Lts Atkey and Gass, two E.A. in flames and three crashed; 2 Lts Gurdon and Thornton, two E.A. in flames and one crashed.

Capt R. N. C. Fenton and Lt P. H. Clarke, 21 Sqn, whilst on patrol were attacked by an E.A. two-seater into which they fired one drum, opening fire at about 70 yards range. The E.A. stopped firing, banked and was lost to sight in the mist. Shortly afterwards an E.A. of the same type was seen lying on its back on the ground in the vicinity of the combat. 3rd Division report that they saw an E.A. crash in the same locality which they think was hit in aerial combat.

Lt F. V. Hall, 210 Sqn, fired 200 rounds into one E.A. scout which went down out of control and was seen to crash by another pilot of 210 Sqn.

Lt K. C. Mills, 1 Sqn, got on the tail of an E.A. scout and kept there for some time, firing continuously. The E.A. dived very steeply and was followed down to 50 feet by Lt Mills, who saw the E.A. crash vertically into some trees about one mile east of Kemmel.

Sopwith Camel fighter of No. 209 Squadron and Handley Page 0/400 night bomber

Top: Albatros D VA fighter

Bottom: Halberstadt CL II fighter reconnaissance aircraft

Lt H. N. Young and 2 Lt H. B. Davis, 8 Sqn, were attacked by two E.A. scouts into one of which they fired about 120 rounds, and the E.A. was observed to crash.

Lts D. H. Phillips and A. J. Ord, 8 Sqn, fired 200 rounds into one E.A. scout which went down in a slow spin and was seen to crash.

Lts Pithey and Rhodes, 12 Sqn, fired three bursts of 10 rounds each into a hostile balloon which immediately burst into flames.

May 8th

The weather was fine, but there was a certain amount of ground mist during the morning, which, however, lifted in the north, but continued thick throughout the day in the south $\sim 10\frac{1}{4}$ tons of bombs were dropped by day $\sim$ There was considerable enemy aircraft activity in the north, but practically none in the south. One E.A. was brought down in our lines by infantry fire.

2 Lts E. C. Bromley and J. H. Umney, 22 Sqn, dived on an E.A. two-seater, then pulled out of the dive and fired two bursts from the back gun into the E.A., which went down in a nose-dive and was seen to crash.

2 Lts G. W. Bulmer and P. S. Williams, 22 Sqn, dived on one E.A. scout, which went down out of control, and finally crumpled up.

Lt S. F. Thompson and Sgt L. Kendrick, 22 Sqn, engaged one E.A. two-seater. The E.A. observer was almost immediately seen to collapse into the cockpit. A burst was then fired into the E.A. from the back gun, and the enemy machine immediately burst into flames and crashed south-east of Arras.

2 Lt S. H. Wallage and Lt G. Thomson, 22 Sqn, engaged a formation of five E.A. scouts, one of which they shot down and observed to crash north of La Bassée.

2 Lts J. E. Gurdon and C. G. Gass, 22 Sqn, fired a burst of about 100 rounds into an E.A. two-seater, which went down steeply and was seen to crash near Cuincy.

Maj A. D. Carter, 19 Sqn, dived on to an E.A. scout and fired a long burst into it at long range. Lt G. B. Irving, of the same squadron, also fired several bursts into the E.A., which went down in a vertical dive, and pieces were seen to come off the fuselage of the E.A.

Lts D. Latimer and T. C. Noel, 20 Sqn, fired about 100 rounds into an E.A. scout, which went down out of control, and later burst into flames.

Lt V. E. Groom and 2 Lt E. Hardcastle, 20 Sqn, fired bursts of 200 rounds from the front gun and 100 rounds from the rear gun into an E.A. triplane which fell completely out of control and crashed near Wervicq.

Capt D. G. Cooke and Lt H. G. Crowe, 20 Sqn, dived on an E.A. triplane and fired 100 rounds into it from the front gun at close range.

They then turned and fired another 50 rounds into it from the rear gun and the E.A. went down out of control and crashed between Comines and Wervieq.

Capts T. P. Middleton and F. Godfrey, 20 Sqn, dived on an E.A. scout, but their front gun jammed. A further 80 rounds were fired into the E.A. from the back gun and it went down out of control, and is confirmed by another pilot of 20 Sqn to have crashed south-east of Bailleul.

Later, they engaged a Fokker triplane and fired 200 rounds into it from the back gun. The E.A. went down in a slow glide which suddenly turned into a nose dive and it was seen to hit the ground east of Dranoutre.

Lts D. Latimer and T. C. Noel, 20 Sqn, fired a long burst at close range into an E.A. triplane, which went down out of control and was seen to crash between Comines and Wervicq.

Lt J. E. Pugh and 2 Lt W. Dixon, 25 Sqn, whilst returning from a long-distance reconnaissance were attacked by a formation of six E.A. They fired 40 rounds into the leader which went down emitting smoke; following it down they fired a further 50 or 60 rounds into the E.A. which continued its dive and burst into flames.

Capt A. Claydon, 32 Sqn, engaged one E.A. scout and fired about 150 rounds into it at point blank range and saw the E.A. pilot fall over in his seat; shortly afterwards the E.A. burst into flames.

Lt K. G. P. Hendrie, 32 Sqn, dived on to the rear machine of a formation of E.A. scouts and fired 80 rounds into it at point blank range; the E.A. was seen to go down in flames.

Lt W. A. Tyrrell, 32 Sqn, fired about 100 rounds at point blank range into an E.A. scout which went down in a steep spiral and afterwards in a vertical nose dive and was seen to crash in the neighbourhood of Sailly-en-Ostrevent.

Lt L. Seymour, 40 Sqn, drove down one E.A. scout to a height of 2,000 feet and finally fired a long burst from both guns into the E.A. which crashed into the ground near Vitry-en-Artois.

Lt J. I. T. Jones, 74 Sqn, observed an enemy two-seater and dived at it from the sun; about 60 rounds were fired into the E.A. from close range and it fell in flames and crashed near the village of Nieppe.

Capts Clarke and St. John, 206 Sqn, fired about 50 rounds into an E.A. scout which went down in a spin and burst into flames, and the wings were seen to break off.

Lt G. A. Cox, 208 Sqn, fired two bursts of 100 rounds each into an E.A. scout which fell out of control and crashed near Provin.

Lt E. G. Johnstone, 208 Sqn, fired a short burst at one E.A. scout at close range. He then attacked it again, firing a further 200 rounds into it, whereupon the E.A. turned on its back, side-slipped and fell completely out of control, finally crashing near Meurchin.

Whilst returning from a bomb raid, a formation of 98 Sqn were attacked by about 20 E.A. scouts. One E.A. dived on to Lt R. E. Dubber and Sgt E. R. Macdonald, who fired one drum into it and the E.A. was seen to burst into flames and fall to pieces about 2,000 feet below. Another E.A. was engaged by Capt E. A. Fawcus and Lt G. D. Dardis. Two bursts were fired at close range into this E.A. which immediately dived and the planes folded back and then broke off. A third E.A. was engaged by Lts C. C. Macdonald and C. P. Harrison who fired one drum into it, the E.A. immediately bursting into flames and falling to pieces in the air.

May 9th
The weather was fine with considerable haze ⌀ 27 tons of bombs were dropped ⌀ Enemy aircraft were fairly active on the whole front, and especially so on the fronts of the 1st and 3rd Brigades.

2 Lt D. W. Beard and Sgt V. H. Davis, 11 Sqn, in a general engagement between a patrol of Bristol fighters and a formation of E.A. scouts, dived on one E.A., fired about 60 rounds into it at 50 yards range and later another 40 rounds at very close range into the same E.A. The E.A. side-slipped and turned on its back and was followed down to 7,000 feet and was then observed to crash one mile west of Combles.

Lts L. M. Price and A. Mills, 20 Sqn, whilst on offensive patrol with nine other Bristol fighters, engaged a formation of E.A. triplanes. One of the E.A. got on to the tail of their machine and two drums were fired into it, whereupon the E.A. burst into flames and fell burning.

Lt D. E. Smith and 2 Lt F. J. Ralph, 20 Sqn, dived on one E.A. triplane which is confirmed by another pilot of the patrol to have crashed near the Canal south-west of Menin.

Lt V. M. Thomson and 2 Lt G. H. Kemp, 20 Sqn, were cut off from their formation by an E.A. scout; they emptied a whole drum into the E.A. which side-slipped and nose dived, eventually crashing into the ground between Comines and Wervicq.

Capt W. Beaver and Cpl E. A. Deighton, 20 Sqn, dived on one E.A. scout and followed it down several thousand feet. The E.A. eventually started spinning and crashed near the Canal east of Warneton.

Capt A. C. Atkey and 2 Lt C. G. Gass, 22 Sqn, fired a short burst into one E.A. scout which immediately went down in flames in a vertical nose dive. On another patrol later on in the day the same pilot and observer dived on a formation of eight E.A. and fired about 50 rounds into one at close range. The E.A. at which they had fired was seen to dive steeply, with flames issuing from behind the pilot's seat, and this is confirmed by another pilot and observer of the same patrol.

2 Lts J. E. Gurdon and A. V. Bollins, 22 Sqn, in an engagement with a formation of seven E.A. scouts, shot down one E.A. in flames.

Capt H. W. Woollett, 43 Sqn, led his patrol against six E.A. scouts. The E.A. almost immediately turned east, chased by the patrol, and Capt Woollett fired 40 rounds into one E.A. which spun and crashed just south of La Gorgue.

Lt G. G. Bailey, 43 Sqn, dived with the rest of his patrol on six E.A. scouts and followed one which was diving east. After a burst had been fired into it the E.A. turned over on its back and broke up in the air.

Two E.A. triplanes dived on a patrol of 46 Sqn. One of the E.A. got on to the tail of Lt R. K. McConnell's machine and fired a burst which shot both spars through and a centre section wire. In order to entice the E.A. down Lt McConnell let his machine fall as though out of control, swerving aside, however, each time the E.A. dived and fired. This ruse having succeeded, Lt H. L. M. Dodson attacked the E.A., firing 150 rounds into it at close range. The E.A. stalled and went down in a spin for about 1,000 feet then came out of the spin and almost immediately went into another as though its controls had been shot away. It went down alternately spinning and recovering, and eventually crashed badly in attempting to land. Lt J. H. Smith, 46 Sqn, also fired a burst of 50 rounds into this E.A.

2 Lt T. G. Jackson and Lt A. E. Ansell, 48 Sqn, fired a long burst into one of several E.A. scouts. The E.A. went down in a spin and was seen to crash close to Vauvillers.

Lts C. H. Arnison and H. E. Merritt, 62 Sqn, fired about 30 rounds into an E.A. scout which was attacking another Bristol fighter. Tracers were seen going into the cock-pit of the E.A. which went down in a dive and was seen to crash south of Herlies.

Lt T. Rose, 64 Sqn, dived into position under the tail of a Rumpler two-seater and fired about 50 rounds at a range of between 75 and 50 yards. The E.A. went down in a spinning nose dive and was seen to crash and burst into flames on hitting the ground.

Capt J. Gilmour, 65 Sqn, dived on two E.A. two-seaters and fired a short burst at one which went down vertically. He then attacked the other E.A. and on turning observed the first E.A. crashing into the ground north-east of Aubercourt.

Lt M. H. Findlay, 201 Sqn, led his flight against eight E.A. scouts. He fired 200 rounds into one E.A. which immediately went down in a spin and crashed near Bapaume.

Lt R. McLaughlin, 201 Sqn, singled out one E.A. and fired a burst of about 50 rounds into it at close range. The E.A. immediately went down in a slow spin and finally broke up in the air. The wreckage of this E.A. was seen by another pilot to crash.

Capt A. T. Whealy, 203 Sqn, got on to the tail of one E.A. scout and fired a good burst into it. The E.A. fell out of control and is reported by the rest of 203 Sqn's patrol to have crashed about one mile east of Herlies.

Capt H. B. Beamish, 203 Sqn, fired a burst of about 100 rounds at close range into an E.A. triplane which was diving on one of our machines. The E.A. fell completely out of control and crashed in the vicinity of Herlies.

Capt O. C. le Boutillier, 203 Sqn, encountered a formation of E.A. triplanes and got on to the tail of one, firing about 150 rounds into it at 50 yards range. The E.A. went down in a vertical nose dive and was later seen crashed on the ground.

Capt A. W. Carter, 210 Sqn, got close to an E.A. two-seater before he was observed. He witheld his fire until within 15 yards and then fired a burst of about 50 rounds into the cockpit of the E.A. which immediately dived vertically. Capt Carter then fired a further 100 rounds into the E.A. and Capt E. S. Arnold and Lt F. V. Hall, of the same squadron, also fired bursts into it as it dived. The E.A. fell completely out of control and is confirmed by all the pilots of the flight to have crashed.

Lt W. Gillman and 2 Lt R. Lardner, 211 Sqn, whilst returning from a bomb raid encountered an E.A. triplane. A few rounds were fired into the E.A. and it went down in flames over Zeebrugge Mole.

Lt J. A. Adam, 2 Sqn, A.F.C., manœuvred to cut off one E.A. scout from its formation. He then dived on it and fired a burst of about 50 rounds whereupon the E.A. turned over on its side. Lt F. R. Smith of the same squadron then engaged the E.A. and fired a burst of about 90 rounds into it. The E.A. went down out of control and crashed near Marcoing.

A patrol of 4 Sqn, A.F.C., were dived on by nine E.A. scouts one of which shot through the petrol tank of Lt P. K. Scharfer's machine and forced it to descend, diving vertically followed by two E.A. scouts. One of the latter broke up in the air and crashed east of St. Eloi and burst into flames on hitting the ground.

Lt J. A. E. R. Daley, 24 Sqn, fired about 180 rounds into an E.A. scout, which spun down through a thin layer of clouds, flattened out, and finally crashed into a wood.

2 Lt T. T. B. Hellett, 24 Sqn, dived on an E.A. scout, firing about 160 rounds into it. 2 Lt W. C. Lambert, of the same squadron, also dived on this E.A. and fired 100 rounds into it. The E.A. went down in a spin from 5,000 feet and was seen to crash in a field.

Capt H. W. Woollett, 43 Sqn, whilst returning from patrol, fired about 50 rounds into a hostile balloon (just north-east of La Gorgue).

The balloon immediately fell in flames—no one was seen to jump out.

May 10th
The weather was fine but very misty, and practically no flying was possible in the North ◇ *21¾ tons of bombs were dropped* ◇ *There was some enemy aircraft activity in the south during the late afternoon.*

Lt R. H. Little and 2 Lt H. F. Lumb, 48 Sqn, whilst on patrol engaged one of a formation of E.A. triplanes, diving upon it and firing a burst of 50 rounds into it. As they came out of the dive two E.A. passed under the tail of their machine; a long burst fired from the back gun into the first of the two E.A. and it fell over on to one wing and went down out of control, emitting smoke and later burst into flames.

Lt H. J. Burden, 56 Sqn, fired a long burst into an E.A. scout which was attacking one of our machines. The E.A. went down in a steep spiral with smoke coming from its cock-pit, and when at about 6,000 feet burst into flames, went down in a spin and was seen to crash.

A patrol of 65 Sqn dived on a single E.A. scout. The whole patrol fired into the E.A. which went down out of control and was last seen spinning below 1,000 feet, and has since been confirmed by A.A. as having crashed. The following officers took part in the combat: Capt J. Gilmour, 2 Lts T. Williams, H. Brown, W. F. Scott-Kerr, H. Spreadbury and M. Newnham.

Capt A. W. B.-Proctor, 84 Sqn, observed an E.A. two-seater getting its height. Capt Proctor stalked the E.A. and waited for it to cross the lines; but the E.A. dived east on observing the formation of 84 Sqn. Capt Proctor immediately dived at the E.A. and fired a burst of 50 rounds into it. The E.A. observer disappeared into the cock-pit and did not fire again. Capt Proctor then got closer to the E.A. and again opened fire, and the E.A. appeared to be out of control. After a further burst had been fired into it the E.A. went down in a vertical nose dive and was watched down to 4,000 feet and was then lost owing to haze, but is confirmed by another pilot of 84 Sqn to have crashed near the River Somme south-east of Bray.

Capt S. M. Kinkead, 201 Sqn, attacked one of three E.A. scouts and fired a burst of about 50 rounds into it at point blank range. Tracers were seen to enter the cock-pit and the E.A. stalled and went down out of control. Capt Kinkead was unable to watch this E.A. crash owing to the presence of other E.A., but A.A. report having seen it crash.

Capt F. W. Knight and Cpl F. Y. McLauchlan, 27 Sqn, whilst returning from a bomb raid with a formation of their squadron were attacked by about thirty E.A. triplanes and scouts. They fired 350 rounds into one triplane which was seen to fall in flames.

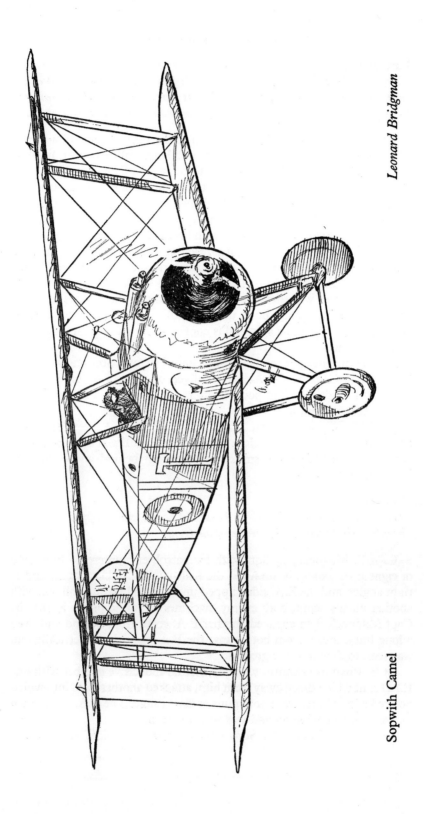

Leonard Bridgman

Sopwith Camel

May 11th

There was thick mist all day on the whole front with the exception of one short clear interval ◌ Over 8 tons of bombs were dropped ◌ Enemy aircraft activity was practically nil until the evening and then it was below normal.

Capt E. Mannock, 74 Sqn, dived on to the rear machine of a formation of E.A. scouts and drove it down to a height of 6,000 feet, firing as occasion offered. The E.A. was seen to burst into flames.

Capt W. M. Fry, 79 Sqn, got on to the tail of one E.A. triplane and chased it down, firing short bursts. When at about 4,000 feet the E.A. turned over and fell out of control and was seen to crash near Bray.

Capt O. C. Bridgeman, 80 Sqn, with his patrol was attacked by a large number of E.A. scouts and triplanes. He immediately turned to meet the attack and engaged one E.A. scout at close range. The E.A. went down in a spin and is confirmed by two other pilots to have burst into flames. Capt Bridgeman was then attacked from above by a triplane and succeeded in getting a good burst into the E.A. at close range, whereupon the E.A. went down in a spin and is confirmed by other pilots of 79 Sqn to have crashed.

During an engagement between a patrol of 210 Sqn and about 30 E.A. scouts, Capt W. M. Alexander dived on the tail of one E.A. and fired 150 rounds into it at point blank range. The E.A. dived vertically and burst into flames.

Lt H. G. Watson, 4 Sqn, A.F.C., engaged one E.A. scout and fired about 50 rounds into it at close range. The E.A. dived vertically for a short distance with black smoke issuing from behind and eventually broke up in the air.

May 12th

There were low clouds all day ◌ 8½ tons of bombs were dropped ◌ Enemy aircraft activity was slight on the whole front.

Capt E. Mannock, 74 Sqn, with his patrol, encountered a formation of eight E.A. scouts; he attacked the rear machine at close range and at right angles, and the E.A. side-slipped underneath him and collided with another enemy scout, both enemy machines falling to pieces in the air. Capt Mannock then engaged another E.A. scout from behind and fired a long burst into it from both guns; the E.A. went down vertically and was seen to dive into the ground.

Lt B. Roxburgh-Smith, 74 Sqn, after an indecisive combat with one E.A. scout which dived away from him, attacked another E.A. into which he fired a long burst from both guns at close range. The E.A. went down in a spin with engine on and was seen to crash.

Capt W. E. Young, 74 Sqn, fired a burst at an E.A. scout which crossed his front; he watched the E.A. down and saw it spinning to the ground north of Wulverghem.

Lt W. B. Giles, 74 Sqn, dived on an E.A. scout and fired bursts from both guns into it. The E.A. turned over on to its back but recovered close to the ground and flew east very low as if to land. Observing this, Lt Giles dived on the E.A. from 5,000 feet and fired a further burst into it. The E.A. dived and made off east. (This E.A. has been confirmed as having crashed in the vicinity of Wulverghem by another pilot of 74 Sqn.)

Enemy machines were also driven down out of control during the period under review by:

Sqn 11 2 Lt D. W. Beard + Sgt V. H. Davis, Lts D. C. M. Brooks + H. R. Kincaid, Lts J. S. Chick + E. C. Gilroy (2), Lts E. S. Coler + C. W. Gladman (3), Lts R. F. Mullins + N. F. Brace. **12** 2 Lts N. Garland + R. Rhodes. **18** 2 Lt H. R. Gould + Capt M. S. E. Archibald. **19** Lt J. D. Hardman. **20** Lts D. Latimer + T. C. Noel (2). **22** Capt A. C. Atkey + 2 Lt C. G. Gass (3), 2 Lts E. C. Bromley + J. H. Umney (2), 2 Lts G. W. Bulmer + H. E. Elsworth, 2 Lts J. E. Gurdon + A. V. Bollins (2), 2 Lts J. E. Gurdon + A. J. H. Thornton, 2 Lts L. W. King + H. E. Elsworth, Lt S. F. Thompson + Sgt L. Kendrick. **24** Capt C. N. Lowe. **25** Lt J. E. Pugh + 2 Lt W. Dixon. **27** 2 Lts G. E. French + F. A. Gledhill, Lt S. W. Taylor + Sgt V. Cummins. **32** Capt A. Claydon, Lt H. C. Leese, Capt S. B. Simpson. **40** Maj R. S. Dallas, Lt R. G. Landis, USA Air Service (attached). **43** Lt C. Banks, Lt G. D. Daly, Capt C. F. King. **46** Capt D. R. MacLaren (2), Lt A. G. Vlasto. **48** 2 Lt T. G. Jackson + Lt A. E. Ansell, Lt R. H. Little + 2 Lt F. H. Lumb. **56** Capt E. D. G. Galley. **60** Lt A. W. Saunders. **62** Lts C. H. Arnison + H. E. Merritt, Capts G. F. Hughes + H. Claye, Lt G. K. Runciman + 2 Lt A. J. Todd. **64** Lt C. A. Bisonette (2), Lt T. Rose. **74** 2 Lt J. I. T. Jones. **80** Lt H. V. Barker, Lt C. S. L. Coulson. **84** Capt J. V. Sorsoleil. **98** Lts F. Smethurst + E. G. T. Chubb, Lts C. D. Taylor + J. R. Jackman. **201** Lt J. H. Forman. **208** Lt G. K. Cooper, Maj C. Draper, Lt H. H. S. Fowler, Lts H. H. S. Fowler/G. A. Whiteman, Capt W. L. Jordan, Lt W. E. G. Mann (2), Lt J. B. White. **2 AFC** Lt J. Adam, Lt J. H. Blaxland.

HONOURS AND AWARDS

VC 2 Lt Alan Arnett McLeod. **DSC** Capt T. F. le Mesurier (2nd Bar), Capt A. R. Brown (Bar). **MC** 2 Lt A. F. McGlasham, Capt I. D. R. MacDonald, 2 Lt G. R. Riley, 2 Lt A. B. Whiteside (Bar), 2 Lt E. F. Howard. **MSM** 1 AM J. I. Hardy, Pte A. Mill.

13 – 19 May

This was a period of considerable activity, with casualties on both sides the heaviest since 1 April.

It was a very successful week for the six two-seat Bristol Fighter squadrons operating on the Front, which together claimed 46 enemy aircraft destroyed or shot down out of control.

Capt P. J. Clayson, 1 Sqn, who claimed a victory on 14 May, was another leading 'ace', whose final score was 21.

The A.E.G. twin-engined bomber which landed in the British lines on 16 May is probably the one later sent to England for evaluation, and based for a time at Biggin Hill.

COMMUNIQUÉ NO. 7

During the period under review we have claimed officially 130 E.A. brought down and 32 driven out of control. In addition, nine E.A. have been brought down by A.A. Fifty-two of our machines are missing. Approximately 193¼ tons of bombs were dropped and 13,964 photographs taken.

May 13th
The weather was fine early, but later rain set in, making flying impossible ◇ *21¾ tons of bombs were dropped* ◇ *Except for enemy two-seaters, which were active on the 3rd Brigade front, enemy aircraft activity was very slight.*

Lt J. H. Jennings and 2 Lt J. H. Hay, 2 Sqn, engaged an E.A. two-seater, which followed them back to their aerodrome. Leaving the ground again they overtook the E.A. and dived on it, firing several bursts into it. Capt I. D. R. Napier, 40 Sqn, then dived on this E.A. and fired a long burst into it, and Lt Jennings fired a further burst. The E.A. stalled, went down in a spin and was seen to crash near Lacouture.

Lt T. Durrant, 56 Sqn, fired about 100 rounds into an E.A. two-seater, which went down in a vertical dive, then turned on its back and crashed on the railway line south-west of Beaucourt.

May 14th
The sky was overcast, with occasional clear gaps ◇ *2¼ tons of bombs were dropped* ◇ *Enemy aircraft activity was slight with the exception of on the*

3rd Brigade front, where a number of two-seater E.A. were encountered. One E.A. was brought down in our lines by A.A. and one by infantry fire from the ground.

Capt P. J. Clayson, 1 Sqn, opened fire at one E.A. scout at long range and closed to 150 yards; when he had fired about 100 rounds at it, the right-hand wings of the E.A. folded back and it started to spin with smoke issuing from the fuselage. The E.A. broke to pieces in the air and the wreckage was seen to hit the ground.

Lt W. Hubbard, 3 Sqn, whilst flying through the clouds, almost collided with an E.A. two-seater which was crossing his front at the same height. He fired a long burst from both guns into it and saw the observer jump to his feet; at the same moment the E.A. banked steeply and began side-slipping. Lt Hubbard then fired another burst at point blank range which caused black smoke to issue from the pilot's seat, and the E.A. nose dived and burst into flames. Lt Hubbard was then attacked by another E.A. two-seater which dived on him but overshot him; he then got on the tail of the E.A. and fired a short burst into it. Immediately the right-hand lower plane folded back and came off and the E.A. went down completely out of control and was seen to crash near Vaux.

Capt A. G. Waller and Lt F. T. R. Kempster, 18 Sqn, fired several bursts into a formation of eight E.A. scouts, one of which was seen to go down out of control and has since been confirmed by A.A. to have crashed.

Lts D. Latimer and T. C. Noel, 20 Sqn, whilst leading a formation of Bristol fighters, encountered eight E.A. scouts; they fired 80 rounds at one E.A. which went down out of control and was seen to crash. A burst was then fired from the back gun into another E.A. which went down out of control, spinning and diving, and crashed in a field.

Lt V. E. Groom and 2 Lt E. Hardcastle, 20 Sqn, followed one E.A. scout down to 3,000 feet and kept on its tail, firing all the while; the E.A. continued to dive and crashed about three miles east of Zillebeke Lake. They were then attacked by an E.A. two-seater into which they fired a whole drum from the back gun, and the E.A. went down and crashed south-west of Polygon Wood.

Lt W. M. Thomson and 2 Lt G. H. Kemp, 20 Sqn, followed one E.A. scout down to 4,000 feet; about 100 rounds were fired at this E.A. at close quarters, and as Lt Thomson pulled his machine out of the dive, his observer (2 Lt Kemp) watched the E.A. down to the ground and saw it crash.

2 Lt H. G. Hegarty, 60 Sqn, observed an E.A. two-seater flying west at a low height. Lt Hegarty attacked the E.A. and fired 300 rounds at a range of 100 yards, closing until he almost collided with the E.A. The

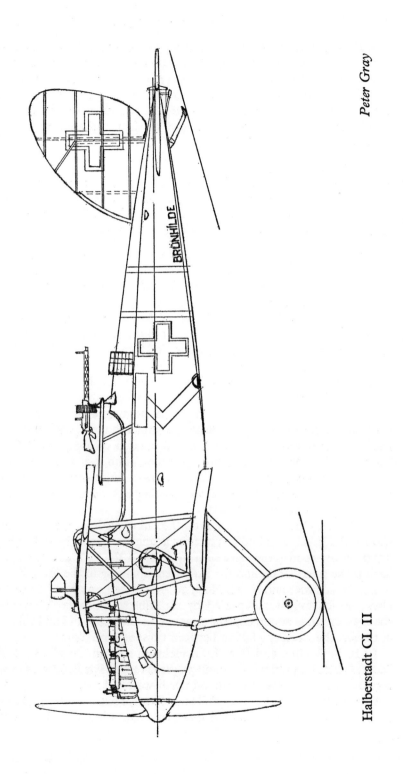

Halberstadt CL II

Peter Gray

E.A. side-slipped to the ground and attempted to land on a small hill
with trenches on the crest, ran into the trenches and half turned over.

Capt A. T. Whealy, 203 Sqn, dived on an E.A. two-seater, which in
turn dived away east. Capt Whealy got to within 100 yards of it and
fired a burst of about 150 rounds. The E.A. fell out of control and was
seen by other pilots of 203 Sqn to have crashed in the vicinity east of
Richebourg.

May 15th

*The weather was fine all day ⌢ 34¾ tons of bombs were dropped ⌢ Enemy
aircraft were active in the early morning and again in the evening, chiefly in
the south. One enemy machine was brought down by machine gun fire from
the ground, in addition to those brought down in combat.*

Capt J. W. Aldred, 3 Sqn, dived under the tail of an E.A. two-seater
and fired good bursts into it. The E.A. turned south and fell out of
control, emitting black smoke. Capt Aldred was unable to follow the
E.A. owing to the presence of two large formations of hostile scouts, but
the E.A. which he attacked is reported by A.A. to have fallen in flames.

Lts J. S. Chick and E. C. Gilroy, 11 Sqn, dived on one E.A. and
opened fire at 100 yards range. A burst of flame was seen in the E.A.
observer's cockpit, followed by clouds of smoke. Immediately afterwards Very lights of many colours were seen to explode and the E.A.
went down in flames.

Lts Chick and Gilroy, 11 Sqn, whilst leading a patrol of Bristol
fighters, observed 16 Fokker triplanes and attacked them, with indecisive
results. Shortly after, they attacked a formation of about 20 E.A. Lt
Chick dived on one E.A. and fired 50 rounds into it at about 30 yards
range and it was seen by Lt Gilroy to crash south-east of Albert. A
burst of 30 rounds was then fired into another E.A. scout which crashed
into a house south-east of Albert.

Maj A. D. Carter, 19 Sqn, got on the tail of an E.A. triplane which
was attacking another Dolphin; he fired a long burst into the E.A. which
dived. Pieces of material were seen flying from the E.A. and the right-
hand plane then fell off and the E.A. went spinning to the ground.

Lts D. Latimer and T. C. Noel, 20 Sqn, dived on one of three triplanes which were accompanied by six Albatross Scouts. They fired
about 100 rounds at one triplane which fell out of control and broke up
in the air, the wreckage falling between Comines and Ypres.

Lt F. E. Boulton and Pbr H. G. Holman, 20 Sqn, dived on a Pfalz
Scout, firing at it until within about 30 yards range. The E.A. went down
vertically and spun into the ground north-west of Lille.

Capt R. H. Rusby, 29 Sqn, while on offensive patrol, dived on to one
of two E.A. two-seaters and fired about 100 rounds into it at close range.

Two large bursts of flame were observed issuing from the pilot's seat and the E.A. went down on fire.

Lt C. W. Usher, 40 Sqn, dived on an E.A. scout which he shot down out of control; his attention was then taken by another enemy machine, but an A.A. battery reports that the first E.A. attacked by Lt Usher crashed.

2 Lts E. R. Stock and W. D. Davidson, 48 Sqn, singled out one of a large formation of E.A. triplanes and scouts and fired 150 rounds into it. The E.A. dived steeply, emitting smoke and then burst into flames. They were then attacked by an E.A. scout which succeeded in shooting away some of their tail wires. Fifty rounds were fired into this E.A. from the back gun and tracers were seen to enter the nose of the E.A. which side-slipped to and fro and then fell into a slow spin. Smoke was seen issuing from the E.A. which was observed to go down in flames.

Lt I. M. Davies, 60 Sqn, attacked one E.A. which had been cut off from its formation; he followed it down for about 4,000 feet, firing short bursts from both guns and tracers were seen to enter the E.A. which dived vertically and is confirmed by another pilot of 60 Sqn's patrol to have continued its dive into the ground in flames.

Capt J. W. Belgrave, 60 Sqn, after manœuvring for position for some time succeeded in getting on the tail of an E.A. scout and fired a burst from both guns into it at less than 50 yards range. The E.A. went down in a spin and was seen to crash near the Arras–Cambrai road.

Capt C. J. P. Scholte, 60 Sqn, attacked an E.A. two-seater and fired several bursts into it from both guns. The E.A. immediately went east, followed by Capt Scholte firing the remainder of the Lewis drum at close range into it, whereupon the E.A. caught fire and was seen to crash north-east of a small wood near Lamotte.

Lts C. H. Arnison and C. D. Wells, 62 Sqn, fired about 100 rounds into one of three E.A. two-seaters. The E.A. went down in a slow flat spin and was seen to crash south of Pys.

Capt T. L. Purdom and 2 Lt P. V. G. Chambers, 62 Sqn, fired 100 rounds into one E.A. two-seater and a further burst from the back gun. The E.A. was seen to go down steeply and crash near Pozières.

2 Lt S. W. Crane, 65 Sqn, whilst on offensive patrol met a large formation of E.A. scouts; he fired about 400 rounds in a series of bursts at one E.A. which went down in a vertical dive and crashed into a wood.

2 Lt G. D. Tod, 65 Sqn, in the same engagement fired a long burst into an E.A. which went down, but Capt Tod was unable to follow this machine, as he was then attacked by several other E.A. Other pilots of the squadron, however, report that the first E.A. engaged by Lt Tod broke in the air.

Capt L. E. Whitehead, 65 Sqn, was driven down from 14,000 to

1,000 feet by six E.A. scouts. When he pulled out of a spin he found that one E.A. was on his tail and another still following. By making a quick turn he got on the tail of the first machine and fired a burst into it a 20 yards range. The E.A. went down vertically and was seen to crash. Capt Whitehead's machine was badly shot about.

Lt W. W. McConnachie, 70 Sqn, attacked an Albatross two-seater and chased it east, firing 800 rounds into it. The E.A. dived steeply and was seen to crash into the ground near Ervillers.

Lt R. J. Cullen and 2 Lt D. Ward, 88 Sqn, dived on one E.A. scout and fired a long burst into it. The E.A. went down in a flat spin and was seen to crash.

A patrol of 201 Sqn attacked a formation of about nine E.A. scouts. Several E.A. were engaged indecisively and one went down completely out of control and was seen by Maj Booker to crash near Mory. The following officers took part in the combat: Maj C. D. Booker, Capt S. M. Kinkead, Lts M. H. Findlay, R. Hemmens, J. H. Forman, R. McLaughlin, H. L. Wallace, B. C. B. Brading and R. S. S. Orr.

Lt F. H. Britnell, 203 Sqn, got close on to the tail of an E.A. two-seater and chased it down to 6,000 feet. A long burst was fired into the E.A. which went down in a vertical nose-dive and was then obscured to view by a cloud, but was later seen by the whole patrol lying crashed in a field.

A formation of 203 Sqn attacked one E.A. two-seater; all the pilots engaged the E.A. which stayed and fought but was eventually shot down and crashed near Salome.

Capt O. Redgate, 209 Sqn, observed a formation of E.A. scouts attacking some D.H.4's; he attacked one E.A. scout, which went down out of control and crashed near Flaucourt.

Capt G. F. Malley, 4 Sqn A.F.C., dived on one E.A. two-seater which was doing wireless; a long burst at close range was fired into the E.A. which immediately turned east and glided very steeply, emitting volumes of smoke, and crashed in the vicinity of Bac St. Maur, smoke still pouring out of the machine.

Capt A. W. B.-Proctor, 84 Sqn, left the ground at 3.25 a.m. to engage E.A. bombing Amiens. He decided to fly east in order to try and intercept the E.A. on their return to their aerodrome. He found the aerodrome by the landing flares and glided down to 3,000 feet and then waited a few miles west of the aerodrome. At about 3.55 a.m., a twin-engined E.A. passed just above him, and Capt Proctor immediately got beneath the E.A.'s tail but was seen by the observer, who opened fire. Capt Proctor then opened fire and the E.A. started to dive down, and the observer stopped firing and did not again fire during the combat. Capt Proctor's gun then jammed and on clearing the stoppage he again attacked the

E.A., firing 150 rounds into it. The E.A. fired a red light, which was answered by another red light from the aerodrome. Capt Proctor was then subjected to very heavy fire from the ground, both by machine guns and 'flaming onions', and broke off the combat at 2,000 feet, having driven the E.A. some distance beyond its aerodrome. When last seen, the E.A. was still diving but probably under control. However, a considerable amount of ammunition had been fired into it and it was probably damaged.

A patrol of 201 Sqn engaged a formation of E.A. scouts which were attacking a patrol of Bristol fighters. All the pilots of 201 Sqn's patrol remarked on the fine performance put up by the Bristol fighters (11 Sqn) against at least 30 enemy machines which were in the vicinity at the time.

May 16th

The weather was fine all day ⌀ A total of 37¾ tons of bombs were dropped ⌀ Enemy aircraft were active but not abnormally so considering the weather. Two hostile machines landed behind our lines and two were shot down by A.A. During the night of the 16th–17th instant, an A.E.G. machine landed in our lines.

Twelve machines of 55 Sqn bombed the railway station and sidings at Saarbrucken. As soon as the formation crossed the lines they encountered 12 hostile scouts and fighting took place up to the objective, by which time 25 hostile machines had collected. Twenty-four 112-lb. bombs were dropped and several bursts were seen on the railway lines and a small fire caused. Three hostile machines were driven down out of control. One of our machines was shot down. The eleven remaining machines returned.

Lts J. P. Seabrook and C. Wrigglesworth, 11 Sqn, fired about 100 rounds at close range into an E.A. two-seater which went down in a spiral and was seen to crash just east of Cambrai.

Lts D. C. M. Brooks and H. R. Kincaid, 11 Sqn, dived on a large formation of E.A. triplanes and scouts. A burst of 50 rounds was fired from the back gun into one of the E.A. which went down in a spin, then a vertical dive, finally crashing in a field north-west of Mametz.

Lt D. J. Weston and Cpl E. A. Deighton, 20 Sqn, dived several times on one E.A. scout which finally turned and endeavoured to get under the tail of the Bristol fighter. A burst of 80 rounds from the back gun was then fired into the E.A. which stalled, dived straight down and was seen crashed on the canal bank near Wervicq.

2 Lts E. C. Bromley and J. H. Umney, 22 Sqn, during a general engagement with a formation of E.A. scouts, fired a burst from the rear gun into one E.A. which was seen to crash and burst into flames. Almost

immediately they fired at another E.A. which went into a spin and was seen to crash.

Lt S. F. Thompson and Sgt R. M. Fletcher, 22 Sqn, dived on one E.A. scout, the right wing of which gave way and the E.A. was seen to crash. They then dived on another E.A. which went down out of control and also crashed.

Lt H. B. Barton, 24 Sqn, engaged one of several E.A. triplanes which were diving on a D.H.4; he fired 50 rounds into one E.A. which went down in a spin and crashed south of Proyart.

Lt C. J. Venter, 29 Sqn, dived on one E.A. two-seater and fired a burst of 200 rounds into it. The E.A. went down out of control followed by Lt Venter who saw it crash.

Lt W. B. Green, 32 Sqn, attacked one of two E.A. scouts and fired 200 rounds into it at point blank range. The E.A. went down on fire and was lost to sight in the clouds.

Lt T. C. Tarbutt, 56 Sqn, attacked one of a formation of E.A. triplanes. He fired a drum into it at close range and was then attacked by the other triplanes. On turning round he saw the E.A. which he had engaged on the ground in flames.

Lt A. W. Saunders, 60 Sqn, drove down one E.A. scout in a spin. At about 3,000 feet the E.A. pulled out of the spin and flew east. Lt Saunders engaged the E.A. again and fired long bursts into it from both guns at close range, whereupon the E.A. dived to the ground and crashed badly near Beaulencourt.

Lt H. G. Hegarty, 60 Sqn, attacked an E.A. two-seater which was being engaged by Lt J. S. Griffith, of the same squadron. They both fought the E.A. for a short time and, when close to the ground, the E.A. went into a vertical dive and crashed at Fampoux and burst into flames.

Lt M. L. Howard, 64 Sqn, during a general engagement between his formation and a formation of E.A. scouts, dived on one E.A. and fired 100 rounds into it from both guns at close range. The E.A. turned on its back and fell completely out of control and crashed near Brebieres.

Lt B. A. Walkerdine, 64 Sqn, engaged another E.A. scout which fell out of control and was seen to crash.

Lt A. C. Hendry, 64 Sqn, fired about 50 rounds into an E.A. scout at close range. The E.A. fell out of control and was seen to crash.

Capt J. A. Slater, 64 Sqn, attacked four E.A. scouts in turn, one of which fell out of control and crashed.

Capt P. S. Burge, 64 Sqn, attacked one E.A. scout and fired 100 rounds into it. The E.A. went down in a steep dive, and at about 2,000 feet the right-hand plane broke off and the E.A. was seen to crash.

2 Lt A. Leitch, 65 Sqn, attacked one E.A. triplane which is confirmed by an A.A. Battery to have crashed.

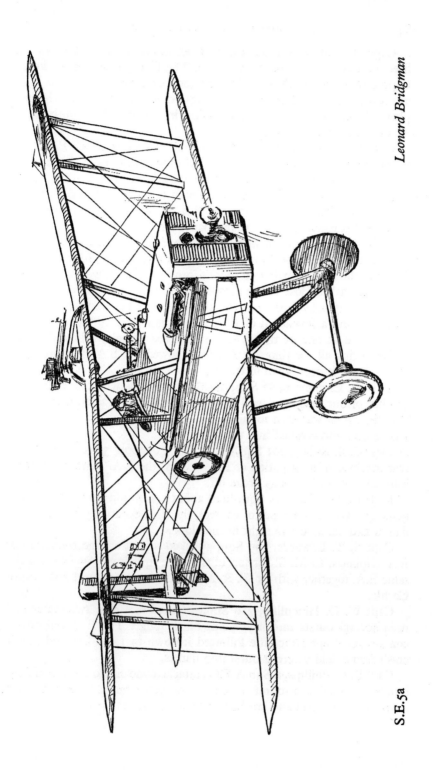

Leonard Bridgman

S.E.5a

Capt M. le Blanc-Smith, 73 Sqn, attacked one of two E.A. scouts and fired a burst into it from under its tail. The E.A. put its nose down and Capt le Blanc-Smith drove it down to 300 feet, firing short bursts into it at short range. The E.A. eventually nose-dived and the two right-hand planes broke off, the wreckage falling in the trenches south of the Arras–Cambrai road.

Capt E. Mannock, 74 Sqn, fired about 40 rounds at one E.A. scout which went down in a vertical dive and broke to pieces in the air.

Lt W. A. Southey, 84 Sqn, dived on one E.A. triplane and fired a long burst into it. He followed the E.A. down to 4,000 feet and then fired another long burst, whereupon the E.A. went into a spin, then nose-dived and crashed in a field near Abancourt.

Lt R. Manzer, 84 Sqn, singled out one E.A. triplane and fired about 100 rounds into it; the E.A. went down in a slow dive, followed by Lt Manzer who fired a further 50 rounds into it. The E.A. went into a nose-dive and crashed close to the cross-roads south of Herleville.

Lt B. Ankers, 87 Sqn, in a general engagement between a patrol of his squadron and a formation of E.A. scouts, got to close range and then opened fire at one of the E.A. which dived steeply, followed by Lt Ankers firing all the time. Lt Ankers followed the E.A. down to 6,000 feet and saw it dive down to the sea.

Lt E. B. Crickmore, 87 Sqn, dived on one E.A. which was attacking another of our machines, and fired a burst of about 20 rounds into it. The E.A. pilot was seen to fall forward and the machine went down in a nose-dive and crashed into the sea.

Capt C. B. Ridley, 201 Sqn, fired a burst of about 50 rounds into the rear machine of a formation of E.A. scouts; the E.A. went down vertically and one of its wings broke off.

Lt J. H. Forman, 201 Sqn, fired about 150 rounds into an E.A. triplane and shot it down out of control, the E.A. eventually bursting into flames and being lost to sight in the clouds.

Capt S. T. Edwards, 209 Sqn, attacked one of a large formation of E.A. triplanes. Lt M. S. Taylor, of the same squadron, also attacked the same E.A. together with Lt W. R. May and forced it to land just west of Corbie.

Capt W. G. Hinchliffe, 210 Sqn, attacked one E.A. two-seater and fired several bursts into it at point blank range. The E.A. fell out of control and Capt Hinchliffe followed it down to 1,500 feet and saw it crash into a field where it burst into flames.

Capt R. C. Phillips, 2 Sqn A.F.C., attacked one of a formation of E.A. scouts and fired 200 rounds into it at 100 yards range. The E.A. went down out of control and crashed near Beaumetz-les-Cambrai.

May 17th

The weather was again fine, but the visibility not so good ∾ 35½ tons of bombs were dropped ∾ Enemy aircraft were by no means so active as on the previous days but several large formations were encountered well east of the lines.

Lt W. M. Thomson and 2 Lt G. H. Kemp, 20 Sqn, while on offensive patrol with other Bristol fighters, engaged a formation of E.A. scouts. They dived on one E.A. and fired a burst of about 200 rounds into it. The E.A. went down in a vertical dive and crashed between Armentières and Lille.

2 Lts G. W. Bulmer and P. S. Williams, 22 Sqn, whilst returning from escort, sighted one E.A. two-seater flying through the clouds; they dived on the E.A., firing about 150 rounds into it. The E.A. commenced to spin, nose-dived to earth and was seen to crash south-east of Douai.

Lt G. Watson, 40 Sqn, dived on one E.A. which was straggling behind its formation, and fired a drum of Lewis and 80 rounds of Vickers into it. The E.A. stalled, commenced a left-hand spin, and as it came out of the spin it burst into flames.

Capt H. G. White, 29 Sqn, managed to cut off an E.A. scout from its formation and after manœuvring for a short time got on to the tail of the E.A. and fired a burst into it, whereupon black smoke was seen issuing from the E.A. which went down out of control, followed by Capt White still firing. The smoke from the E.A. gradually increased and when last seen the E.A. was still going down out of control and on fire.

Lt W. H. Farrow, 64 Sqn, dived on a Fokker triplane which appeared to be quite alone. The E.A. was obviously unaware of Lt Farrow's presence and allowed him to get within close range. Lt Farrow fired 50 rounds into the E.A. which did a half roll and then burst into flames which rapidly increased as the E.A. went down.

Capt L. E. Whitehead, 65 Sqn, attacked one E.A. scout which went down in a spin to 3,000 feet and then came out and dived away. Capt Whitehead followed the E.A. and fired at it again; the E.A. then dived vertically and its wings came off in the air.

Capt G. M. Cox, 65 Sqn, whilst on offensive patrol was attacked by two E.A. scouts. He climbed up and fired a drum at one of these from underneath and something was seen to fall from the E.A. which fell out of control. Three other E.A. scouts then attacked Capt Cox, who was forced to break off the combat with the E.A. which he had shot down, but A.A. confirm this E.A. as having crashed.

Capt E. Mannock, 74 Sqn, attacked the rear machine of a formation of E.A. scouts and fired a long burst from both guns into it, and the E.A. spun down out of control. Capt Mannock was then attacked by another

E.A. and forced to spin away, but 210 Sqn confirm the first E.A. attacked by Capt Mannock as having crashed in flames. Later in the day Capt Mannock observed an E.A. two-seater crossing the line near Ypres. He climbed north and then east and approached the E.A. at which he fired approximately 200 rounds at close range during a fight which lasted about one minute, the E.A. going down alternately diving and spinning. At about 4,000 feet the E.A. burst into flames and was seen to crash and to burn itself out on the ground.

Lt J. I. T. Jones, 74 Sqn, when with his patrol attacked 10 E.A. During the fight he observed one two-seater slightly in front and just below him and fired from both guns into it. Hits were observed on the engine and cockpits and the E.A. went down vertically, emitting smoke, and later burst into flames, falling near Estaires.

Lt H. W. L. Saunders, 84 Sqn, whilst leading a patrol dived on a formation of E.A. scouts and got on to the tail of one, firing several good bursts. The E.A. did a half roll and eluded Lt Saunders for a few seconds. He, however, again got on to the E.A.'s tail and fired several bursts, whereupon the E.A. stalled and eventually went down in a vertical dive and crashed south-east of Hangest.

Capt H. P. Smith, 84 Sqn, while escorting back a formation of D.H.4's observed several E.A. scouts about to attack. He dived on the nearest E.A. and fired 400 rounds, chasing it down to 6,000 feet. He followed it down and saw it crash near Rosieres. He then zoomed up and started back to our lines alone. While returning, he suddenly felt a blow in the right ankle and found that he was wounded by a bullet from an E.A. triplane which was attacking from behind; almost at the same moment his petrol tank was hit and his engine stopped. He at once dived for our lines, kicking his rudder as he went, eventually crossing the enemy's trenches at Villers-Bretonneux at a height of 100 feet and crashing in 'No man's land'. While extricating himself from his machine he was hit in the left ankle, and his left arm was broken badly by a machine gun bullet. He, however, managed to roll over into a slight depression in the ground and was finally pulled into a sap-head by some Australians, one of whom was badly wounded while attempting to rescue Capt Smith.

Lt M. H. Findlay, 201 Sqn, attacked an E.A. scout and drove it down from 18,000 to 10,000 feet, firing 500 rounds into it. The E.A. fell in a spin on its back and after about two turns its tail fell off and it crashed to earth.

Capt H. F. Beamish, 203 Sqn, attacked one E.A. which had detached itself from its formation. Capt Beamish fired 400 rounds into the E.A., which fell out of control and crashed into a house south of Merville.

Capt L. H. Rochford, 203 Sqn, attacked one of three E.A. scouts and

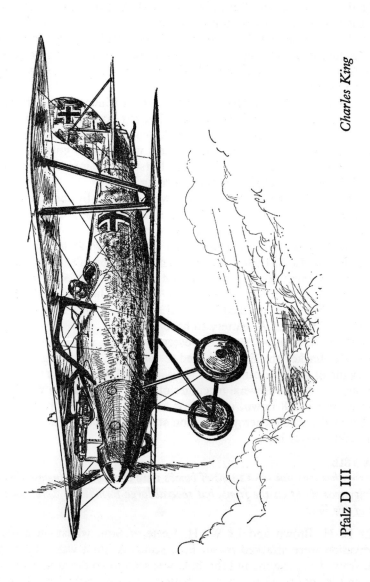

Pfalz D III

Charles King

got to within about 10 yards of it. The E.A. went down out of control and crashed into a field near Beaupre.

Lt E. T. Hayne, 203 Sqn, observed an E.A. two-seater proceeding towards our lines. He dived at it from the east and fired two good bursts before he was observed. The E.A. went down steeply, flying a somewhat zig-zag course. Lt Hayne chased it, firing several times, and at about 4,000 feet the E.A. stalled and side-slipped out of control and was seen to crash near Steenwerke.

A patrol of 203 Sqn attacked one E.A. scout which fell in flames.

Lt R. Chalmers and 2 Lt S. H. Hamblin, 205 Sqn, on returning from a bomb raid, were attacked by three E.A. scouts; 200 rounds were fired from the back gun at one E.A. and tracers were seen to enter its front. The E.A. immediately nose-dived and burst into flames and was seen several thousand feet below rapidly burning.

Lt Burn and 2 Lt Duncan, 206 Sqn, were attacked by about nine E.A scouts; 200 rounds were fired at these E.A. and one was seen to go into a flat spin and burst into flames and dive down on fire.

Lt H. A. Patey, 210 Sqn, dived on an E.A. two-seater, firing 200 rounds into it. Lt A. L. Jones, of the same squadron, also dived on this E.A., firing a burst of 100 rounds into it. The E.A. started to go down, followed by Lts Patey and Jones who, however, had to break off the combat as they were attacked by five E.A. scouts. The E.A. two-seater is confirmed by an A.A. battery to have crashed.

Lt W. J. A. Duncan, 60 Sqn, observed 15 E.A. scouts attacking an R.E.8. He attacked the E.A. and fired at one which was diving vertically and a wing of the E.A. came off as it disappeared through the clouds. Lt Duncan then fired at several machines of the E.A. formation which had followed the R.E.8 down, and was eventually forced to break off the combat as the whole enemy formation started to attack. The R.E.8 got back safely to our lines.

May 18th

The weather was fine ∽ 32 tons of bombs were dropped ∽ Enemy aircraft activity was slight on the front, but several large formations were met well east of the lines.

Lt L. H. Brown and Lt W. H. Leete, 7 Sqn, whilst on artillery observation were attacked by an E.A. scout. A burst was fired at the E.A. from the rear gun, and the E.A. was seen to go down in a straight dive and is confirmed by an A.A. battery to have crashed north of St. Julien.

Lt G. V. Howard and 2 Lt L. Harrison, 7 Sqn, were engaged by 5 E.A. scouts, two of which dived on them. A burst was fired at one of the E.A., which was seen to dive away rapidly in the direction of Houthulst, and is confirmed by the Belgian Mission to have crashed near St. Julien.

Lt D. A. Latimer and Lt D. C. Noel, 20 Sqn, dived on the rear machine of a formation of six E.A. scouts and fired 100 rounds into it at close range. The E.A. dived completely out of control and was seen to crash in Comines.

Lt J. H. Colbert and 2 Lt R. W. Turner, 20 Sqn, whilst on offensive patrol with a formation of Bristol fighters, encountered a large number of E.A. scouts. They engaged one of the E.A. and fired a burst into it from the back gun. The E.A. was seen to go down out of control and crash north of Neuf Berquin.

Capt H. G. White, 29 Sqn, whilst leading an offensive patrol, engaged one of a formation of E.A. scouts and fired 50 rounds into it, following it down and firing further bursts into it at 50 yards range. The E.A. went down completely out of control. Capt White followed it down to within 500 feet of the ground, and was then forced to break off the combat owing to his gun jamming. Another pilot of the same patrol confirmed the E.A. as having crashed $1\frac{1}{2}$ miles west of Estaires.

Lt C. J. Venter, 29 Sqn, dived on another E.A., firing 70 rounds into it. The E.A. went down emitting smoke which gradually increased, and eventually burst into flames. This is confirmed by Capt White as going down in flames.

Lt R. H. Rusby, 29 Sqn, got on to the tail of an E.A. scout which was following down another of our machines. He fired a burst of about 150 rounds into the E.A. which went down completely out of control. This is confirmed to have crashed by Maj C. H. Dixon.

Maj R. S. Dallas, 40 Sqn, observed an E.A. getting height over its own lines. Maj Dallas was unable to get to the E.A.'s height, so he followed under its tail for an hour. A Camel passed below the E.A. which it is thought the E.A. mistook for Maj Dallas breaking off the combat, and the E.A. then started to lose height over Lille. Maj Dallas then fired a drum of Lewis into the E.A. which went down emitting volumes of smoke and flame.

Capt J. D. Belgrave, 60 Sqn, engaged an E.A. scout and fought it down for several thousand feet. The E.A. went down in a spin, followed by Capt Belgrave. At 8,000 feet, the E.A. came out or the spin and dived vertically and was seen to crash near Carnoy.

Capt J. Gilmour, 65 Sqn, whilst leading an offensive patrol, attacked a formation of about 12 E.A. scouts. He dived on one E.A. and fired a long burst into it at close range, whereupon the E.A. dived vertically and two wings were seen to break up in the air. Capt Gilmour shortly afterwards dived on an E.A. two-seater and fired a long burst into it at close range. The E.A. turned east and went down in a slow dive, and was observed to crash and burst into flames on the ground.

2 Lt T. Williams, 65 Sqn, dived on three E.A. two-seaters, one of which he chased to just west of Wiencourt, losing height all the time, and after firing about 300 rounds it went down out of control and crashed just west of Wiencourt.

Lt J. I. T. Jones, 74 Sqn, attacked one E.A. two-seater, which was being engaged by A.A. fire. He got into position under the E.A.'s tail and fired 250 rounds into it, causing an explosion, and the E.A. burst into flames and was seen to crash. Shortly afterwards Lt Jones observed another E.A., which was being engaged by our A.A. fire. He attacked this E.A. from under its tail, but was fired at by the enemy observer, who was firing through a hole in the fuselage. Lt Jones then attacked the E.A. from directly underneath and fired up. The E.A. banked steeply, and after a few rounds had been fired into it, the observer was seen to fall overboard. Lt Jones was then forced to break off the combat owing to lack of ammunition and gun jam.

Capt E. Mannock, 74 Sqn, engaged an E.A. two-seater at right angles, firing a burst of 40 rounds into it. The E.A. went down in a vertical dive and crashed near Steenwerck, and burst into flames on hitting the ground.

Capt R. A. Grosvenor, 84 Sqn, attacked an E.A. two-seater, which was being engaged by French A.A. guns. He dived on the E.A. and fired several long bursts into it. The E.A. dived vertically and was followed by Capt Grosvenor for about 1,000 feet, who saw the E.A. crash just north-east of Moreuil.

Lt C. W. B. Martin and 2 Lt H. R. Goss, 88 Sqn, in a general engagement with several E.A. scouts, were attacked by one E.A., into which they fired a burst from the back gun, and the E.A. was seen to go down in flames.

Capt H. F. Beamish 203 Sqn, dived on an E.A. two-seater, firing a burst of about 250 rounds into it. Lt J. D. Breakey, 203 Sqn, also dived on this E.A. and fired a burst of 500 rounds into it. The E.A. went down in a steep nose dive and was seen to fall in flames.

Lt E. T. Hayne, 203 Sqn, observed 10 E.A. about to attack three Dolphins. Lt Hayne led his formation against the E.A. and attacked three separate machines. The second E.A. attacked went down in a steep spiral and burst into flames at about 3,000 feet.

Capt Euan Dickson and Aerial Gunner C. V. Robinson, 205 Sqn, whilst on a bombing raid, were attacked by a formation of seven E.A. scouts and triplanes. They fired a burst at one triplane and succeeded in driving it off. At the same time they were attacked by an E.A. scout, into which they fired about 50 rounds at close range. The E.A. burst into flames and then broke up in the air.

Lt H. B. Maund, 210 Sqn, attacked one of a formation of E.A. scouts,

R.E.8   Leonard Bridgman

firing 500 rounds into it at close range. The E.A. went down vertically out of control in the vicinity of Bac St. Maur. This machine is confirmed to have crashed by a flight of 203 Sqn.

Capt W. M. Alexander, 210 Sqn, in the same engagement, fired 200 rounds at 100 yards range into one E.A. scout and tracers were seen to enter its fuselage. The E.A. went down in a spin out of control. Capt Alexander was then attacked by several other E.A. scouts and was not able to observe the result of the first combat, but a patrol of 203 Sqn, confirmed that the first E.A. he attacked crashed.

Lt R. C. Nelson, 4 Sqn A.F.C., dived on the rear machine of four E.A. triplanes and fired a long burst. The E.A. went down completely out of control. A.A. Battery confirm this machine as crashed.

May 19th

The weather was fine throughout the day ⌀ A total of 29¼ tons of bombs were dropped ⌀ Enemy aircraft activity was nowhere above normal.

Capt J. W. Aldred, 3 Sqn, while on wireless interception attacked an E.A. two-seater and fired two bursts at short range from under its tail. The machine dived steeply and was seen to crash by an A.A. battery.

Lt W. Hughes and 2 Lt F. C. Peacock, 10 Sqn, were attacked by two Fokker triplanes near Zillebeke. The observer fired at one of them at close range and it was seen to crash on a Nissen hut.

An offensive patrol of 20 Sqn engaged about 20 E.A.

Lt D. J. Weston and Sgt E. A. Deighton fired 150 rounds at one E.A. which burst into flames and went down in a spin. They then attacked another E.A. which went down in a vertical dive and crashed north of Frelinghem.

Lt P. T. Iaccaci and Sgt W. Sansome dived on a triplane and fired 25 rounds at 200 yards range. The E.A. went down in a steep dive and crashed.

Lt A. T. Iaccaci and 1 AM A. Newlands attacked another triplane. One drum was fired from the back gun at close range and the E.A. crashed near Vieux Berquin.

Capt D. G. Cooke and Lt S. H. P. Masding dived on a Pfalz Scout which went down in flames. They were then attacked by another E.A. from behind. After 30 rounds had been fired into it, this machine went down out of control and was seen to crash at Laventie.

Lt W. M. Thomson and 2 Lt G. H. Kemp dived on a Pfalz Scout. The observer fired three drums into this machine which crashed on a house at Estaires.

Capt A. C. Atkey and 2 Lt C. G. Gass, 22 Sqn, while on escort duty attacked an E.A. two-seater and fired 75 rounds into it, and the E.A. spun down and flattened out at 2,000 feet. The observer then fired 50 more rounds and the E.A. went down and crashed near Douai.

Lt F. J. Davies, 29 Sqn, attacked an E.A. scout at 30 yards range. After 50 rounds had been fired the E.A. turned on its back and was observed to crash near La Creche.

Lt C. J. Venter, 29 Sqn, attacked an E.A. two-seater over Nieppe Forest and fired 400 rounds. The E.A. dived east with smoke issuing from it and was confirmed to have crashed by an anti-aircraft battery.

Capt H. G. White, 29 Sqn, dived on a Pfalz Scout. After firing 50 rounds he zoomed up and collided with the E.A. which rolled over and went down vertically, followed by Capt White, who, after firing another 100 rounds into it, saw the wings fall off in the air, Capt White's engine stopped and he crashed on attempting to land as his machine was more or less out of control.

Lt C. O. Rusden, 40 Sqn, whilst leading an offensive patrol, dived on a formation of E.A. He fired first a short burst into one of them at very close range; the E.A. went down in a spin and was seen to crash near Provin.

Lt R. G. Landis (U.S.A.), 40 Sqn, on offensive patrol, attacked one of a formation of E.A. scouts. After several bursts from both guns, the E.A. started to spin and then went into a vertical dive and crashed near Provin.

Lts R. C. Stokes and R. A. V. R. Scherk, 49 Sqn, while returning from a bomb raid, were attacked by one of eight E.A., which got on to their tail. Fifty rounds were fired into it from the back gun, when it went down like a falling leaf, emitting smoke, and was eventually seen burning on the ground.

Capt C. J. F. Scholte, 60 Sqn, attacked an E.A. artillery machine east of Arras. After firing a burst into it from below, the E.A. burst into flames and broke up in the air.

Capt J. A. Slater, 64 Sqn, attacked the rear machine of a formation of Albatross scouts. After 150 rounds had been fired, the E.A. went down out of control and was observed to crash. Capt Slater then attacked another formation and fired a drum at close range into one of them, which fell out of control and was seen to crash.

Lt J. White, 65 Sqn, attacked an E.A. two-seater and followed it down in a steep spiral, firing short bursts. The E.A. crashed near Villers-Bretonneux.

Capt A. W. B. Proctor, 84 Sqn, while leading his patrol, with the assistance of three S.E.5's, engaged one of five Albatross scouts and got on to its tail and fired 100 rounds at 50 yards range. The E.A. nose-dived and crashed on our side of the lines near Cachy.

Lt H. O. MacDonald, 84 Sqn, also attacked another of the above Albatross scouts and got on to its tail, firing 200 rounds at close range.

The E.A. dived steeply and crashed near Villers-Bretonneux.

During the above two combats, two E.A. were seen to collide in the air and crash in the same place.

Capt R. N. G. Atkinson and Lt F. A. Shaw, 98 Sqn, fired half a drum into a Pfalz Scout which dived vertically; the remainder of the drum was then fired into another Pfalz Scout which had got on to their tail and this machine went into a spin. Both machines were seen burning on the ground near Becelaere.

Lt E. T. Hayne, 203 Sqn, attacked one of a formation of Pfalz Scouts from above and in front. After firing a burst at close range the E.A. went into a nose-dive and crashed east of Merville.

Lt Burn and A./G. H. W. Williams, 206 Sqn, while on a bomb raid, were attacked by one of a formation of 10 Albatross Scouts. Fifty rounds were fired at the E.A. from the back gun, when it went into a spin and then broke up in the air.

Capt W. G. Hinchliffe, 210 Sqn, fired 90 rounds at an E.A. two-seater over Armentières. The E.A. observer's gun jammed, and he held up his hands. The E.A. then went down in a spin, followed by Capt Hinchcliffe to 2,000 feet, when he saw it crash.

Lt J. S. Forgie and 2 Lt J. S. Muir, 211 Sqn, were attacked by several E.A. while on a bombing raid over Blankenburghe. The observer fired 30 rounds into one E.A., which nose-dived and caught fire on hitting the ground.

A hostile kite balloon was attacked by Lt H. S. Preston, 46 Sqn; 150 rounds were fired at long range, when the balloon burst into flames.

Lt Birkbeck and 2 Lt Susman, 206 Sqn, were attacked by five E.A. The observer fired a drum at one of the machines, which rolled over and went into a vertical dive. The top plane of this machine was seen to break away in the air.

Maj McClaughry, 4 Sqn A.F.C., went up at 10.15 p.m. after enemy bombing machines. He attacked two but had to break off the combat, owing to the glare of our searchlights.

Enemy machines were also driven down out of control during the period under review by:

Sqn 3 Capt J. W. Aldred/Lt Brotheridge, Lt L. Hamilton (USAS). **8** Lts F. M. F. West + J. A. G. Haslam. **11** Lts J. S. Chick + E. C. Gilroy, Lts J. T. Seabrook + C. Wrigglesworth. **18** Capts A. G. Waller + F. T. R. Kempster, Capt A. G. Waller + Lt Ayres/2 Lt A. Green + Lt F. Loly/2 Lt G. Darvill + Lt E. Collis. **19** Lt A. W. Blake, Maj A. D. Carter, Maj A. D. Carter/Lt J. D. Hardman, Lt N. W. Hustings, Lt F. McQuistan, Lt P. J. E. Pierce. **20** Capt J. W. Belgrave, Lt F. E. Boulton + Pbr H. G. Holman, Lts D. Latimer + T. C. Noel. **22** Capt A. C. Atkey + 2 Lt C. G. Gass (4), Lt S. F. Thompson + Sgt R. M. Fletcher, 2 Lt S. H. Wallage + Lt G. Thompson. **24** Lt C. M. G. Farrell,

Capt I. D. R. MacDonald. **32** Lt H. L. W. Flynn. **40** Maj R. S. Dallas, Lt I. F. Hind (2), Lt D. F. Murmann, Lt C. O. Rusden, Lt G. Watson. **41** Lt A. S. Hemming, Capt R. W. Chappell. **43** Capt H. W. Woollett. **46** Capt D. R. MacLaren/Lt A. G. Vlasto/Lt V. M. Yeates. **48** 2 Lt L. A. Payne + Lt C. J. R. Gibson. **49** Lts N. Braithewaite + F. P. Bellingan, Lts F. W. Lowen + F. B. Denison, Lts F. D. Nevin + H. P. Roberts, Lts H. L. Rough + V. Dreschfeld. **55** Lt A. S. Keep + 2 Lt W. R. Patey (2), 2 Lts C. E. Reynolds + J. E. Reynolds, 2 Lts H. E. Townsend + W. F. Roaks, 2 Lts C. R. Whitlock + G. Bryer-Ash, 2 Lts E. J. Whyte + W. F. Robins, Capts F. Williams + W. H. Mason-Springgay. **60** Capt J. D. Belgrave. **62** Capt T. L. Purdom + 2 Lt P. V. G. Chambers, Capt T. L. Purdom + Sgt W. M. Holmes, Lts D. A. Savage + E. W. Collis. **64** Capt P. S. Burge, Lt A. C. Hendry, Lt G. A. Rainier, Lt B. A. Walkerdine. **65** Lt J. L. M. White. **70** Lt S. T. Liversedge/Lt G. C. Morris, Lt W. W. McConnachie, Capt H. N. C. Robinson. **74** Lt J. I. T. Jones. **80** Capt H. A. Whistler. **84** Capt A. W. Beauchamp-Proctor (3), Lt E. E. Biccard, Capt R. A. Grosvenor, Lt H. O. MacDonald, Lt A. F. Mathews (USAS), Capt H. W. L. Saunders (2). **87** Lt C. E. Worthington. **88** Lt T. E. Duffy + 2 Lt F. A. Lewis, Capt Hepburn + 2 Lt Lambert, Lt E. C. Johnston + 2 Lt J. Rudkin (2). **201** Lt R. B. Brading, Lt G. B. Gates, Lt H. P. Guard, Capt S. M. Kinkead, Lt H. L. Wallace (2). **203** Capt H. B. Beamish, Lt J. D. Breakey, Lt Britnell, Capt R. A. Little/Lt E. T. Hayne, Capt L. H. Rochford, Capt L. H. Rochford/2 Lt Brown. **208** Capt G. K. Cooper, Capt W. C. Debenham, Lt H. H. Fowler. **209** Capt O. C. le Boutillier/Lt R. M. Foster, Capt S. T. Edwards, Lt J. W. Sidall. **3 AFC** Capt E. J. Jones + R. Hainsworth.

HONOURS AND AWARDS

DSC Capt T. A. Batchelor. **MC** Capt I. P. R. Napier, Capt M. R. N. Jennings, Lt E. L. O'Leary, Lt F. W. McChisney, Lt F. W. Burdick, Capt K. R. Napier, 2 Lt W. A. Tyrrell.

20 – 26 May

During a week of relatively little activity Mannock had a successful day on 20 May, destroying four of the enemy.

Structural failures of the type experienced by Lt Mark, 24 Sqn, in an S.E.5a, were not infrequent with the wooden aircraft of the period.

COMMUNIQUÉ NO. 8

During the perod under review we have claimed officially 58 E.A. brought down and 10 driven down our of control. In addition, five E.A. were brought down by A.A. fire. Sixteen of our machines are missing. Approximately 190 tons of bombs were dropped, 242,120 rounds fired at ground targets, and 6,653 photographs taken.

May 20th
Weather fine; visibility fairly good ⌀ 37 tons of bombs dropped ⌀ Enemy aircraft inactive considering weather ⌀ One hostile machine brought down by A.A. fire.

Hostile kite balloons were shot down by the following: Capt D. R. MacLaren, 46 Sqn (two); Capt J. S. Stubbs and 2 Lt C. C. Dance, 105 Sqn; 2 Lt W. F. J. Harvey and Lt G. Thomson, 22 Sqn (two).

Lt R. T. Mark, 24 Sqn, dived on an E.A. and his right-hand top plane commenced to break up. Another E.A. attacked him and he dived west. Seeing Capt Lowe, 24 Sqn, going down with an E.A. on his tail, Mark turned and dived on this machine, firing 30 rounds and frightening the E.A. away. This E.A. then attacked Lt Mark, and Capt Lowe, seeing Lt Mark's predicament, fired 60 rounds at the E.A. and forced it to land, thus enabling both machines to return home. Owing to the condition of his machine Lt Mark crashed on landing and his machine caught fire.

May 21st
Weather fine ⌀ 13 tons of bombs dropped by night and 29¾ tons by day, including 2,688 lb., 2,016 lb. and 2,068 lb. respectively on railway stations at Coblenz, Thionville and Metz ⌀ E.A. activity same as last two days.

Lt J. S. Boult and 2 Lt J. L. Brown, 12 Sqn, on photographic reconnaissance, were attacked by eight E.A. Lt Brown fired at the leader, who went down in flames.

A patrol of 48 Sqn, met 13 E.A. In the combat which ensued, three E.A. were crashed by Capt H. C. Sootheran and 2 Lt P. A. Cockeram, Lt J. E. Drummond and 2 Lt C. C. Walmsley and 2 Lts H. A. Oaks and C. S. Bissett.

A patrol of 74 Sqn encountered six Pfalz Scouts, upon whom they dived, shooting down five of them—one of which Maj K. L. Caldwell destroyed one, Capt E. Mannock three, and Capt W. E. Young one. Capt Mannock also destroyed another E.A. earlier in the day.

Lt R. F. C. Metcalfe and 2 Lt D. R. Bradley, 211 Sqn, were attacked on returning from bomb raid by five E.A. scouts and one two-seater. The two-seater was shot down by 2 Lt Bradley and one of the scouts by Lt Metcalfe.

Hostile kite balloons were destroyed by Lts S. C. Joseph, A. L. Jones, C. W. Payton, 210 Sqn (one); Capt H. B. Maund, Lt H. A. Patey, Lt G. B. Wootten, 210 Sqn (one); Lt A. H. Cobby, 4 Sqn A.F.C. (one).

May 22nd
Weather fine ∽ *57½ tons of bombs dropped* ∽ *Enemy aircraft inactive considering weather.*

Capt R. A. Little 203 Sqn, having been forced to leave his patrol owing to pressure failure, met a two-seater Albatross on the way home, which he attacked at close range, shooting it down at St. Leger, where it crashed into a railway cutting. Capt Little had just shot down another E.A. before leaving his formation.

Lt J. I. T. Jones, 74 Sqn, left his formation to attack six Pfalz Scouts over Lille. After firing at one of them which evaded him, he turned on a second, which fell vertically. The wings of this machine were seen to fall off in the air, and the fuselage burst into flames on hitting the ground.

A patrol of 22 Sqn attacked 10 E.A. scouts near Cambrai. In the fight which ensued, 2 Lts S. H. Wallage and A. P. Stoyle crashed one machine and drove down another out of control, and Lt S. F. H. Thompson and Sgt R. M. Fletcher crashed one.

Lt Straw and 2 Lt Watson, 25 Sqn, during the course of a long-distance reconnaissance, had an engine failure on approaching Tournai. Being obliged to return, Lt Straw turned west, intending to photograph Valenciennes and Douai, but when over the former saw 10 E.A. scouts approaching. He therefore turned north-west; petrol gave out over Lille, and he was attacked at 8,000 feet by E.A. scout when gliding without engine. He turned round and his observer fired one and a-half drums into E.A., which made off. The lines were finally crossed south of Poperinghe at a few hundred feet, under heavy fire. Machine landed in shell holes just behind our front lines, after a flight of four hours.

May 23rd

Weather fine in morning; later overcast, high wind ○ 26½ tons of bombs dropped ○ E.A. activity very slight.

A patrol of nine machines, 27 Sqn, destroyed one E.A. scout.

Capt H. D. Belgrave, 60 Sqn, destroyed an Albatross Scout near Fricourt.

During the course of night operations, Capt Vickers and 2 Lt McConville, and Lt Macdonell and 2 Lt Murray, 101 Sqn, both attacked hostile bombing machines which had been caught in our searchlights. Several hundred rounds were fired at these machines until they were lost sight of.

May 24th

Weather: rain throughout the day ○ 12 tons of bombs dropped ○ Enemy aircraft activity nil.

May 25th

Weather: sky overcast, bright intervals ○ 6½ tons of bombs dropped ○ E.A. activity slight.

A patrol of 22 Sqn, led by Capt A. C. Atkey and 2 Lt C. G. Gass, while escorting D.H.4's of 18 Sqn, encountered a large formation of about 40 E.A. A fierce fight ensued, in the course of which so many E.A. were seen spinning and diving away that it was impossible to tell whether they were out of control or not. At the conclusion of the fight four E.A. were seen crashed on the ground, and, in addition, one Albatross Scout, attacked by Lt S. F. H. Thompson and Sgt R. M. Fletcher, was seen to go down in flames.

May 26th

Weather: clouds, bad visibility ○ 7½ tons of bombs dropped ○ Enemy aircraft activity slight.

Enemy aircraft were also brought down during the period under review by:

Sqn 1 Lt E. M. Forsyth. **18** 2 Lt G. Darvill + 2 AM L. Vredenburg, 2 Lt G. Leitch + Capt D. Gale. **19** Lt J. D. de Pencier. **20** Lts D. Latimer + T. C. Noel (2), Capt T. P. Middleton + Lt A. Mills, Lt W. M. Thomson + 2 Lt H. D. Kemp. **22** 2 Lt H. H. Beddow + Sgt J. Goodman, Capt W. J. Mostyn + Sgt J. H. Jones, Lt S. F. H. Thompson + Sgt R. M. Fletcher, 2 Lts S. H. Wallage + A. P. Stoyle. **27** Capt S. Anderson + Lt W. I. Crawford, Capt A. E. Palfreyman + Lt W. G. Hurrell, Lt G. E. Wait + 2 Lt F. Gledhill. **29** Capt R. H. Rusby/Lts J. Davies/S. G. Ross, Lt L. C. Tims/Lt C. H. R. Lagesse. **40** Capt G. H. Lewis. **46** 2 Lt G. A. Lamburn/Lts W. A. Burkitt/H. S. Preston (2), Capt D. R. MacLaren/Lt C. R. Chapman, Lts A. G. Vlasto/J. R. Cote/V. M. Yeates/N. Bruce. **48** Lt E. A. Foord + Pte L. James. **62** Capt G. E. Gibbons + Lt S. A. W. Knights, Capt W. E. Staton + Lt J. R. Gordon, Lt

W. K. Swayne + 2 Lt T. Elliott. **64** Capt P. S. Burge, Lt T. Rose/Lt A. D. Pate (4 AFC), Capt J. A. Slater. **65** Capt J. Gilmour, Capt J. Gilmour/Lt E. C. Eaton. **70** Lt G. C. Morris. **73** Lt G. L. Graham, Capt W. H. Hubbard. **74** Capt E. Mannock, Lt B. Roxburgh-Smith. **79** Maj N. W. Noel. **203** Capt L. H. Rochford/2 Lt Berlyn. **205** Formation from. **210** Lt C. W. Payton. **4 AFC** Lt G. Nowland, See also under Sqn 64.

HONOURS AND AWARDS

DSO Capt E. Mannock, MC, Capt H. W. Woollett. **DSC** Capt S. T. Edwards (Bar), Capt O. W. Redgate, Capt A. T. Whealy (Bar). **MC** Capt A. C. Atkey (Bar), Capt J. Todd, Capt J. R. Duigan, 2 Lt C. G. Gass, Capt J. Gilmour (2nd Bar), Capt A. W. Beauchamp-Proctor (Bar), 2 Lt T. M. Williams, 2 Lt H. W. L. Saunders, MM.

27 May – 2 June

This communiqué recorded the first action by 85 Sqn, which had arrived in France on 22 May under the command of Maj W. A. Bishop, V.C., who had built up a victory score of 45 in 60 Sqn. During 85 Sqn's first week at the Front Bishop shot down nine enemy aircraft. He remained with the squadron until 19 June, by which time his score had risen to 72, the highest achieved by any British 'ace'.

COMMUNIQUÉ NO. 9

During the period under review we have claimed officially 111 E.A. brought down and 38 driven down out of control. In addition, two E.A. were brought down by anti-aircraft. Twenty-five of our machines are missing. Approximately 222½ tons of bombs were dropped, and 9,760 photographs taken.

May 27th
Weather fine but cloudy; visibility bad ⌒ *17 tons of bombs dropped* ⌒ *Enemy aircraft activity slight.*

Capt W. Beaver and Sgt E. A. Deighton, 20 Sqn, while on offensive patrol, dived on nine E.A., one of which Capt Beaver shot down near Armentieres. Shortly afterwards he dived on several triplanes, four of which got on to his tail. Sgt Deighton fired 50 rounds at close range at one of these which went down out of control. After firing 200 rounds into another it crashed near Perenchies. They were now separated from the patrol, and as the observer had run out of ammunition they shook off the remaining E.A. with great difficulty and returned. The machine was badly shot about.

A patrol of 40 Sqn, led by Maj R. S. Dallas, dived on a formation of eight Pfalz scouts. In the combat which ensued, three E.A. were shot down by Maj Dallas, Capt G. H. Lewis and Lt I. F. Hind—one each.

Maj W. A. Bishop, 85 Sqn, dived on an E.A. two-seater over Houthulst Forest. E.A. dived east with Maj Bishop on its tail. The left top and bottom planes fell off, and a little later the right-hand planes and also the tail. E.A. crashed east of Passchendaele.

May 28th

Weather fine ∽ 49¼ tons of bombs dropped ∽ Enemy aircraft activity considerable in morning, slight in afternoon.

Lts H. N. Young and H. B. Davies, 8 Sqn, were attacked by seven E.A. while proceeding on a bomb raid. After keeping the E.A. off till the objective was reached, they were attacked at close range by a scout firing from below. Lt Davies fired at this machine, which did an 'Immelmann' turn breaking into an uncontrolled spin and eventually being seen to crash. They were then attacked by two more E.A. which they succeeded in evading by manouevring their machine, eventually reaching the lines in safety.

Lt L. Manzer, 84 Sqn, dived upon a formation of E.A. scouts. After shooting one down out of control he turned to attack another E.A. which was on his tail. Lt Manzer succeeded in getting on to this machine's tail and firing at it from close range, when E.A. turned to the left and then sharply to the right, causing Lt Manzer to collide with it. The E.A.'s right top plane was carried away by the under-carriage of the S.E.5, which was turned upside down by the shock. E.A. fell to the ground.

A hostile kite balloon was brought down in flames by Lt L. I. Lord, 79 Sqn.

May 29th

Weather fine but cloudy ∽ 16 tons of bombs dropped ∽ Enemy aircraft activity very slight till evening.

May 30th

Weather fine, visibility good ∽ 16 tons of bombs dropped by night and 36½ tons by day ∽ Enemy aircraft activity considerable.

Capt T. P. Middleton and Lt A. Mills, 20 Sqn, while leading a patrol, attacked nine E.A. Capt Middleton fired at one Albatross Scout at close range, which fell into the Canal at Lille. He then side-slipped on to one of seven Pfalz Scouts at which Lt Mills fired. This machine broke up in the air. During this combat Lt Weston and Lt Noble, of the same squadron, also shot down another E.A.

A patrol of 43 Sqn attacked a formation of Albatross Scouts. In the course of this combat, four of the enemy machines were shot down by the following: Lt G. G. Bailey (two), Lt H. Daniel (one), Lt G. D. Daly (one).

Maj W. A. Bishop, 85 Sqn, was attacked by two E.A. two-seaters. He zoomed and fired at one of them which fell in flames near Roulers. He then got on the tail of the second one, which, after several bursts had been fired, fell to pieces in the air. Maj Bishop also destroyed an Albatross Scout later in the day.

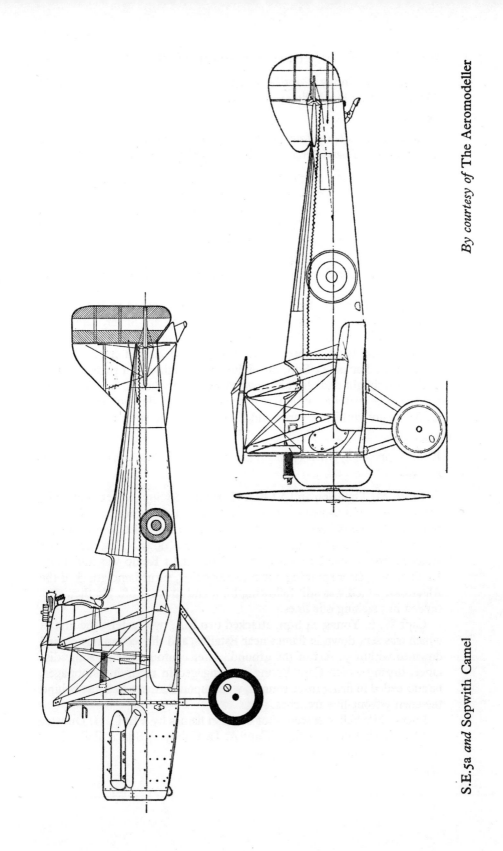

By courtesy of The Aeromodeller

S.E.5a *and* Sopwith Camel

Capt A. H. Cobby, Capt G. F. Malley, 4 Sqn A.F.C., each brought down an enemy kite balloon.

May 31st

Weather fine, visibility fair ⌀ 18 tons of bombs dropped by night and 32 tons by day ⌀ Enemy aircraft active in morning, slight in afternoon.

A patrol of nine machines of 20 Sqn met two formations of E.A. scouts. Lt P. T. Iaccaci and 1 AM A. Newlands attacked five of the enemy machines which were diving on another Bristol Fighter. 1 AM Newlands fired at two of the E.A., one of which burst into flames, and the other crashed near it at Merville. During this combat, Capt T. P. Middleton and Lt A. Mills, Lt J. H. Colbert and 2 Lt P. W. Wilson, Lt L. H. T. Capel and Pbr F. J. Ralph each destroyed an enemy machine.

A patrol of 64 Sqn, led by Capt J. A. Slater, engaged 11 E.A. scouts. During a fierce fight, four E.A. were crashed by Capt Slater, Capt E. R. Atkinson, Lt D. Lloyd-Evans, and Lt W. H. Farrow. In addition, two Albatross Scouts were observed to collide in the air and crash.

Lt C. C. Banks, 43 Sqn, on night patrol, sighted a Friedrichshafen in the searchlight and climbed towards it. Greatly helped by the searchlights, which switched off him at once and succeeded in holding the E.A. Lt Banks got within 25 yards and shot the E.A. down in flames.

June 1st

Weather fine ⌀ 47½ tons of bombs dropped ⌀ Enemy aircraft activity was normal.

Lt W. M. Thomson and 2 Lt G. H. Kemp, 20 Sqn, were cut off from their patrol and attacked by four E.A. Lt Thomson turned and fired 200 rounds into one of these which was seen to crash. 2 Lt Kemp fired at another at very close range which was also shot down. They were then attacked from above by an Albatross Scout. 2 Lt Kemp was killed and Lt Thomson, after spinning down to 2,000 feet, turned and attacked the Albatross, which was still following him, and drove it off. He then succeeded in reaching our lines.

Capt W. E. Young 74 Sqn, attacked two E.A. two-seaters, the first of which was sent down in flames near Estaires, and the second one chased down to within 50 feet of the ground. After contour chasing some distance, during which Capt Young was engaged in rectifying stoppages, he succeeded in firing three rounds, whereupon E.A. crashed just behind the enemy front-line trenches.

Enemy kite balloons were shot down in flames by 2 Lt C. H. Dunster and Sgt J. H. Jones, 22 Sqn; Capt A. H. Cobby, 4 Sqn A.F.C.; Capt A. W. Beauchamp-Proctor, 84 Sqn.

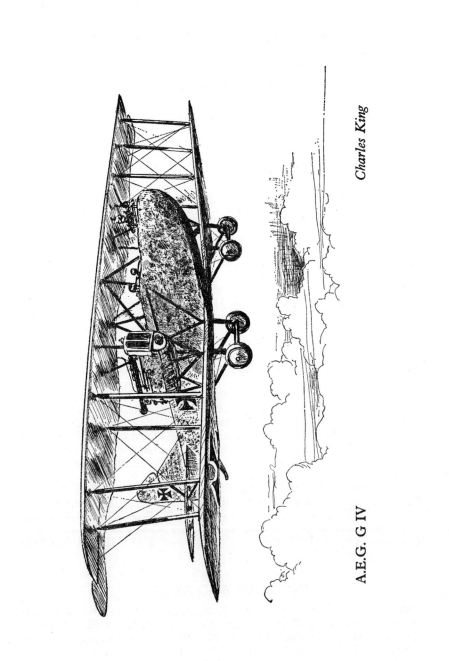

A.E.G. G IV

Charles King

June 2nd

Weather fine; visibility indifferent ↷ 30 tons of bombs dropped ↷ Enemy aircraft activity was slight.

Enemy aircraft were also brought down during the period under review by:

Sqn 1 Capt P. J. Clayson (3), Capt P. J. Clayson/Lt A. F. Scroggs, patrol led by Capt P. J. Clayson, Capts Henderson/P. J. Clayson/Lts Knight/Kullberg/Owen/Scroggs, Lt E. T. S. Kelly. **18** Capts D. Stewart + L. Collins, Capt D. A. Stewart + Lt W. Miller, Capt A. G. Waller + Lt B. J. Blackitt. **20** Capt W. Beaver + Sgt E. A. Deighton, Lts J. H. Colbert + A. Mills, Lt V. E. Groom + 2 Lt E. Hardcastle (2), Lt A. T. Iaccaci + **1** AM A. Newlands, Capt D. Latimer + Lt T. C. Noel, Lt E. Lindup + Sgt E. A. Deighton, Lt W. M. Thomason + 2 Lt H. G. Kemp. **22** Capt A. C. Atkey + 2 Lt C. G. Gass (2), 2 Lts E. C. Bromley + J. H. Umney, 2 Lts C. H. Dunster + Sgt J. H. Jones, Lt F. G. Gibbons + 2 Lt J. H. Umney (2), 2 Lt W. F. J. Harvey + Lt G. Thomson (2), 2 Lts A. W. King + J. McDonald, Lt S. F. H. Thompson + Sgt R. M. Fletcher (3). **23** Lts H. A. F. Goodison/H. F. Faulkner, Lt R. A. Way. **24** Lt J. A. E. R. Daley, Lt J. J. Darve, Lt W. C. Lambert, Capt I. D. R. MacDonald (2). **29** Lt F. J. Davies, Lt C. H. R. Lagesse, Lt C. G. Ross, Capt R. H. Rusby, Capt R. H. Rusby/Lts C. G. Ross/H. M. Hutton. **41** Lt F. R. McCall. **46** Capt D. W. Forshaw, Lts G. Hudson, D. H. Robertson, P. M. Tudhope (this patrol of 46 led by Capt D. W. Forshaw also sent 2 E.A. down out of control), Capt D. W. Forshaw/Lts D. H. Robertson/E. R. Watt/C. R. Chapman. **48** Lt R. H. Davies + Cpl H. F. Watson, Capt L. A. Payne + Lt A. E. Ansell, Capt F. Ransley + 2 Lt G. Dixon. **60** Capt J. W. Belgrave. **62** Capt G. E. Gibbons + Lt S. A. W. Knights, Capt H. Rees-Jones + 2 Lt C. Wealthall, Capt W. E. Staton + Lt J. R. Gordon. **64** Capt E. R. Alkinson (2), Lt H. G. Ross, Capt J. A. Slater (2), Capt E. R. Tempest, Lt B. A. Walkerdine (2). **65** Lt C. L. Morley. **70** Lt W. W. McConnachie, Capt J. Todd (3), Capt J. Todd/Lt V. C. Chapman, Lt K. B. Watson. **74** Lt H. G. Clements, Lt J. I. T. Jones (4), Capt E. Mannock (3). **80** Capt H. A. Whistler (2). **84** Lt E. A. Clear. **85** Maj W. A. Bishop (5). **87** Maj J. C. Callaghan, Capt C. J. W. Darwin, Capt A. D. Pentland. **88** Capt A. Hepburn + **1** AM Proctor, Lt J. P. West + 2 Lt N. M. Dales. **201** Capt S. M. Kinkead/Lt R. E. Bright. **208** Capt W. L. Jordan/Lts R. L. Johns/P. M. Dennett/McDonald. **209** Capt R. M. Foster (2), Lt W. R. May (in our lines). **210** Capt A. W. Carter, Lts L. P. Coombes/C. W. Payton, Lt W. S. Jenkins, Lt E. Swale. **2 AFC** Lt W. Q. Adams, Capt A. T. Cole, 2 Lt G. Cox, Lt E. D. Cummings, Capt H. G. Forrest, Lt R. L. Manuel. **4 AFC** Capt A. H. Cobby (2), Capt G. F. Malley.

HONOURS AND AWARDS

DSO Maj A. D. Carter (Bar), Capt E. Mannock (Bar), MC. **MC** Capt J. D. Belgrave (Bar), Capt J. W. Aldred (Bar), Capt D. R. MacLaren (Bar), Capt The Hon R. A. Grosvenor (Bar), Lt T. C. Noel (Bar), Lt D. Latimer, 2 Lt A. A. Leitch, 2 Lt E. F. Peacock, Lt S. F. H. Thompson, 2 Lt J. H. Umney, Lt G. W. Bulmer, 2 Lt H. G. Hegarty, Lt W. J. A. Duncan (Bar), Lt R. St. J. Dix (Bar), 2 Lt K. W. Payne, Lt J. I. T. Jones, MM. **DSM** Pte C. V. Robinson. **MM** Sgt G. R. Smith.

3 – 9 June

The award of the D.C.M. to Sgt E. A. Deighton, 20 Sqn, was a reminder of the magnificent work performed by the air gunners of the Bristol Fighter squadrons. Flying with various pilots, Deighton had taken part in air combats which resulted in the destruction of 10 enemy aircraft, and later added at least two to this score.

COMMUNIQUÉ NO. 10

During the period under review we have claimed officially 56 E.A. brought down and 26 driven down out of control. In addition, one E.A. was brought down by anti-aircraft. Twelve of our machines are missing. Approximately $174\frac{3}{4}$ tons of bombs were dropped and 6,933 photographs taken.

June 3rd
Weather fine; cloudy in morning ↶ 24 tons of bombs dropped ↶ E.A. inactive until evening.

June 4th
Weather overcast all day ↶ 13¾ tons of bombs dropped ↶ Enemy aircraft activity very slight.

One E.A. was shot down in flames into the sea by Maj W. A. Bishop, 85 Sqn.

June 5th
Weather fine ↶ 27¼ tons of bombs dropped ↶ Enemy aircraft activity slight below normal.

Lt E. C. Bromley and 2 Lt C. G. Gass, while leading a patrol of 22 Sqn, sighted a Halberstadt two-seater, which on their approach fired a green light. Lt Bromley, suspecting a trap, waited, and in a short time some Albatross scouts appeared and joined the Halberstadt. Almost at once, six Albatross scouts dived out of the sun on to the others, apparently mistaking them for one of our patrols. Lt Bromley then led the patrol into the melée and shot down the Halberstadt. Lt S. F. H. Thompson and Sgt R. M. Fletcher shot down two of the Albatross scouts while the E.A. continued to fight among themselves, several of them being seen to go down out of control. Lt Bromley's good leadership thus led the Huns into their own trap.

Enemy balloons were shot down in flames by Lt A. L. Jones, 210 Sqn and Lt E. Swale, 210 Sqn.

June 6th
Weather fine ⌒ 37¾ tons of bombs dropped ⌒ Enemy aircraft activity considerable.

Capt P. J. Clayson, while leading a patrol of 1 Sqn, attacked formation of Pfalz and Albatross scouts, two of which he shot down in flames.

Lt E. E. Owen and Lt C. B. Henderson, of the same patrol, also each shot down an E.A. in flames.

Two hostile balloons were shot down in flames by Capt A. W. Beauchamp-Proctor, 84 Sqn, and one by Lt H. G. Watson, 4 Sqn A.F.C.

June 7th
Weather fine; cloudy in afternoon ⌒ 34¾ tons of bombs dropped ⌒ Enemy aircraft activity slight.

Lt C. R. Pithey and 2 Lt H. Rhodes, 12 Sqn, while on photographic work were attacked by nine Pfalz scouts. Of the two first pairs to attack Lt Rhodes drove two down out of control. He then fired at one of the third pair and shot away its tail. The remaining E.A. then made off.

A formation of 49 Sqn on bomb raid were attacked by about 45 E.A. Lts L. R. Charron and F. B. Denison were attacked by two of them at close range, both of which Lt Denison shot down and crashed.

June 8th
Weather, cloudy with fair intervals ⌒ 8¾ tons of bombs dropped ⌒ Enemy aerial activity was very slight.

June 9th
Weather, fine in morning, rain in afternoon ⌒ 28½ tons of bombs dropped ⌒ Enemy aircraft activity slightly below normal, except on battle front.

Lt F. R. McCall, 41 Sqn, dived on an E.A. two-seater which opened fire on him at 1,000 yards range, hitting a longeron and the petrol tank. After considerable manœuvring, Lt McCall got within 100 yards of E.A., whose observer then ceased firing, and the machine was seen by ground observers to crash at Mezieres. Lt McCall's machine was badly damaged, two cylinders being blown off the engine during the combat.

Lts R. C. Armstrong and F. J. Hart, 3 Sqn A.F.C., on returning from the line had their attention attracted by anti-aircraft bursts to an E.A. two-seater which was making for the line. Lt Armstrong cut the E.A.

F.E.2b

Leonard Bridgman

off and by skilful manœuvring forced it to land intact on his own aerodrome.

A hostile balloon was shot down in flames by Lt C. J. Shackell, 210 Sqn.

The following information was obtained from a German prisoner:

> On 28th May a British single-seater was forced to land near Morcourt. The Germans who took him prisoner questioned him, but he refused to answer. Thereupon they threatened to shoot him; but as he still refused to reply to their questions he was taken to the rear. Subsequently the Battalion Commander told the men to imitate his example, if captured.

Enemy aircraft were also brought down during the period under review by:

Sqn 3 Lts A. W. Franklyn/W. Hubbard. **19** Lt C. V. Gardner, Lt N. W. Hustings. **20** Lt A. T. Iaccaci + Cpl A. Newlands, Capt D. Latimer + Lt T. C. Noel, Capts T. P. Middleton + F. Godfrey (2), Lt W. M. Thomson + Pbr F. J. Ralphs. **22** Lt J. E. Gurdon + Sgt J. Hall. **23** Lt H. A. Goodison, Lt J. W. Pearson. **24** Lt G. D. Foster, Capt C. N. Lowe (2), Capt I. D. R. MacDonald (2). **25** Capt J. E. Pugh + Lt S. C. Eschmann. **29** Capt C. H. R. Lagesse (our side of the lines), Lts A. E. Reed/C. G. Ross, Lt B. R. Rolfe, Lt C. J. Venter. **32** Capt W. A. Tyrrell, Capt W. A. Tyrrell/Lt J. W. Trasler. **43** Lt J. Paine, Capt C. F. King. **46** Capt D. R. MacLaren. **54** Lt J. H. Spence/Sgt P. H. Williams. **56** 2 Lt C. Parry (2). **60** Capt J. D. Belgrave (2), Capt W. J. A. Duncan. **62** Lts G. K. Runciman + A. J. Todd, Capt W. E. Staton + Lt J. R. Gordon (2), Lt W. K. Swayze + 2 Lt E. M. Nicholas. **73** Capt M. le Blanc-Smith, Lt W. B. Probart. **74** Squadron patrol, Capts W. E. Young/E. Mannock/Lts A. C. Kiddie/H. G. Clements. **79** Lt F. I. Lord. **84** Capt A. W. Beauchamp-Proctor/ Lt A. W. Southey, Capt J. V. Sorsoleil. **87** Capt C. J. W. Darwin, Lt A. W. Vigers. **88** Lt K. B. Conn + 2 Lt B. Digby-Worsley (2). **103** Formation led by Capt J. S. Stubbs + 2 Lt C. C. Dance. **206** Capt Stevens + Lt Christian/Lt Eaton + 2 Lt Tatnell. **209** Lt C. G. Edwards, Lt W. R. May, Lt J. H. Siddall, Lts J. H. Siddall/C. G. Edwards. **210** Capt A. W. Carter/Lt Baird, Lt S. C. Joseph, Lt S. C. Joseph/Lt K. T. Campbell, Capt J. G. Manuel, Capt J. G. Manuel/Lt W. S. Jenkins. **3 AFC** Lts R. C. Armstrong + J. H. Jeffrey/T. L. Baillieu + F. A. Sewell.

HONOURS AND AWARDS

DSC Capt J. H. Forman, 2 Lt L. R. Shoebottom. **MC** Capt F. Hyde, 2 Lt S. H. Wallage, Capt B. E. Catchpole, Capt P. S. Burge, MM, Capt E. J. Jones, Capt C. N. Lowe, 2 Lt C. A. Sundy, 2 Lt B. L. Lindley, Capt D. E. Gibbons, Lt H. S. P. Walmsley, Capt E. Williams, Lt A. S. Keep, Lt W. McK. Thomson. **DCM** Sgt E. A. Deighton.

10 – 16 June

This week saw the return to operational flying of Maj R. Collishaw (now Air Vice-Marshal, retired), one of the leading R.N.A.S. 'aces'. He was credited with a victory score of 60 by the end of the war.

Capt E. J. McClaughry, 4 Sqn Australian Flying Corps (22 victories), also reached the rank of Air Vice-Marshal, and is known for his writings on air strategy.

Capt G. J. C. Maxwell, returning to 56 Sqn for a combat refresher course, was credited with 27 victories by the end of the war.

COMMUNIQUÉ NO. 11

During the period under review we have claimed officially 63 E.A. brought down and 31 driven out of control. In addition, 2 E.A. were brought down by anti-aircraft. Thirty-one of our machines are missing. Approximately $115\frac{3}{4}$ tons of bombs were dropped, and 4,104 plates exposed.

June 10th
Weather, rain; some bright intervals ∽ $10\frac{1}{2}$ tons of bombs dropped ∽ Activity was slight.

Capt G. Fox-Rule and Lt E. H. Tredcroft, 49 Sqn, while on low bombing were attacked by five E.A., who cut them off from the line. Capt Fox-Rule dived through the E.A., singling out the leading machine, at which he fired until within 30 yards, whereupon it burst into flames and was seen to hit the ground. They were then attacked by three E.A. from the rear, at which the observer fired 100 rounds, sending one down out of control and forcing another to break off. Owing to their tail plane bracing wires being shot through, the combat was not continued with. During a bomb raid on Bapaume Dump, Lt C. W. Peckham and Sgt J. Grant, 57 Sqn, were attacked by eight Fokker triplanes at the first of which Sgt Grant fired, sending it down in flames. The remaining E.A. then headed off the D.H.4, compelling it to fly north. A little later another of the E.A. opened fire from below; Lt Peckham dived on it, and after firing 80 rounds saw it crash to the ground. The D.H.4 then returned home.

June 11th

Weather, overcast; clearing in afternoon ∽ *21¾ tons of bombs dropped* ∽ *Activity was below normal, except on the battle front.*

Patrols of 73 Sqn destroyed 6 E.A. in the course of the day, the following pilots accounting for one each: Lt G. Pilditch, Lt O. M. Baldwin, Capt G. A. H. Pidcock, Lt R. N. Chandler, Lt A. V. Gallie, Capt W. H. Hubbard.

June 12th

Weather, overcast; visibility fair ∽ *27 tons of bombs dropped* ∽ *Activity generally slight, except on battle front.*

Patrols of 73 Sqn destroyed five E.A. during the day, two of which were shot down in our lines—both by Capt M. le Blanc-Smith, who had also previously destroyed, another E.A. The remaining two E.A were accounted for by Lt G. N. Anderson and Lt J. H. Drewry.

Capt R. C. Phillipps, 2 Sqn A.F.C., while on offensive patrol, dived on six triplanes which were attacking another of our patrols, and shot down two of them. Shortly afterwards he attacked an enemy two-seater, which he shot down, the E.A. bursting into flames on hitting the ground. Capt Phillipps also destroyed another E.A., thus accounting for four in one day, all of which were confirmed by pilots.

A hostile balloon was shot down in flames by Capt E. J. McClaughry, 4 Sqn A.F.C.

June 13th

Weather, cloudy; visibility poor ∽ *9½ tons of bombs dropped* ∽ *Inactive, except for a brief spell on the Third Army front.*

Lt H. A. Gordon, 60 Sqn, in company with Lt R. G. Lewis and Capt J. D. Belgrave, dived on an E.A. two-seater which went out of control, closely followed by Capt Belgrave into the mist. Lt Gordon then followed Lt Lewis, who was losing height, and landed beside him between Ablaincourt and Chaulnes—Lt Lewis smashing his undercarriage. Some soldiers soon appeared, who opened fire on them. Lt Gordon ran to his machine, calling to Lt Lewis to get in with him, but the latter, apparently mistaking the soldiers for friends, walked towards them. As they were still firing, Lt Gordon took off and then circled back over the body of men, intending to fire on them, but seeing Lt Lewis in their midst refrained from doing so, as he was afraid of hitting him. Lt Gordon then returned home, having had one wire of his rudder control shot through and a longeron practically shot away.

June 14th

Weather overcast, low clouds, high winds ∽ *4½ ton of bombs dropped* ∽ *Activity very slight; no decisive combats.*

ARTILLERY OBSERVATION BIPLANES

Top: Armstrong Whitworth F.K.8

Bottom: R.E.8

The Fokker Dr I triplane

June 15th

Weather, cloudy; fair intervals ∽ 10 tons of bombs dropped ∽ Activity slight.

A hostile balloon was shot down in flames by Capt P. J. Clayson, 1 Sqn.

Three machines of 83 Sqn left at 11.5 p.m., 11.10 p.m. and 11.12 p.m. to carry out a reconnaissance of the area Cambrai–Le Cateau–St. Quentin–Peronne. All machines had to be sent together as a clear interval occurred in the weather at 11 p.m. The machines returned respectively at 1.55 a.m., 1.10 a.m. and 2.12 a.m. Reconnaissances were carried out from heights varying from 800 to 2,500 feet, but were greatly hindered owing to severe rain storms and low clouds. Several Michelin flares were dropped; a number of lights were seen in woods west of Estrees, and a considerable amount of transport was observed on the road at the S.W. edge of Manancourt Wood. Another column of transport was seen on the main road three miles west of Cambrai proceeding in the direction of Bapaume. Observation in the majority of cases was rendered very difficult owing to machines having to alter their altitude very frequently through running into banks of clouds.

June 16th

Weather variable—some rain, fair intervals ∽ 32½ tons of bombs dropped ∽ Active on French battle front and north of British front.

Lts E. A. Coghlan and H. M. Stewart, on a bomb raid of 27 Sqn, were attacked by about 20 E.A. Lt Stewart shot one of them down in flames, but was then killed. The E.A. continued to attack, and Lt Coghlan was wounded. Another D.H.4 of the formation closed up on Lt Coghlan's tail and escorted him safely to the lines.

Enemy aircraft were also brought down during the period under review by:

Sqn 1 Capt P. J. Clayson. **11** Lts N. B. Scott + H. E. Power. **20** Capts T. P. Middleton + F. Godfrey, Lt D. E. Smith + 2 Lt J. Hills. **32** Capt A. Claydon (2). **41** Lt W. G. Claxton, Lt F. R. McCall (2). **43** Lt C. C. Banks (2), Lt J. G. Beck, Capt C. L. E. Geach, Capt C. F. King (2), Lt C. B. Ridley. **48** Patrol led by Capt C. R. Steele. **49** Lts H. Ford + H. H. Jones, Capt F. W. Lowen + Lt V. Dreschfeld. **56** Capt G. C. Maxwell (2). **57** Lt A. D. R. Jones + Sgt J. T. Ward. **64** Capt E. R. Tempest. **65** Capt J. Gilmour. **73** Lt G. L. Graham, Capt G. A. H. Pidcock/Lt E. R. Trendell. **74** Lt S. Carlin, Lt H. G. Clements, Lt P. F. C. Howe (2), Capt E. Mannock. **80** Lt L. K. Baker, Capt H. A. Whistler (2). **84** Capt A. W. Beauchamp-Proctor, Lt G. A. Vaughn (USAS). **85** Capt W. A. Bishop (3), Lt L. H. Callahan, Capt S. B. Horn. **201** Lt G. B. Gates. **203** Maj R. Collishaw (2). **206** Capt Stevens + Lt Christian. **2 AFC** Lt T. J. Hammond, Lt R. L. Manuel. **4 AFC** Capt E. J. McClaughry.

17–23 June

The first awards of the new R.A.F. decorations, the Distinguished Flying Cross and Medals were made on 23 June. In the original ribbon the purple and white stripes ran horizontally, but for various practical reasons the design was shortly afterwards changed to the current diagonal pattern.

Lts Springs and Grider, 85 Sqn, were Americans serving in the R.A.F. Grider's diary, edited after his death by Springs, formed the basis of the well-known book *War Birds*.

COMMUNIQUÉ NO. 12

During the period under review we have claimed officially 53 E.A. brought down and 10 driven down out of control. Nineteen of our machines are missing. Approximately 107 tons of bombs were dropped, and 3,626 plates exposed.

June 17th

Weather, fine in morning; some thunder in afternoon ⟟ 34¾ tons of bombs dropped ⟟ Activity was considerable on north of British front.

85 Sqn destroyed five E.A. in the course of the day, of which Maj. W. A. Bishop crashed two and sent one down in flames, Lt A. Cunningham-Reid shot down one, and Lts J. D. Canning, E. W. Springs, J. M. Grider accounted for the fifth.

A hostile balloon was shot down in flames by Lt W. G. Claxton, 41 Sqn.

Capt Gamon, 205 Sqn, during a bomb raid on Chaulnes was wounded in the head by A.A. fire, and fainted. The engine was hit and, the main petrol pipe being severed, went on fire. The machine fell for 1,000 feet when the fire went out. Maj Goble (observer) regained control of the machine and released his bombs; he then glided to the lines, which he crossed at 6,000 feet, when Capt Gamon recovered and brought his machine safely back to the aerodrome although a Pfalz scout attacked them on the way.

June 18th

Weather, fair, overcast in afternoon ⟟ 28½ tons of bombs dropped ⟟ Active in morning, very slight in afternoon.

Lts F. M. F. West and D. R. Sharman during a bomb raid of 8 Sqn, were attacked by four of a formation of Pfalz scouts. Lt West turned and dived on one E.A. which he shot down and crashed. Four more Pfalz scouts then attacked them; Lt Sharman fired at the leading one which went down out of control. They were again attacked, but succeeded in shaking off the E.A. Lts F. A. Whittall and A. J. Ord, on the same raid. also sent down a Fokker triplane out of control and returned with their machine badly shot about.

A patrol of 56 Sqn attacked six Albatross scouts over Suzanne aerodrome. Lt H. J. Burden attacked one which he shot to pieces in the air. Lt C. Parry shot down another and drove a third down compelling it to land about a mile from the aerodrome, where Lt Burden saw it and fired several bursts into it.

Capt A. Pentland, 87 Sqn, while flying alone attacked four enemy two-seaters. He fired at the straggler, which dived east very steeply, and then climbed back to the other three. He attacked the leader, which went down east, with his engine stopped, followed by one of the others. Capt Pentland then attacked the remaining E.A. which he shot down out of control.

June 19th
Weather, low clouds and rain ⌒ *7¾ tons of bombs dropped* ⌒ *Enemy aircraft activity was very slight.*

Lts J. E. Gurdon and J. J. Scaramanga, 22 Sqn, dived on one of a formation of Pfalz scouts and fired into it at close quarters, whereupon the E.A. side-slipped steeply and crashed into the centre-section of another hostile scout just below it. Both of them were seen to go down locked together.

Maj W. A. Bishop, 85 Sqn, while flying alone attacked three Pfalz scouts which were immediately joined by two others. After firing a short burst into one of them it went down vertically and crashed near Ploegsteert. Two of the other E.A., while circling round, collided and fell together. Maj Bishop then attacked one of the remaining two E.A. which had started to dive east and shot it down. The last escaped in the clouds. Ten minutes later Maj Bishop attacked an enemy two-seater and shot it down in flames.

Capt A. H. Cobby, 4 Sqn A.F.C., shot down a Pfalz scout on our side of the lines.

Capt C. H. R. Lagesse, 29 Sqn, shot down an enemy balloon in flames.

Lt Smith and F/Sgt Shepherd, 29 Balloon Section, had their balloon set on fire by a hostile machine during a shoot. They both jumped but Lt Smith's parachute failed to open. His fall was broken by a tree and he landed on marshy ground none the worse except for a shaking. F/Sgt

Charles King

Friedrichshafen G III

Shepherd's parachute opened, but he was unfortunately seriously wounded in the back.

A raid was carried out on Bancourt aerodrome by a patrol of 201 Sqn, consisting of Lts Brading, Gates, Nightingale, Bright, Riddell and McLaughlin, protected by two flights of 60 Sqn. Twenty-four 25-lb. bombs were dropped from 500 feet, bursts being observed among the hangars, after which the machines descended lower and over 3,000 rounds were fired into the hangars and huts believed to be officers' quarters. A Hannoveraner two-seater which was on the aerodrome was set on fire. All the machines returned, though most of them were hit.

June 20th
Weather, low clouds and rain ⌀ *8½ tons of bombs dropped* ⌀ *Enemy aircraft activity very slight.*

A hostile machine was brought down by Lt M. A. Newnham, 65 Sqn.

June 21st
Weather, low clouds, occasional rain-storms ⌀ *7 tons of bombs dropped* ⌀ *Enemy aircraft activity was very slight.*

One hostile machine was brought down by Capt J. I. T. Jones, 74 Sqn.

June 22nd
Weather, low clouds and high wind ⌀ *2½ tons of bombs dropped* ⌀ *Practically no E.A. seen. No decisive combats.*

June 23rd
Weather, overcast, fair intervals, high wind ⌀ *18 tons of bombs dropped* ⌀ *Enemy aircraft activity very slight.*

E.A. were brought down by Lt L. H. T. Capel and Sgt E. A. Deighton, 20 Sqn, and Capt L. P. Coombes, 210 Sqn.

Enemy aircraft were also brought down during the period under review by:

Sqn 18 Capts D. Stewart + L. I. Collins. **20** Lt L. H. T. Capel + Sgt E. A. Deighton, Lt A. I. Iaccaci + Cpl A. Newlands, Lts P. T. Iaccaci + W. Noble, Lt L. M. Price + 2 Lt E. Hardcastle. **23** Capt H. V. Puckeridge, Lt C. L. A. Sherwood. **24** Lt W. C. Lambert, Capts I. D. R. MacDonald/G. O. Johnson/Lt H. D. Barton (in our lines). **29** Capt F. J. Davies, Lt A. G. Reed, Lt C. J. Venter. **41** Lt W. G. Claxton. **54** Lt M. G. Burger, Capt F. M. Kitto, Lt J. H. Spence. **65** Lt E. G. Brookes. **74** Lt J. I. T. Jones, Capt E. Mannock, Lt B. Roxburgh-Smith. **84** 2 Lt R. Manzer. **85** Maj W. A. Bishop (2), Capt A. C. Randall/Lt A. Cunningham-Reid, Lt E. W. Spriggs. **98** Capt F. A. Laughlin + 2 Lt H. Tasker, Lt C. H. Roberts + Sgt G. W. Slater. **209** Capt R. M. Foster/Lt R. D. Gracie (USAS). **210** Lts K. T. Campbell/C. H. Strickland, Capt H. A. Patey,

Lt E. Swale. **4 AFC** Capt A. H. Cobby, Capt E. J. McClaughry, Maj F. I. Tanner, Lt H. G. Watson.

HONOURS AND AWARDS

DFC 2 Lt W. F. J. Harvey, Capt H. A. Whistler, 2 Lt G. G. Bailey, Capt R. H. Rusby, Capt A. H. Cobby, Capt E. D. Atkinson, Capt M. H. Findlay, DSC, Lt H. Fall, Capt R. Affleck, Capt W. E. Young, Capt T. P. Middleton, Capt A. R. Churchman, Lt W. H. Leete, Capt C. H. Darley, DSC, Capt S. N. Pike, Capt H. G. Forrest, Lt R. L. Manuel, 2 Lt A. McGregor, 2 Lt J. M. Glaisher, 2 Lt G. A. King, Capt P. J. Clayson, MC, Capt D. Gilley, Capt J. A. Slater, MC, Capt S. M. Kinkead, DSC, Capt I. D. R. MacDonald, Capt T. L. Simpson, 2 Lt H. N. Young, 2 Lt H. B. Davies, Lt H. Briggs, Capt G. E. Siedle, Lt A. Mills. **DFM** Pte W. J. Middleton.

24–30 June

Successful pilots during this week included Maj K. R. Park, 48 Sqn, (Air Marshal Sir Keith Park, A.O.C. No. 11 Fighter Group, during the Battle of Britain), and Lts Claxton and Shields, 41 Sqn, who were credited with victory scores of 37 and 24 respectively by the end of the war.

COMMUNIQUÉ NO. 13

During the period under review we have claimed officially 90 E.A. brought down and 39 driven down out of control. Thirty-six of our machines are missing. Approximately 206½ tons of bombs were dropped and 8,196 plates exposed.

June 24th
Weather, clouds and strong wind; rain in afternoon ∽ 30 tons of bombs dropped ∽ Enemy aircraft activity slight.

June 25th
Weather overcast. Visibility bad ∽ 6¾ tons of bombs dropped ∽ Enemy aircraft activity was slight except on the southern part of the front.

June 26th
Weather cloudy, with bright intervals ∽ 18¼ tons of bombs dropped ∽ Enemy aircraft activity was slight.

June 27th
Weather fine ∽ 36 tons of bombs dropped ∽ Enemy aircraft activity was considerable.

A patrol of 79 Sqn, led by Capt F. S. Wilkins, attacked a formation of 15 E.A. In the combat which ensued, Capt Wilkins shot down one E.A. Lt H. J. MacDonald, Lt V. G. Snyder and Lt C. L. Lindberg also shot down one E.A. each. Lt F. I. Lord, of the same squadron, flying alone later in the day, attacked a triplane and 4 Pfalz scouts, the former of which broke up in the air. Shortly afterwards he shot down another E.A.

Capt J. S. Ralston, while leading a squadron formation of 15 machines of 84 Sqn, engaged a formation of E.A., which were reinforced by a large number of others. After a fight of about one and a half hours, during which Capt Ralston had shot down an E.A. out of control, his machine was hit in the petrol tank, and, being blinded by the petrol, he was obliged to spin down. On coming out of the spin, Capt Ralston was attacked in the rear, but as he turned to engage the E.A. his engine cut out and caught on fire at 2,000 feet. He managed, however, to land and get clear of his machine before it went up in flames.

Lt N. F. McKenna and Lt W. P. Heslop, 3 Sqn A.F.C., while on artillery observation, were attacked on all sides by 12 Albatross Scouts, one of which Lt Heslop shot down out of control.

June 28th
Weather fine ○ 27½ tons of bombs dropped ○ Enemy aircraft activity was considerable.

Capt A. H. Cobby, 4 Sqn A.F.C., dived on an E.A. two-seater near Merris, which he shot down. Soon after, he attacked a Pfalz Scout which went down in flames. Later in the day, Capt Cobby also shot down an Albatross two-seater, which was observed to crash.

Capt G. E. H. McElroy, 40 Sqn, shot down a hostile balloon in flames.

June 29th
Weather fine, visibility not good ○ 30 tons of bombs were dropped ○ Enemy aircraft activity was not great.

A patrol of 41 Sqn encountered several E.A. in the neighbourhood of Bray. In the fighting, two hostile machines were brought down and three driven down out of control.

Whilst patrolling over the lines at night, Capt Armstrong, 101 Sqn, encountered a large tractor machine, at which he fired several hundred rounds. It went down vertically, but could not be followed owing to the bad visibility.

June 30th
Weather fine, visibility good ○ 47½ tons of bombs dropped ○ Enemy aircraft activity was considerable.

Maj A. W. Keen, 40 Sqn, dived on one of three Fokker triplanes, which turned very sharply to the left in an attempt to get on the S.E.'s tail. Maj Keen looped, coming out 100 feet above the E.A., and fired a burst of 10 rounds before he overshot it. The E.A. went into a flat spin and, after several bursts had been fired at it, broke up in the air, both its wings being seen to fall off.

A patrol of 20 Sqn attacked two formations of E.A., one of nine, the other of seven, machines, two of which were shot down by Capts T. P. Middleton and F. Godfrey. Lt A. T. Iaccaci and Sgt A. Newland, Capt D. Latimer and Lt T. C. Noel, Lts D. J. Weston and W. Noble, Capt

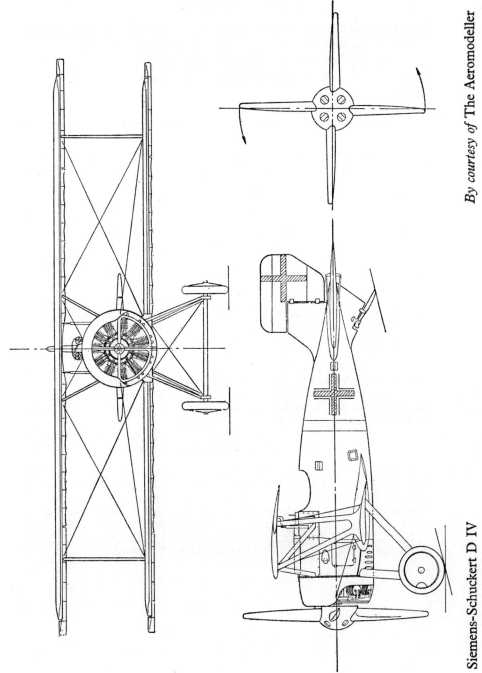

By courtesy of The Aeromodeller

Siemens-Schuckert D IV

H. P. Lale and 2 Lt E. Hardcastle, of the same patrol, also accounted for an enemy machine each, making a total of six E.A. destroyed.

Hostile balloons were shot down in flames by: Lt A. Buchanan, 210 Sqn (1); Capt G. E. H. McElroy, Lts G. J. Strange, A. R. Whitten, 40 Sqn (1).

Enemy aircraft were also brought down during the period under review by:

Sqn 1 'C' Flight, Capt P. J. Clayson. **22** Lts F. C. Gibbons + V. St. B. Collins. **23** Sqn Patrol. **24** Lt W. C. Lambert, Capt C. N. Lowe. **29** Lt P. S. Harrison, Lt C. J. Venter. **32** Capt A. Claydon. **40** Capt G. E. H. McElroy. **41** Lt W. G. Claxton (2), Lt F. R. McCall (5), Lt S. A. Puffer (2), Lt W. E. Shields (2), Lts E. Stephens/F. R. McCall, Lt H. E. Watson. **48** Capt J. E. Drummond + 2 Lt J. A. Galbraith, Maj K. R. Park + 2 Lt H. Knowles, Capt F. C. Ransley + 2 Lt C. W. Davies, 2 Lts N. Roberts + W. F. Hanna, 2 Lts N. Roberts + C. C. Walmsley. **49** Lt E. D. Asbury + 2 Lt W. N. Hartley, Lts A. J. P. Estlin + E. H. Tredcroft. **54** Capt R. A. Jones. **55** Capt A. A. Leitch. **56** Capt W. O. Boger, Lt W. R. Irwin (2), Capt G. C. Maxwell (2). **62** Lts L. W. Hudson + H. E. Merritt. **64** Lt Barrett. **65** Capt J. Gilmour. **70** 2 Lt O. A. P. Heron, Capt J. Todd (2). **74** Lt H. G. Clements, Capt J. I. T. Jones (4). **84** Capt H. W. L. Saunders, Capt J. V. Sorsoleil. **85** Lt A. Cunningham-Reid, Lt J. Dymond, Lt M. C. McGregor, Lt E. W. Springs. **87** Maj J. C. Callaghan. **88** Lt K. B. Conn + 2 Lt E. H. Smyth (2), Lt K. J. Cullen + 2 Lt E. H. Ward, Lt J. P. West + Sgt E. Antcliffe, Lt W. A. Wheeler + 2 Lt T. S. Chilton, Lt A. Williamson + A. G. E. Hoare (2), Patrol 88. **203** Maj R. R. Collishaw. **209** Capt E. B. Drake, Capt R. M. Foster. **210** Lt W. G. Claxton (4), Capt L. P. Coombes/Lts K. R. Unger/J. C. Saunderson, Lt S. C. Joseph (2), Capt H. A. Patey, Capt Patey/Lt W. W. Gyles. **4 AFC** Capt A. H. Cobby (2), Lt G. S. Jones Evans, Lt R. King (3), Capt E. J. McClaughry, Lt H. G. Watson (2).

HONOURS AND AWARDS

DFC Capt C. F. King, MC, Capt R. C. Phillipps, MC, Capt A. Claydon, Capt W. H. Hubbard, Capt M. le Blanc-Smith, Capt H. L. Rough, Lt V. Dreschfeld, Lt C. R. Pithey, 2 Lt H. Rhodes, Lt J. M. Todd, Capt A. W. Beauchamp-Proctor, MC, Maj W. A. Bishop, VC, DSO, MC, Capt A. O. Lewis-Roberts, 2 Lt E. N. Lohmeyer, Lt R. Wilson, 2 Lt E. H. Hobson, Lt C. C. White, 2 Lt G. N. Sellers, Lt H. N. Hampton, Lt C. J. Venter, Lt C. Parry, Lt F. J. Lain, Lt M. McConville, MC, 2 Lt R. J. Hook, 2 Lt W. E. F. Jones.

1 – 7 July

Although the Fokker D.VII biplane had been in service with German squadrons since May, the communiqué for 4 July was the first to give it specific mention. The D.VII was not a particularly fast aeroplane, but it retained remarkable manœuvrability at high altitudes and is considered by some authorities to be the best fighter produced by either side during the war.

On the same day was the first recorded instance of an air-drop of supplies to advanced infantry formations.

COMMUNIQUÉ NO. 14

During the period under review we have claimed officially 67 E.A. brought down and 44 driven down out of control. Twenty-one of our machines are missing. Approximately 167 tons of bombs were dropped and 7,685 plates exposed.

July 1st
Weather fine, visibility good ⌒ 38¾ tons of bombs dropped ⌒ Enemy aircraft active, especially in morning.

Capt J. Gilmour, 65 Sqn, while leading a patrol, dived on a Fokker triplane, and, getting on its tail, shot it down in flames. Shortly after, he attacked another E.A., which dived steeply, but could not be followed. A little later Capt Gilmour led his patrol to attack 40 E.A., at one of which he fired at point blank range; the E.A. dived steeply, and its wings were seen to fall off in the air. Another E.A. which was attacked dived over the vertical, and appeared to be out of control. On his way back to the lines Capt Gilmour was attacked by four Albatross scouts. By doing an Immelmann turn and the half-roll he succeeded in getting on the tail of the leader, which he shot down in flames. Having by this time exhausted all his ammunition, Capt Gilmour returned home.

Capt E. J. McClaughry, 4 Sqn A.F.C., was dived on by three Pfalz scouts, two of which, however, collided in the air during their dive; the third scout fired on him, but when attacked dived east. One of the E.A. which collided immediately fell to the ground, while the other went down in a slow spiral. Capt McClaughry then dived on the latter, which, after 100 rounds had been fired into it, burst into flames.

Hostile balloons were shot down in flames by: Lt J. A. E. R. Daley, 24 Sqn; D. S. Poler (U.S.A.), 40 Sqn; Capt G. E. H. McElroy, 40 Sqn.

July 2nd
Weather fine ☞ *13 tons of bombs dropped by night and 16 tons by day* ☞ *Enemy aircraft not active considering weather.*

Capt P. J. Clayson, 1 Sqn, attacked a Hannoveraner over Armentieres. On opening fire the E.A. machine suddenly went into a steep dive, the observer's map fell overboard quickly followed by the observer himself, who caught hold of the gun mounting and lay along the top of the fuselage. The machine caught fire and finally crashed.

Five machines of 60 Sqn, led by Lt A. W. Saunders, saw a formation of six Pfalz scouts 7,000 feet below flying over Villers Bretonneux. The patrol went down and attacked the E.A. at the tail end of the left-hand side of the formation. A drum of Lewis and a long burst of Vickers were fired at it by Lt Saunders, whereupon it went down vertically and was seen to crash by an A.A. battery. The second E.A. on the left of the leader suddenly turned to the right and collided into the E.A. leader, both machines collapsing and crashing in the Bois de Pierret. A Hannoveraner which was firing at one of our S.E.s was then attacked; it dived to within 50 feet of the ground when it flattened out, flying east. Lt Saunders then became separated from his patrol and saw three Pfalz scouts, which he attacked and chased east. On coming home he saw an E.A. attacking an S.E.5 and joined in, whereupon this E.A. also flew east. Lt Saunders was fighting altogether 45 minutes.

July 3rd
Weather, cloudy ☞ *3 tons of bombs dropped by night and 10 tons by day* ☞ *Enemy aircraft activity slight all day.*

Capt A. H. Cobby, 4 Sqn A.F.C., attacked a hostile balloon which was a height of 4,000 feet from above; it was hauled down smoking, but when at a height of 700 feet burst into flames.

July 4th
Weather fine, with strong west wind ☞ *8 tons of bombs dropped by night and 12 tons by day* ☞ *Low-flying E.A. fairly active on the Fourth Army front; otherwise activity slight.*

Combats on a large scale took place between 10 machines of 24 Sqn and 20 hostile machines, consisting of 14 Fokker biplanes, 2 Pfalz scouts and 4 D.V.'s. One E.A. was brought down by Capt W. Selwyn and two by Lt W. C. Lambert, while one other was driven down out of control.

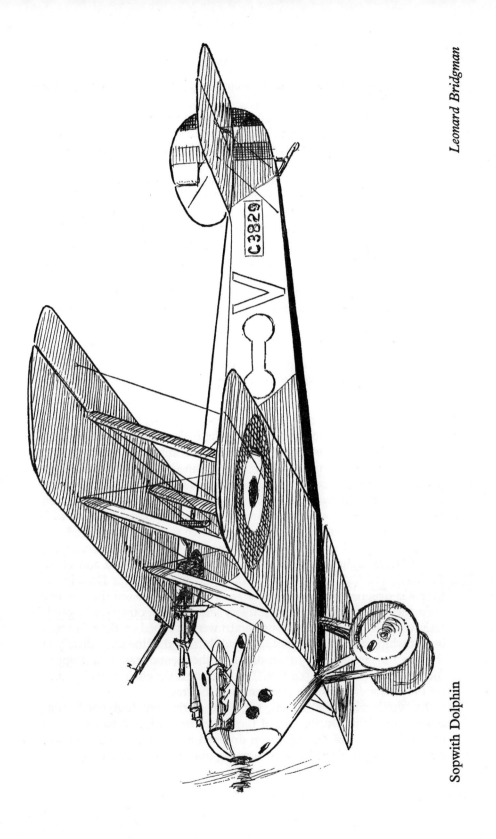

Leonard Bridgman

Sopwith Dolphin

In addition, there were 10 indecisive combats. All our machines returned undamaged.

Lt T. N. Harrison, 29 Sqn, on wireless interruption, shot down an enemy two-seater, which burst into flames. He was then attacked by three Pfalz scouts and a two-seater, and succeeded in shooting down one of the former.

Pilots of 23, 41 and 209 Sqns fired a large number of rounds and dropped a great many bombs on hostile batteries and troops from a low height in conjunction with the successful operations by the Fourth Army north-east of Villers Bretonneux. At the same time 9 Sqn dropped 100,000 rounds of ammunition in 83 boxes to our advanced infantry.

In spite of bad weather, machines of 101 Sqn patrolled a line east of the Fourth Army front continuously from dark till dawn. Machines of the same squadron dropped 350 25-lb. bombs. All pilots carried out three raids, while Lt Anderson, with Lt Lovell as observer, made four trips.

July 5th
Weather fine ◇ 17½ tons of bombs dropped by night and 20¼ tons by day ◇ Enemy aircraft fairly active in the evening.

Lt S. A. Puffer, 41 Sqn, on diving through the clouds whilst on offensive patrol almost collided with a hostile balloon; he fired 50 rounds at it from a range of 40 yards, causing the balloon to burst into flames.

In the middle of a low reconnaissance, Lts Dunlop and Scott, 53 Sqn, had their petrol tank pierced by machine gun fire from the ground. Lt Scott (observer) climbed out on to the wing of the machine to investigate the extent of the damage. He then climbed back into his seat, removed his cloche, stepped out on to the wing again and blocked the rent with his stick and leather cap. The reconnaissance was then completed and messages dropped at Divisional Headquarters on the return journey.

Whilst on night reconnaissance, Lts A. J. E. Broomfield and G. B. Nicholas, 102 Sqn, observed two trains moving west near Hermies. A flare was dropped from a height of 800 feet which showed that the one train was loaded with carts or artillery and that the other was a goods train with about 50 trucks. Four bombs were dropped on the first train, one of which was an OK, another bomb hitting the line immediately in front of the engine. They then dived on the second train and dropped four 25-lb. bombs from 500 feet. The truck next the engine was knocked off the line and also one in the centre of the train.

Lt Welsh with Maj Mason, 101 Sqn, carried out four bomb raids during the night. During one of these they succeeded in blowing up a dump. Machines of this squadron dropped altogether over 400 bombs during the night, in addition to carrying out six reconnaissances.

DAY BOMBERS

Top: De Havilland D.H.4

Bottom: De Havilland D.H.9

P.R.M. 728.

Top: F.E. 2b night bomber of No. 100 Squadron

Bottom: A group of No. 92 Squadron pilots, against S.E.5a's, which illustrates the variety of uniforms worn after the formation of the R.A.F.

July 6th

Weather cloudy all day ⌒ 1½ tons of bombs dropped by night and 16 tons by day ⌒ Enemy aircraft activity slight.

Lt C. J. Heywood and 2 Lt E. A. Dew, 205 Sqn, when flying on the rear of a bombing formation, were attacked by five Pfalz scouts. The pilot fired 200 rounds with the front gun, while the observer opened fire on two of the E.A. which had got on their tail. After firing 450 rounds at a close range, he was very badly wounded in the leg, but fired a further 50 rounds, which sent one of the hostile machines down in flames. The observer then fainted and fell on the dual control lever, causing the machine to go into a very steep nose-dive from which the pilot had great difficulty in pulling it out. The machine landed O.K. at Bertangles.

July 7th

Weather fine, visibility bad ⌒ 1½ tons of bombs dropped by night and 11½ tons by day ⌒ Enemy aircraft activity slight.

Enemy aircraft were also brought down during the period under review by:
Sqn 1 Lts J. C. Bateman/Kullberg/Smart. **19** Capt R. A. Del'Haye, Lt M. S. Gregory, Capt G. Irving/Lts J. D. Hardman/J. A. Aldridge. **20** Lt P. T. Iaccaci + 2 Lt R. W. Turner (2), Lt E. W. Sweeney + Pbr C. G. Boothroyd, Lts D. J. Weston + W. Noble. **22** Lts J. E. Gurdon + J. J. Scaramanga. **23** Lt H. N. Compton, Capt A. B. Fairclough (2), Capt A. B. Fairclough/Lt H. M. Sinclair, Lt J. W. Pearson, Lts G. W. R. Pidsley/J. Adam, Capt H. V. Puckridge, Lt C. E. Watson. **27** Lt B. M. Bowyer-Smythe + Sgt W. B. Harold. **29** Capt F. J. Davies, Lt T. S. Harrison, Capt R. C. L. Holme, Lt C. J. Venter, Lt H. A. Whittaker. **40** Capt G. E. H. McElroy (3), Capt I. P. R. Napier (2). **41** Lt W. G. Claxton (2), Lt E. F. H. Davis, Capt F. R. McCall (2), Lt W. E. Shields (3). **46** Capt D. R. MacLaren. **48** A Flight (Pilots: Capt H. A. Oaks, Lt E. D. Shaw (USAS), 2 Lt N. Y. Lewis), Capt J. E. Drummond + 2 Lt J. A. Galbraith, Capt H. A. Oaks + Lt G. J. Maynard, Capt C. R. Steele + Lt A. E. Ansell. **56** Capt C. M. Crowe, Capts G. C. Maxwell/C. M. Crowe. **60** Lt J. S. Griffith (2), Capt H. G. Hegarty. **65** Lt H. Browne, Capt J. Gilmour (3), Capt E. F. Peacock, Lts T. M. Williams/D. M. John. **74** Lt W. B. Giles, Capt J. I. T. Jones. **85** Lt A. Cunningham-Reid. **87** Capt A. Pentland. **88** Lt K. B. Conn + 2 Lt B. Digby-Worsley. **203** Lt N. C. Dixie, Lt W. A. W. Carter. **205** Lt E. H. Johnson + 2 Lt A. R. Crosthwaite. **209** Lt W. R. May. **210** Capt L. P. Coombes. **2 AFC** Lt F. R. Smith. **4 AFC** Capt A. H. Cobby.

HONOURS AND AWARDS

DSO Maj E. Mannock (2nd Bar), MC. **DFC** 2 Lt E. F. Van der Riet, Capt O. L. Beater, Capt J. M. Mason, DSC, Capt S. Anderson, Capt F. C. Ransley, Capt J. I. Jones, MC.

8 – 14 July

Maj Edward Mannock, who assumed command of 85 Sqn following Bishop's posting to an administrative job, celebrated his promotion with a victory on 8 July.

148 Sqn, United States Air Service, which scored its first victory on 13 July, operated with 17 Sqn on the British Front. Both flew Sopwith Camels. Most of the American squadrons were on the French Front, where the first had arrived in February.

COMMUNIQUÉ NO. 15

During the period under review we have claimed officially 47 E.A. brought down and 19 driven down out of control. In addition, one E.A. was brought down by A.A. Twenty-two of our machines are missing. Approximately 102 tons of bombs were dropped, and 3,662 plates exposed.

July 8th
Weather overcast in morning, heavy thunderstorms in afternoon ⌒ 5 tons of bombs dropped by night and 19 tons by day.

A formation of machines of 103 Sqn whilst on a bomb raid was attacked by about 15 E.A. at a height of 15,000 feet. Lt J. G. H. Chrispin and 2 Lt E. A. Wadsworth fired three bursts at one of the machines which was attacking their tail; it dived down vertically and was observed to crash.

July 9th
Weather cloudy with occasional showers ⌒ 14 tons of bombs dropped by day ⌒ Enemy aircraft fairly active.

Lts C. F. Galbraith and G. W. Parlee, 5 Sqn, whilst engaged on a shoot, saw an Albatross single-seater on the tail of one of our scouts; they dived on it, but the pilot's gun jammed after 10 rounds had been fired. The hostile single-seater left our scout and turned east. The pilot of the R.E.8 side-slipped his machine, the observer firing a burst of about 20 rounds; at the same time a second Camel dived at the E.A., which then turned west. The R.E.8 side-slipped once again, allowing the observer to fire three bursts at close range. The hostile machine burst into flames and crashed to the ground.

Whilst machines of 107 Sqn were releasing their bombs in formation, three hostile machines attacked them in the rear. 2 Lt J. R. Brown and AM J. P. Hazell fired 40 rounds at one of the E.A., which burst into flames.

July 10th

Weather cloudy, with rain storms ◇ 3½ tons of bombs dropped by night and 10 by day ◇ Enemy aircraft fairly active in the north during the morning; otherwise slight.

Patrol of 9 Bristol Fighters of 22 Sqn encountered a hostile formation of between 15 and 20 Fokker Triplanes and Pfalz scouts. Lt J. E. Gurdon dived on one of the Pfalz Scouts and sent it down in flames. Two E.A. then got on to the tail of his machine. Lt J. J. Scaramanga (observer) shot them both down out of control, himself being severely wounded.

Lt F. C. Stanton then dived on another of the Pfalz Scouts, when 5 got on his tail, all of which the observer, 2 Lt C. J. Tolman, engaged, sending one down out of control. Lt Stanton brought down two other machines, while Capt W. F. J. Harvey and Lt Thomson, his observer, shot down a third, and sent a fourth down out of control.

Lt T. W. Martin and Capt D. E. Waight fired a long burst at a Pfalz Scout, which went down out of control.

Lt F. G. Gibbons (pilot) and Lt V. St. B. Collins (observer) were attacked by 3 E.A. who got on the tail of their machine. One of these the observer shot down out of control. During the fight other hostile machines were shot down, but it was impossible to say by whom.

July 11th

Weather, low clouds and rain ◇ 9 tons of bombs dropped by day ◇ Enemy aircraft activity very slight, only a few combats taking place.

July 12th

Weather, low clouds and rain ◇ 1 ton of bombs dropped by day ◇ Enemy aircraft activity practically nil—no combats.

July 13th

Weather, clouds and rain with occasional bright intervals ◇ 3 tons of bombs dropped by night and 4½ tons by day ◇ Enemy aircraft fairly active in the north during morning.

A patrol of 74 Sqn had a combat with six enemy scouts. Several of the patrol opened fire at close range. One hostile machine was shot to pieces in the air and another driven down out of control.

A patrol of 40 Sqn attacked an enemy two-seater, which was shot down and seen to crash.

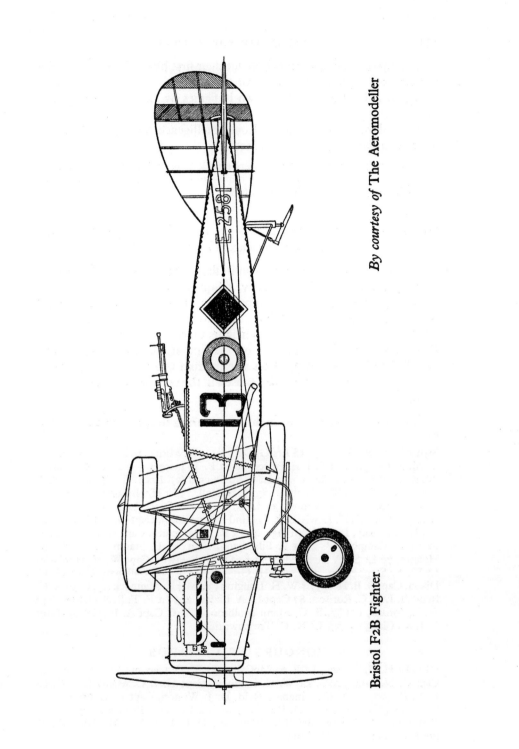

Bristol F2B Fighter

By courtesy of The Aeromodeller

The 148th American Squadron got their first blood, Lt F. E. Kindley shooting off the tail plane of an Albatross scout.

A hostile balloon was shot down in flames by Lt T. S. Harrison, 29 Sqn.

The following is an extract from Intelligence Summary of the 1st Australian Division, dated 12th instant:

> Several prisoners stated they were unable to offer any resistance owing to one of our aeroplanes, which by machine-gun fire forced them to keep their heads down in their shell hole position.

July 14th

Weather, fine early; overcast later ∽ 33¼ tons of bombs dropped ∽ Enemy aircraft fairly active in early morning, otherwise quiet.

Hostile balloons were shot down in flames by Capt R. C. L. Holme, 29 Sqn, and by Capt A. H. Cobby, 4 Sqn A.F.C.

During the night 207 Sqn dropped 132 112-lb. and 33 25-lb. bombs on the railway between Blanc Misseron and Thulin and on the Valenciennes–Mons railway from heights varying from 300 to 3,500 feet. Eight direct hits were obtained on the line at Blanc Misseron. Eight 112-lb. bombs were dropped on a train from 900 feet, causing several explosions. Explosions were also caused in the railway works at Quievre-chain.

Enemy aircraft were also brought down during the period under review by:

Sqn 1 Lt H. A. Kullberg. **18** Lts G. Darvill + W. Miller. **19** Lt C. V. Gardner, Lt M. S. Gregory, Lt P. J. E. Pierce. **20** Lt P. T. Iaccaci + 2 Lt R. W. Turner (2). **22** Capt G. W. Bulmer + 2 Lt J. McDonald (2), Lts J. E. Gurdon + J. J. Scaramanga, Lt T. W. Martin + Sgt J. H. Hall. **23** Lt H. N. Compton. **29** Capt F. J. Davies, Lt C. J. Venter. **32** Lt R. E. L. MacBean. **40** Lt R. G. Landis (USAS), Capt G. H. Lewis/Lt I. F. Hind (in our lines), Capt G. E. H. McElroy (4), Lt I. L. Roy, Lt G. J. Strange. **43** Lt R. E. Meredith, Capt H. W. Woollett. **62** Lt L. Campbell + 2 Lt P. Pilkington, Capt W. E. Staton + Sgt W. N. Holmes. **70** Lt S. T. Liversedge. **73** Lt O. M. Baldwin, Capt W. H. Hubbard, Lt W. S. Stephenson. **74** Lt R. H. Gray. **85** Lt L. K. Callahan, Capt G. C. Dixon, Capt S. B. Horn, Lt W. H. Longton (3), Maj E. Mannock (2), Capt A. C. Randall, Lt J. C. Rorison. **87** Capt H. A. Biziou. **203** Lt F. T. S. Sehl. **208** Capt W. L. Jordan, Lts W. E. G. Mann/Mollison. **4 AFC** Capt A. H. Cobby, Capt E. J. McClaughry (3), Lt N. C. Trescowthick.

HONOURS AND AWARDS

DFC Lt H. G. Watson, Lt F. R. McCall, 2 Lt W. G. Claxton, Lt J. E. Gurdon, Capt C. N. Lowe, MC, Lt W. C. Lambert, Capt G. J. C. Maxwell, MC, Lt L. L. Brown, Lt A. Cunningham-Reid, D. J. Weston, Capt F. Godfrey, 2 Lt W. Noble, Capt A. A. N. D. Pentland, MC, 2 Lt E. G. Brookes, Capt R. M. Foster, Capt G. Irving, Maj G. L. Thomson, DSC, Lt J. A. E. R. Daley. **DFM** Pte J. Chapman, Sgt W. Jones.

15 – 21 July

Low-level attacks on enemy aerodromes, such as those of 16 and 19 July, were intensified during the closing months of the war.

Lt Indra Lal Roy, 40 Sqn, who gained two victories, was the only World War I 'ace' from India. He claimed nine victories and won the D.F.C. before he was killed in action.

Sgt A. Newland, awarded the D.F.M. on 21 July, was another of 20 Sqn's leading air gunners. He had shot down six enemy aircraft by the end of the war.

COMMUNIQUÉ NO. 16

During the period under review we have claimed officially 56 E.A. brought down and 8 driven out of control. In addition, 2 E.A. were brought down by A.A. Forty-two of our machines are missing. Approximately 125 tons of bombs were dropped, and 10,160 plates exposed.

July 15th
Weather, low clouds and ran ⌒ 3¼ tons of bombs dropped ⌒ Enemy aircraft inactive.

Lts J. Gould-Taylor and B. G. Thomson, 3 Sqn A.F.C., while on artillery observation, attacked an enemy two-seater, which dived steeply after 50 rounds had been fired at it by the pilot, and burst into flames on hitting the ground.

Capt A. H. Cobby, 4 Sqn A.F.C., while flying with Lt H. G. Watson, attacked five Pfalz scouts, one of which he shot down in flames and another broke up in the air after being attacked.

A hostile balloon was shot down in flames by Capt H. W. Woollett, 43 Sqn.

July 16th
Weather, low clouds in morning, afterwards fine; thunderstorms in evening ⌒ 4½ tons of bombs dropped by night and 13 tons by day ⌒ Enemy aircraft inactive, except for a brief spell in afternoon.

Capt E. J. McClaughry, 4 Sqn A.F.C., and Lt G. S. Jones-Evans, of the same squadron, attacked two balloons on the ground, which they had located the previous evening, and set them both on fire.

Capt H. W. L. Saunders, 84 Sqn, Capt J. S. Ralston, 84 Sqn, and Lt W. V. Thomas and 2 Lt H. T. G. Robey, 98 Sqn, each shot down an enemy balloon in flames.

A bomb raid was carried out on Foucaucourt aerodrome by 65 and 209 Sqns, escorted by 23, 24 and 84 Sqns. 105 25-lb. bombs were dropped and 8,300 rounds fired from 500 feet and lower on the sheds and huts. Many direct hits were obtained, and two hangars set on fire. All machines returned. Two hostile balloons were shot down in flames on the way back.

July 17th

Weather, low clouds in early morning, then fine; thunderstorms in evening ∞ *8$\frac{1}{2}$ tons of bombs were dropped by night and 16$\frac{1}{4}$ tons by day* ∞ *Enemy aircraft inactive.*

Hostile balloons were shot down in flames by Capt T. F. Hazell, 24 Sqn; Lt N. W. R. Mawle, 84 Sqn; Lt R. G. Smallwood, 4 Sqn A.F.C.

July 18th

Weather fine, high wind, some clouds ∞ *15$\frac{1}{2}$ tons of bombs dropped by day* ∞ *Enemy aircraft activity very slight.*

Lt I. L. Roy, 40 Sqn, saw a D.F.W. pointed out by A.A. fire which he dived on and shot down near Arras.

Lt R. K. Whitney, 60 Sqn, attacked an enemy two-seater at 1,000 feet which broke up at the third burst and crashed in pieces. Lt Whitney crossed the trenches at 600 feet and had his cowling and longeron shot through by fire from the ground.

Capt H. W. Woollett, 43 Sqn, shot down two hostile balloons in flames.

July 19th

Weather fine, cloudy ∞ *13$\frac{3}{4}$ tons of bombs dropped by night and 13$\frac{3}{4}$ tons by day* ∞ *Enemy aircraft active for a short time in morning, otherwise few seen.*

Hostile balloons were shot down in flames by: 2 Lt H. Manzer, 84 Sqn; Lt S. Carlin, 74 Sqn; Capt D. R. MacLaren, 46 Sqn.

A bomb raid was carried out by 209 Sqn on Cappy aerodrome from a height of 500 to 100 feet. A direct hit was obtained on a hangar and casualties were inflicted on personnel in machine gun emplacements on the aerodrome. Lt Edwards actually landed on the aerodrome during the course of the raid. Two hangars were seen to be smoking. On the way home troops and transport were scattered by machine gun fire, and Lt Siddall attacked trenches from 50 feet. Four of a party of men who

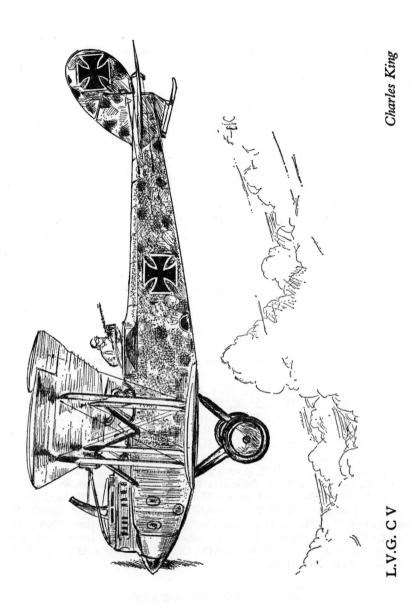

Charles King

L.V.G. C V

attempted to run into a dug-out were seen to fall. Fifteen machines took part in this raid.

July 20th

Weather fine in morning, thunderstorms afternoon and evening ○ *$14\frac{1}{2}$ tons of bombs dropped by night and $16\frac{1}{4}$ tons by day* ○ *Enemy aircraft active during morning, otherwise few seen.*

Capt W. F. J. Harvey and Lt G. Thomson, 22 Sqn, while escorting a bomb raid encountered 15 E.A., which they engaged, and Lt Thomson shot down two of them and sent a third down out of control.

Lt N. W. R. Mawle, 84 Sqn, dived on one of three Fokker biplanes, which evaded him by rapid manœuvring. He then attacked a second at very close range, which spun down and was seen to crash. On the way home Lt Mawle shot down a balloon in flames.

Hostile balloons were shot down in flames by Capt J. S. Ralston, 84 Sqn; Lt J. E. Boudwin (U.S.A.S.), 84 Sqn (one); Lt S. Carlin, 74 Sqn.

July 21st

Weather, high wind and low clouds ○ *$4\frac{1}{2}$ tons of bombs dropped by day* ○ *Practically no hostile machines were seen, except on the French battle-front.*

E.A. were brought down by Lt E. J. Salter, 54 Sqn (three), and a patrol of 73 Sqn led by Maj R. H. Freeman.

Enemy aircraft were also brought down during the period under review by:

Sqn 3 Lt C. G. Brock/2 Lt J. G. Fleet. **19** Capt R. A. De L'Haye. **20** Capt D. Latimer + Lt T. C. Noel, Lt W. M. Thomson + Sgt J. D. C. Summers. **23** Lt H. F. Faulknor. **25** Lts F. Ollenbittle + A. R. Watts. **29** Lt C. J. Venter. **40** Capt G. E. H. McElroy (2), Lt I. L. Roy. **43** Capt C. F. King. **46** Capt D. R. MacLaren, Lt J. Taylor. **64** Capt P. S. Burge (2), Lt M. L. Howard. **70** 2 Lt A. Webster. **73** Lt O. M. Baldwin, Lt G. L. Graham (2), Lt W. S. Stephenson. **74** Maj K. L. Caldwell, Lt B. Roxburgh-Smith. **79** Capt J. D. Canning. **80** Lt J. R. Orr. **84** Capt H. W. L. Saunders. **85** Maj E. Mannock (2). **87** Lt R. A. Hewat, Lt R. M. Macdonald. **98** Lt W. G. Davis + Sgt J. K. Ison, Capts O. W. C. Johnsen + G. H. P. Whitfeld (2), Lt C. H. Roberts + Sgt G. W. Slater, Lts F. C. Wilton + C. P. Harrison (3). **203** Maj R. Collishaw, Capt L. H. Rochford/Lt W. Sidebottom, Lt A. E. Rudge. **208** Capt W. J. Jordan. **209** Capt J. K. Summers/Lt K. M. Walker. **2 AFC** Capt A. T. Cole. **4 AFC** Capt E. J. McClaughry, Lt L. E. Taplin.

HONOURS AND AWARDS

DFC Lt A. T. Iaccaci, Capt J. Todd, MC, Capt P. H. Cummings, Capt W. G. Preston, 2 Lt G. H. Welsh, Lt J. S. Griffith, Lt A. J. E. Broomfield, Capt E. J. McClaughry, Capt W. L. Jordan, DSC. **DFM** Sgt A. Newland.

22 – 28 July

This communiqué recorded the death of Mannock, shot down by enemy ground fire after he and Lt D. C. Inglis had destroyed a Junkers CL-1 two-seater monoplane. Mannock, who was credited with 50 victories, was awarded a posthumous V.C. on 18 July 1919.

Another notable event was the destruction of an enemy night bomber by Capt Yuille, 151 Sqn. This unit was the first specialist night-fighter squadron on the Western Front. It flew Sopwith Camels modified for night operations, and for the remainder of the war mounted many successful patrols and intruder sorties against enemy night-bomber bases.

Capt J. M. Robb, who opened scoring for the newly arrived 92 Sqn, retired from the R.A.F. after World War II as Air Chief Marshal Sir James Robb.

COMMUNIQUÉ NO. 17

During the period under review we have claimed officially 75 E.A. brought down and 12 driven out of control. Seven enemy balloons were destroyed. In addition, two E.A. were brought down in our lines by anti-aircraft. Thirty-three of our machines are missing. Approximately 135 tons of bombs were dropped and 4,194 plates exposed.

July 22nd
Weather fine ☁ 16 tons of bombs dropped by night and 16 tons by day ☁ Enemy aircraft active in morning, otherwise slight.

Maj R. Collishaw, and Capt L. H. Rochford, 203 Sqn, left at 3.40 a.m. to attack Dorignies Aerodrome. Capt Rochford attacked first, firing all his ammunition into buildings and hangars from 200 feet. He then dropped three bombs on the living quarters on the aerodrome and a fourth on a hangar, which went on fire. Maj Collishaw then attacked three machines, which were being brought out of a hangar, with machine gun fire and dropped four bombs from 150 feet which burst among the huts. Before returning, Maj Collishaw attacked a hostile machine at 800 feet, which was going to land on the aerodrome, and shot it down in flames. Returning about two hours later to see what damage had been done, he was attacked by three Albatross scouts, one of which was shot down and seen to crash. Later in the day Capt Rochford led his patrol to attack five Fokker biplanes, one of which he shot down; the remainder were either shot down or driven down out of control by the rest of his patrol—Lt W. Sidebottom and Lt A. E. Rudge destroying one each.

Capt J. M. Robb scored first blood for 92 Sqn by destroying one of four Fokker biplanes.

Hostile balloons were shot down in flames by: Capt T. F. Hazell, Lt G. B. Foster, 24 Sqn (1); Capt H. W. L. Saunders, 84 Sqn; Lt R. H. Youdale, 4 Sqn A.F.C.

July 23rd
Weather, high wind and rain ∽ 11½ tons of bombs dropped by day ∽ Enemy aircraft—practically none seen. No combats took place.

July 24th
Weather fine, high wind; cloudy in morning ∽ 5¾ tons of bombs dropped by day ∽ Enemy aircraft active in evening, otherwise slight.

A patrol of 85 Sqn flying in two layers saw six E.A., which the lower flight decoyed towards our lines. The higher flight then attacked from the east, with the result that four of the enemy machines were shot down, Capt M. C. McGregor, Lt W. H. Longton, Capt A. C. Randall, and Lt O. A. Ralston (U.S.A.S.) accounting for one each.

July 25th
Weather fine, some showers ∽ 21½ tons of bombs dropped by night and 16½ tons by day ∽ Enemy aircraft not particularly active, except on the French battle-front in the evening.

Capt A. B. Yuille, 151 Sqn, while on night patrol, sighted an enemy twin-engine machine at 12.45 a.m., into which he fired a burst of 50 rounds at 30 yards range. He then fired a second burst of 30 rounds, but was upset in the backwash as the E.A. dived away. Picking the machine up again he attacked it a second time and then lost sight of it. The enemy machine came down in our trenches. According to the prisoners' statements, Capt Yuille had wounded the observer with his first burst, put one engine out of action with his second, and the other engine out of action in his last attack.

A patrol of 20 Sqn encountered about 20 E.A. on returning from a bomb raid on Menin. In the fight which ensued four hostile machines were shot down—one by Lt Smith and Pbr Hills, one by Lt Thomson and Sgt Summers, one by Capt H. P. Lale and 2 Lt F. J. Ralph, and one by the patrol collectively.

Capt J. S. Ralston, 84 Sqn, attacked and set on fire a hostile balloon

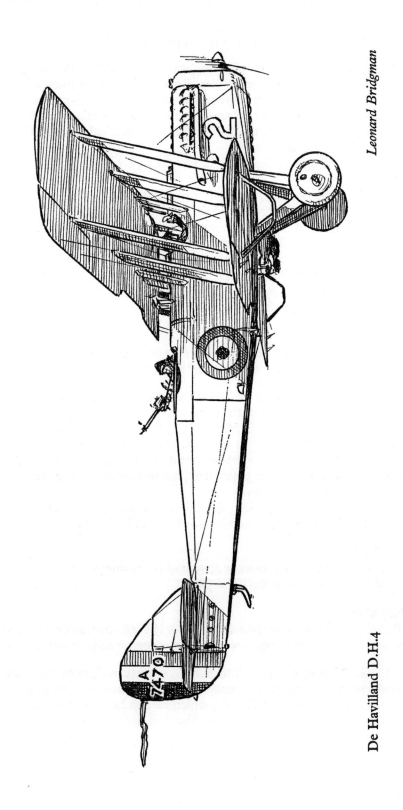

Leonard Bridgman

De Havilland D.H.4

near Warvillers. He was heavily fired at from the ground and was hit in the buttock. At 200 feet, near Villers Bretonneux, Capt Ralston fainted and came to at 900 feet over Warfusee-Abancourt, still flying east and being shot at. He then turned west, and his vision becoming blurred a second time landed on our side of the lines and crashed, having fainted just as he was flattening out.

Lt H. G. Watson, 4 Sqn A.F.C., also shot a hostile balloon down in flames.

Capt W. A. Southey, 84 Sqn, while attacking a Fokker biplane became lost in clouds, through which he dived from 15,000 to 300 feet, and being unable to see his instruments he flew through the rain towards what he thought was the sun, but it turned out, however, to be the moon. He then glided down to land. As his machine was running on the ground he was fired at from all sides, so he took off again, and managing to switch on his lights for five minutes succeeded in getting his direction and returning home at 300 feet.

July 26th
Weather cloudy, rainstorms ○ 9 tons of bombs dropped by night and 18½ tons by day ○ Very few enemy aircraft were seen.

A patrol of 24 Sqn, led by Lt H. D. Barton, forced an enemy two-seater to land on our side of the lines.

Lt D. C. Inglis and Maj E. Mannock, 85 Sqn, attacked an enemy two-seater, which they shot down in flames. On returning at 200 feet, Lt Inglis saw Maj Mannock's machine shot down from the ground, and his own machine was hit in the petrol tank, but he succeeded in landing five yards behind our front lines.

Capt J. I. T. Jones, 74 Sqn, also brought down a hostile machine.

Capt T. F. Hazell, 24 Sqn, shot down a hostile balloon in flames.

July 27th
Weather, low clouds and rain ○ 2¼ tons of bombs dropped by day ○ No aerial activity and no combats took place.

July 28th
Weather, fine early coming overcast ○ 2 tons of bombs dropped by night and 12 tons by day ○ Few enemy aircraft seen, except in early morning.

Lt G. S. Jones-Evans, 4 Sqn A.F.C., on returning from dropping bombs on train, attacked and brought down an enemy two-seater, when he was fired on by a second E.A., which he also brought down after a short burst. He was then hit by machine gun fire from the ground but returned safely.

Hostile balloons were shot down by Capt E. J. McClaughry, 4 Sqn A.F.C., and Lt S. Carlin, 74 Sqn.

On the 16th July, Lts G. B. Gates and R. S. S. Orr, 201 Sqn, both attacked the same enemy balloon, which they shot down in flames.

On the 19th, the same officers each shot down an enemy balloon in flames.

Enemy aircraft were also brought down during the period under review by:

Sqn 18 Lts J. Gillanders + E. Walker. **20** Lt J. H. Colbert + 2 Lt R. W. Turner, Lts L. M. Price + A. Mills, Lts G. E. Randall + G. V. Learmond. **25** Lt L. Young + 2 Lt H. Pullen. **29** Lt T. S. Harrison, Lt A. E. Reed, Lt C. G. Ross. **32** Lt A. A. Callender, Lt J. O. Donaldson (USAS). **40** Lt P. V. Burwell (USAS), Lt I. F. Hind, Lt R. G. Landis (USAS), Capt G. E. H. McElroy (2), Lt G. J. Strange. **46** Capt D. R. MacLaren (2). **49** Capt L. R. Charron + Lt W. A. Owens. **54** Capt H. H. Hackwill. **56** Capt W. O. Boger. **64** Capt P. S. Burge, Sgt Cowlishaw, Lt A. G. Donald, Lt W. R. Henderson, Lt M. L. Howard, Lt D. Lloyd-Evans. **73** Lt R. N. Chandler, Lt G. L. Graham (2), Lt E. J. Lussier, Lt W. S. Stephenson (3), Lt W. S. Stephenson/2 Lt N. Cooper. **74** Lt G. R. Hicks, Capt J. I. T. Jones (3), Lt O. M. Baldwin (2). **84** Lt C. F. Falkenberg, 2 Lt W. J. B. Nel, Capt J. S. Ralston/Lt N. W. R. Mawle, Lt G. A. Vaughn (USAS)/2 Lt R. Manzer. **85** Maj E. Mannock. **92** Lt E. F. Crabb. **98** Sgts H. W. Bush + E. R. McDonald. **203** Capt L. D. Bawlf, Capt L. H. Rochford. **206** Lt H. D. Stier (USAS) + Cpl J. Chapman. **208** Lts White/Howell/Wightman. **2 AFC** Capt R. C. Phillipps. **4 AFC** Lt R. King, Capt E. J. McClaughry (3), Lt R. Moore.

HONOURS AND AWARDS

DFC Capt A. H. Cobby (1st and 2nd Bar), 2 Lt W. G. Claxton (Bar), Capt R. Hilton, MC, Capt F. A. Laughlin, Capt R. G. D. Francis, 2 Lt E. A. Dew, Capt C. E. Williamson-Jones, Capt E. Waterlow, MC, Capt W. E. Staton, MC, Capt E. Dickson, DSC, Capt G. H. Harrison.

29 July – 4 August

The ratio of enemy aircraft destroyed to British losses made this a very satisfactory week.

Successful night operations were continued by 151 Sqn. Maj Brand, the C.O., who had a short while before shot down a Gotha over England, remained in the R.A.F. after the war, and as Air Vice-Marshal Sir Christopher Brand commanded No. 10 Fighter Group during the Battle of Britain.

The week's victorious pilots included Maj C. D. Booker, 201 Sqn, formerly of 8 Sqn, R.N.A.S., who ended the war with a victory score of 22.

COMMUNIQUÉ NO. 18

During the period under review we have claimed officially 73 E.A. brought down and 19 driven down out of control. Five enemy balloons were destroyed. In addition, two E.A. were brought down by A.A. Fifteen of our machines are missing. Approximately $134\frac{1}{4}$ tons of bombs were dropped and 9,207 plates exposed.

July 29th
Weather fair, misty, visibility bad ⟳ 1 ton of bombs dropped by night and 10 tons by day ⟳ Enemy aircraft active in the north, otherwise quiet.

A patrol of 206 Sqn on returning from a bomb raid were attacked by about 20 Pfalz scouts. Capt L. R. Warren and Lt L. A. Christian shot down one E.A. which was seen to crash, and sent down another in flames. Lt G. A. Pitt and Cpl G. Betteridge also shot down one of them in flames.

July 30th
Weather fine, ground mist, visibility indifferent ⟳ $1\frac{1}{4}$ tons of bombs dropped by night and $16\frac{3}{4}$ tons by day ⟳ Enemy aircraft active in morning, and in northern sector in evening.

Lt N. W. R. Mawle, 84 Sqn, dived on one of seven enemy scouts at which he fired 300 rounds, sending it down in a series of stalls and spins. He was then attacked from above by another machine, but succeeded in getting on its tail by a series of climbing turns when he was attacked by three more E.A. to avoid which he put his machine into a spin, and on coming out saw that two of them had collided. A third E.A. made off east.

July 31st

Weather fine, visibility poor ↦ 3½ tons of bombs dropped by night and 15½ tons by day ↦ Enemy aircraft active, especially in evening.

Capt E. J. McClaughry, 4 Sqn A.F.C., shot down an enemy two-seater, which was observed to crash, in the morning. Later in the day he was attacked by three Fokker biplanes, one of which he destroyed, but was himself hit by one of the others, so after driving the remaining two E.A. east he returned home.

A patrol of 19 Sqn attacked five E.A., three of which were shot down and seen to crash, the pilots responsible being Lts L. H. Ray, C. V. Gardner and A. W. Blake. Lt W. Northridge, of the same squadron, also destroyed a Fokker biplane earlier in the day.

A formation of 18 Sqn, led by Capt H. R. Gould and 2 Lt E. Jinman, while returning from a bomb raid, were attacked by 10 Pfalz scouts. In the combat which ensued several E.A. were seen to fall, but only one, engaged by Lt J. Gillanders and 2 Lt S. Walker and Lt E. Peskett and 2 Lt W. Clarke, was actually seen to crash, though another fired at by the same observers was seen to partially break in the air.

August 1st

Weather fine, visibility fair ↦ 21¼ tons of bombs dropped by night and 24¼ tons by day ↦ Enemy aircraft fairly active.

During the night, two machines of 151 Sqn carried out offensive patrols over Estrees and Guizancourt aerodromes. Capt S. Cockerell arrived at Estrees just as a machine was landing and dropped a bomb which was seen to burst 50 yards from the E.A. He then fired 200 rounds at close range at an E.A. which was attempting to land. All lights being extinguished, no result could be observed. After dropping two more bombs Capt Cockerell returned. Capt W. H. Haynes, when over Estrees, saw three, Gothas approaching, so dropped his bombs on the searchlights to put them out and attacked one of these machines, but later lost it. His gun having failed, he returned home.

Lts A. E. Grigson and H. B. James, 3 Sqn A.F.C., while on artillery patrol observed two of our balloons shot down by an enemy scout, at which they dived. Lt Grigson having fired 150 rounds in bursts, turned away, allowing Lt James to fire 100 rounds into the E.A., which they followed down to within 200 feet of the ground, where they saw it crash.

A bomb raid was carried out on Epinoy aerodrome by 3 and 56 Sqns, escorted by 60 and 11 Sqns. One hundred and four 25-lb. bombs were

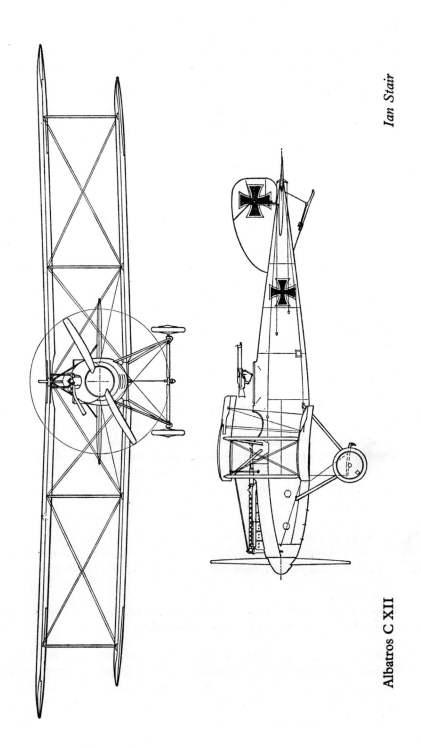

Ian Stair

Albatros C XII

dropped and a large number of rounds fired into the hangars, billets, officers' mess and workshops on the aerodrome, six hangars being observed to go on fire and two to be hit by bombs. Sixteen machines are also believed to have been set on fire, and one machine was blown to pieces. Maj Gilchrist, 56 Sqn, dived to within 10 feet of one Pfalz scout which was standing on the ground, whereupon it burst into flames. Two very large fires were also started which are believed to be from two workshops, the volumes of smoke—very clearly seen on photographs—ascended to 10,000 feet in one case.

August 2nd
Weather fine early, becoming overcast with rain ∽ 10 tons of bombs dropped by night and 12¾ tons by day ∽ Very few enemy aircraft seen.

Two machines of 151 Sqn carried out offensive patrols over Estrees and Guizancourt aerodromes during the night. Maj C. J. Q. Brand was the first to arrive over Guizancourt where he dropped two bombs on hangars. He then fired into a large two-seater machine which was landing and observed his bullets richochet from cockpit and engine. Seeing white lights being placed round the machine on the ground he fired 100 more rounds into it, and all lights were put out. A little later he dropped two more bombs in the path of another machine which was landing. After having fired at hangars and searchlights, he attacked another E.A. but was himself attacked from behind by an enemy scout. He then returned home, having been over the aerodromes for 40 minutes.

Capt S. Cockerell dropped four bombs on the hangars at Guizancourt which were lit up by searchlights, and then attacked each searchlight in turn till they were extinguished. A little later he attacked a Gotha which was preparing to land, all lights being extinguished at once. The Gotha landed or crashed about two miles from the aerodrome.

Lt G. W. G. Gauld and Lt F. S. Gordon, both of 74 Sqn, attacked an enemy two-seater which they shot down on our side of the lines.

Lt S. T. Liversedge, 70 Sqn, also brought down an enemy two-seater.

Lt S. Carlin, 74 Sqn, shot down a hostile balloon in flames.

August 3rd
Weather, fine early, becoming overcast, with rain ∽ 5¾ tons of bombs dropped by day ∽ Enemy aircraft activity slight.

A patrol of 46 Sqn, led by Lt R. K. McConnell, attacked five Fokker biplanes, of which the one attacked by Lt McConnell broke up in the air. Lts C. H. Sawyer, and V. M. Yeates sent two of the remainder down spinning, and they were afterwards observed lying crashed on the ground.

A hostile balloon was shot down in flames by Lt F. W. Gillet, 79 Sqn.

August 4th

Weather, low clouds and rain in morning, fair in afternoon ◌ 5 tons of bombs dropped by night and 6½ tons by day ◌ Enemy aircraft activity slight.

A hostile balloon was set on fire by Lt N. W. R. Mawle, 84 Sqn.

Enemy aircraft were also brought down during the period under review by:
Sqn 1 Lt H. A. Kullberg. **3** Capt H. L. Wallace. **20** Lt J. H. Colbert + 2 Lt R. W. Turner, Lts Groom + Hardcastle (2), Capts T. P. Middleton + F. Godfrey. **23** Lt J. W. Pearson. **24** Lts H. D. Barton/C. M. G. Farrell/W. C. Lambert/T. Hellet, Capt T. F. Hazell, Capt T. F. Hazell/Lts G. V. Foster/E. P. Crossen. **29** Capt R. C. L. Holme, Capt C. H. R. Lagesse. **41** Lt W. G. Claxton (2), Capt F. R. McCall, Capt F. R. McCall/Lt W. G. Claxton. **43** Capt L. G. Loudoun. **46** 2 Lt J. Taylor. **48** Capt H. A. Oaks + 2 Lt H. Knowles. **56** Lt T. J. Herbert (USAS). **62** Lt N. N. Coope + 2 Lt H. S. Mantle (2). **70** Capt W. M. Carlaw (3), 2 Lt J. S. Wilson. **73** Lt R. N. Chandler, Lt G. L. Graham, Lts E. J. Lussier/A. McConnell-Wood/2 Lt N. Cooper. **74** Lt S. Carlin, Capt J. I. T. Jones (3), Lt A. C. Kiddie, Lt H. E. Shoemaker (USAS). **79** Lt R. B. Bannerman. **80** Capt H. A. Whistler. **84** 2 Lt R. Manzer (2), Lts N. W. R. Mawle/A. C. Lobley, Capt H. W. L. Saunders, Capt W. A. Southey, 2 Lt C. R. Thompson, Lt G. A. Vaughn (USAS)/2 Lt R. Manzer. **85** Capt M. C. McGregor, Capt A. C. Randall. **88** Lt J. P. Findlay + 2 Lt R. E. Hasell, Capt H. Hepburn + Sgt E. Antcliffe, Lts H. R. Little + F. W. Addison, Lt W. G. Westwood + 2 Lt W. Tinsley. **92** Lt O. J. Rose, Lt E. Shapard. **201** Maj C. D. Booker, Capt R. C. Brading. **205** Lt R. L. Barbour + 2 Lt J. H. Preston. **206** Lt E. Bailey + 2 Lt R. Milne, 2 Lts Percival + Paget, Lt Schlotzhauer (USAS) + Cpl H. W. Williams, Capt L. R. Warren + Lt L. A. Christian. **208** Lt M. C. Howell, Lts Mann/Green, Lt J. B. White. **209** Capt R. M. Foster/Lt W. R. May. **2 AFC** Capt R. C. Phillipps, Lt J. J. Wellwood. **4 AFC** Lt T. R. Edols, Lt L. E. Taplin, Lts H. G. Watson/R. King. **17 Amer.** Lt W. J. Armstrong, Lt M. L. Campbell, 2 Lt R. M. Todd.

HONOURS AND AWARDS

DSO Maj R. Collishaw (Bar), DSC, DFC. **DFC** Capt G. E. H. McElroy, MC (Bar), Capt E. J. McClaughry (Bar), Capt J. I. T. Jones, MC (Bar), MM, Lt C. G. Edwards, Lt E. H. Tredcroft, 2 Lt R. Manzer, Lt G. Thomson, Capt D. R. MacLaren, MC, Lt G. S. Jones-Evans, Lt F. W. Smith, Capt J. S. Ralston, MC, Lt N. Roberts, Capt L. R. Warren, Capt G. Fox-Rule, Lt J. C. Wilson, Lt I. L. Roy, Lt R. S. Bell, Capt F. J. Davies, Lt O. M. Baldwin, Lt W. Grossart, Lt L. A. Christian, Lt T. S. Harrison.

5 – 11 August

Aircraft losses this week, on both sides, were the highest in the period covered by the R.A.F. communiqués. Most of them occurred during the very active four days, 8–11 August. British bomber formations were heavily attacked by enemy fighters, of which more than 20 were shot down by our bombers.

The first reference to the use of parachutes in enemy aircraft was on 11 August. They had been employed by balloon observers on both sides for a considerable time. Britain was developing a parachute for aircraft use, but its introduction was opposed in some quarters on the grounds that pilots would be tempted to use it unnecessarily. The number of German airmen saved by parachutes is not known.

COMMUNIQUÉ NO. 19

During the period under review we have claimed officially 177 E.A. brought down and 90 driven out of control. Nine enemy balloons were destroyed. In addition, four E.A. were brought down by A.A. Ninety-three of our machines are missing. Approximately 242 tons of bombs were dropped and 5,862 plates exposed.

August 5th
Weather stormy, some rain ⌒ 9¾ tons of bombs dropped ⌒ Very few enemy aircraft seen—no combats took place.

August 6th
Weather, low clouds, rain showers ⌒ 1½ tons of bombs dropped by day ⌒ Enemy aircraft activity very slight.

Capt J. I. T. Jones, 74 Sqn, observed a formation of nine E.A. climbing from their aerodrome and, closing up behind the rear machine, joined the enemy formation with whom he remained for five minutes without being observed. Soon after, two of the enemy machines left the formation to attack an R.E.8. Capt Jones dived at one of these, firing a short burst, whereupon one E.A. side-slipped into the other and they became interlocked. After a long burst had been fired at them, Capt Jones saw them go down together in flames.

A hostile machine was brought down by Capt A. H. Cobby, 4 Sqn A.F.C.

August 7th

Weather fine, ground mist, visibility poor ᐤ 22½ tons of bombs dropped by night and 17 tons by day ᐤ Enemy aircraft activity slight, except on 10th Brigade front.

Capt A. H. Cobby, and Lt N. C. Trescowthick, 4 Sqn A.F.C., while on special mission, saw five Pfalz scouts on which they dived. Lt Trescowthick shot one of these down in flames, and the second he attacked broke up in the air. Capt Cobby shot a third down in flames. Later in the day Capt Cobby destroyed another hostile machine.

Lt M. L. Campbell, and Lt L. A. Hamilton, 17 American Sqn, encountered five E.A. over Armentieres. Lt Campbell shot two of these down, which were both seen to crash by other pilots. Lt Hamilton also accounted for one of the E.A.

Capt W. Armstrong, 151 Sqn, while carrying out an offensive patrol over Estrees aerodrome during the night, accompanied by Maj C. J. Q. Brand, followed an E.A. round the aerodrome for some time which was attempting to land, and eventually shot it down in flames. Both pilots also dropped bombs on lights and hangars on the aerodrome.

August 8th

Weather fair, rain and clouds in morning ᐤ 1¼ tons of bombs dropped by night and 36 tons by day ᐤ A large number of combats took place on the battle front.

Sgts H. W. Bush and E. R. McDonald, 98 Sqn, were attacked by six Pfalz scouts on returning from a bomb raid. Sgt McDonald's gun having jammed after a short burst he fired a Very's light at one of the scouts (which was attacking at close range), which frightened it away. Having rectified the jam, he shot the E.A. down and it was seen to crash.

Lt R. G. Landis (U.S.A.S.), 40 Sqn, after a combat with a hostile machine which he sent down in a cloud of smoke, attacked a hostile balloon, but, observing an enemy two-seater near, diving east, engaged and shot it down. Returning to the balloon, he fired into it at very close range, whereupon it went down in flames.

A patrol of 22 Sqn, led by Capts W. F. J. Harvey and D. E. Waight, while escorting a bomb raid, engaged 10 hostile machines which were attempting to attack the D.H.4's. Two of the enemy machines were shot down by Capt Harvey and his observer, and two by Lt T. H. Newsome and Sgt H. C. Hunt. Lt S. F. H. Thompson and Sgt R. M. Fletcher also destroyed one of the E.A.

A patrol of 65 Sqn, consisting of Lts J. White, G. D. Tod, F. Edsted,

Leonard Bridgman

Handley Page o/400

C. Tolley, D. Oxley and Capt E. Brookes, forced two Fokker biplanes to land on our side of the lines.

Capt A. W. Saunders, 60 Sqn, dived on a Fokker biplane, which he observed to go down in a spin and crash. Soon afterwards he attacked another enemy machine, which fell through the clouds out of control, and on following it down he saw a train, into which he fired from 50 feet, circling twice round the engine. Though heavily fired at from the ground and shot in the seat of his machine, and having fired all his ammunition away, Capt Saunders returned.

One E.A. was forced to land on our sides of the lines by 2 Lts C. Imeretinsky and A. Urinowski, 48 Sqn.

Lt N. W. R. Mawle, 84 Sqn, attacked two enemy balloons which were being towed by a team of horses. Having fired at the first without result, in spite of heavy machine gun fire he successfully attacked the second, which was at a height of 25 feet, and set it on fire. Having again attacked the first one unsuccessfully, he turned his attention to an anti-tank gun, which was hastily limbered up, but the horses scattered and the gun was observed to upset into a ditch. After having attacked various parties of infantry on the ground, Lt Mawle returned to his aerodrome having been wounded in the stomach and the arm by fire from the ground.

Hostile balloons were also shot down in flames by Capt A. W. Beauchamp-Proctor, 84 Sqn; and Lt C. G. Ross, 29 Sqn.

Capt T. M. Williams, 65 Sqn, attacked the rear train of three, on which he dropped two bombs from a low altitude. The train was observed to break in half.

Lt Misener, 201 Sqn, attacked a train which caught fire. He then dived on enemy troops who were attacking an A.W. machine which had landed in 'No Man's Land' and drove them off.

Lt Rollasson, 209 Sqn, dropped four bombs from 100 feet on parties of enemy troops—in one case on a group which had collected round a Bristol Fighter near Beaucourt. His machine was so badly damaged by fire from the ground that he was compelled to land opposite our cavalry outposts, where he remained firing with a rifle, eventually obtaining a horse and returning to his aerodrome.

Capt T. F. Hazell, 24 Sqn, fired a large number of rounds into guns and limbers which were galloping along a road to Rosieres. Several units broke away into the fields and got bogged.

August 9th
Weather fine, with some clouds ◇ *7 tons of bombs dropped by night and 40½ tons by day* ◇ *Enemy aircraft active.*

Lt J. A. Keating (U.S.A.S.) and 2 Lt E. A. Simpson, 49 Sqn, on returning from a bomb raid were attacked by two large formations of enemy scouts. The first E.A. to attack at close range was shot down in flames by 2 Lt Simpson. A little later, a second E.A. which was attacking from the rear was also shot down in flames, and during the course of the combat two more hostile machines were seen to spin down and crash, all of which had been fired at by the observer. Lt Keating's machine had been very badly shot about and he was obliged to land soon after crossing our lines.

Patrols of 29 Sqn shot down five hostile machines during the day, the following pilots accounting for one each: Lts C. M. Wilson, A. E. Reed, H. C. Rath, T. S. Harrison, and Capt F. J. Davies.

Four hostile machines were brought down by pilots of 60 Sqn, Capt A. W. Saunders, 2 Lt H. Buckley, and Lt G. M. Duncan each brought down one, and Capt J. E. Doyle, and Lt R. K. Whitney accounted for one between them.

A hostile balloon was shot down in flames by Lt W. G. Claxton, 41 Sqn.

Lt Lambert, 24 Sqn, fired 300 rounds from a low height at an Anti-Tank gun which was holding up armoured cars, silencing it and allowing the cars to proceed.

Lt Barton, 24 Sqn, seeing Lt Watkins of the same squadron shot down, attacked the machine gun battery and silenced them. On attacking a second time, he was shot down by fire from the ground and landed just behind our Cavalry. His machine being shelled, he went forward and met Lt Watkins who was being brought in from 'No Man's Land' and assisted him to be taken back in a Tank.

Lt McKay, 201 Sqn, while firing at enemy infantry, was shot down by four Fokker biplanes 300 yards behind the enemy's lines. He made a dash for one of our Tanks and got into it, but on learning that it was about to go into action got out again and escaped to our lines under heavy machine gun fire.

August 10th

Weather fine, clouds in morning ∽ *18½ tons of bombs dropped by night and 28½ tons by day* ∽ *Enemy aircraft active.*

Capt H. J. Burden, 56 Sqn, on offensive patrol during the morning engaged a formation of hostile machines, of which he shot down two which were observed to crash. Attacking a second formation a little later, he fired at one E.A. from close range which broke up in the air. In the evening, Capt Burden brought down two more hostile machines.

Capt A. B. Yuille, 151 Sqn, saw a hostile machine caught by several searchlights, and, getting to close range, fired a burst of 75 rounds. The E.A. opened fire on him from below the fuselage. Capt Yuille then fired three more bursts at 25 yards range when the E.A. caught fire under the observer's seat. Shortly afterwards the whole machine burst into flames and fell on our side of the lines.

Capt J. E. Gurdon and 2 Lt C. G. Gass, Lts L. W. King and V. St. B. Collins, 22 Sqn, engaged a hostile formation of 12 Fokker biplanes. The pilots and observers of each machine brought down one hostile machine, thus accounting for four in all.

Lt M. C. Kinney, 3 Sqn, forced a hostile machine to land intact on our side of the lines.

Capt H. L. Wallace, and Lt L. H. McIntyre, of the same squadron, each brought down a hostile machine, and Lt W. H. Boyd and Lt J. R. Montgomery one between them.

Lt F. L. Munslow and 2 Lt W. A. Mercer, 8 Sqn, while on contact patrol in co-operation with Tanks, were attacked by a Fokker biplane, which 2 Lt Mercer brought down.

Hostile balloons were shot down in flames by: Lt R. King, 4 Sqn A.F.C.; Lt R. G. Smallwood, 4 Sqn A.F.C.; 2 Lt W. L. Dougan, 29 Sqn.

Lt Cowper Cole and 2 Lt Pargeter, 53 Sqn, while on reconnaissance had their petrol tank pierced by A.A. fire which saturated the pilot. The observer climbed out on to the left-hand bottom plane and stopped the hole with his glove. Though the machine was banked and side-slipped steeply, Lt Pargeter remained on the wing until just before landing.

August 11th
Weather fine ⌁ 31 tons of bombs dropped by night and 29½ tons by day ⌁ Enemy aircraft active on the battle front; flying in large formations.

Lt C. V. Gardner, 19 Sqn, attacked one of four Pfalz scouts, which fell in flames. The pilots of this machine was seen to jump out and go down in a parachute. A little later, Lt Gardner shot down another E.A.

A bomb raid of 205 Sqn were attacked by some Pfalz scouts on approaching their objective, one of which was shot down by Lt G. Matthews and Sgt L. Murphy; Lt W. Grossart and 2 Lt J. S. Leach dropped a 112-lb. bomb on another of them, which broke one of the wings of the E.A. without exploding, and is believed to have burst on the ground. On returning from the raid, a third hostile machine was destroyed by Lt R. L. Barbour and Sgt F. G. Manning.

A patrol of 88 Sqn engaged a formation of about 25 Fokker biplanes. A fierce fight ensued and five of the enemy machines were brought down, accounted for by Lt C. Findlay and 2 Lt B. Digby-Worsley (who also destroyed another E.A. later in the day), Lt G. R. Poole and Sgt E. Antcliffe, Lt A. Stedman and 1 AM A. Proctor, Capt E. C. Johnston and 2 Lt J. Rudkin, Lt A. Williamson and AM E. Hoare.

Hostile balloons were shot down in flames by: Capt H. P. Lale and 2 Lt J. Hills, 20 Sqn; Lt E. W. Sweeney and 2 Lt C. G. Boothroyd, 20

Sqn; Capt F. J. Davies, 29 Sqn; Lt R. G. Robertson, 29 Sqn.

A bomb raid was carried out from a low height on Courtrai railway station and sidings by 20 and 29 Sqns, escorted by 74 and 85 Sqns. 20 Sqn attacked with 112-lb. bombs, obtaining a direct hit on the station, one on an engine, one on the line, and five on trucks and buildings. 29 Sqn attacked with 25-lb. bombs, obtaining 20 direct hits on the station and sidings and one on a lorry. The average height of attack was from 900 to 400 feet. A large number of rounds were also fired into transport and troops near the station. A large fire was caused in the sidings and three fires in the station. All our machines returned from this enterprise.

Enemy aircraft were also brought down during the period under review by:

Sqn 1 Lt H. A. Kullberg, 2 Lt C. G. Pegg, Lt E. E. Owen. **3** Lt D. J. Hughes. **9** Lt D. S. Ogilvie + 2 Lt P. V. Kilby, Lt S. T. H. Roberts + 2 Lt West, Lts Sawyer + Williams. **11** Lt H. A. Hay + 2 Lt E. J. Norris. **13** Lts F. Belway + F. P. J. Travis. **19** Capt F. McQuistan. **24** Lt C. M. G. Farrell, Lt T. M. Harriss, Capt T. F. Hazell, Lt W. C. Lambert. **27** Lt B. M. Bowyer-Smythe + 2 Lt L. J. Edwardes, 2 Lts I. L. Dutton + T. Brown. **29** Lt A. E. Reed, Lt B. R. Rolfe. **32** 2 Lt J. O. Donaldson (USAS) (2). **40** Lt G. B. Gates (2), Maj A. W. Keen, Lt D. F. Murmann. **41** Lt W. G. Claxton (3), Capt F. R. McCall (2), Lt W. E. Shields, Capt F. O. Soden. **43** Lts P. Arundel/C. LeFroy, Lt J. H. Forbes, Capt H. W. Woollett. **46** Lts M. M. Freehill/A. L. Aldridge, Lt R. Moore. **48** 2 Lt D. T. Turnbull + Sgt T. R. Turner. **49** Lt H. Ford + 2 Lt J. Whitehead, Lt J. A. Keating + 2 Lt E. A. Simpson, Lt S. B. Welch + 2 Lt D. C. Roy. **54** Lt J. C. MacLennan. **56** Lt T. J. Herbert, Capt W. R. Irwin. **57** Capt F. McD. C. Turner + 2 Lt H. S. Musgrave. **60** Lt G. F. Caswell, Lt G. M. Duncan (2), Capt Doyle, Capt Doyle/Lt R. Whitney, Lt R. Whitney. **64** Capt E. R. Tempest (2). **65** Lt J. L. M. White. **73** Lts G. L. Graham/R. N. Chandler/E. J. Lussier. **74** Lt S. Carlin, Capt J. I. T. Jones (2), Capt B. Roxburgh-Smith. **80** Lt T. S. Nash. **84** Capt D. Carruthers, Lt C. F. Falkenberg, 2 Lt R. Manzer, Lt N. W. R. Mawle, Capt W. A. Southey, 2 Lt C. R. Thompson. **85** Lt W. H. Longton, Capt A. C. Randall (2). **87** Lt R. A. Hewat, Lt L. N. Hollinghurst (2), Lt L. C. K. Oliver, Capt A. Pentland (2), Lt A. W. Vigers (2). **88** Capt E. C. Johnston + 2 Lt J. Rudkin, Lt H. R. Little + 1 AM W. J. Spaulding. **92** Maj A. Coningham, Lt E. F. Crabb, Lt H. B. Good (2), Lt W. S. Rogers. **98** Lt F. Carpenter + 2 Lt N. C. MacDonald, Lt P. C. Wilton + Capt G. H. Gillis. **103** 2 Lt G. L. P. Drummond (Obs), Sgt E. G. Stevens (Obs). **107** Lt G. Beveridge + 2 Lt S. L. Dunlop, Capt F. M. Carter + Lt A. W. K. Arundell, Capt A. J. Mayo + 2 Lt J. W. Jones, Lt F. T. Stott + 1 AM W. J. Palmer. **201** Capt S. M. Kinkead. **203** Maj R. Collishaw (2). **205** Lt A. R. McAfee + Sgt L. Murphy, Capt J. M. Mason + Sgt W. J. Middleton. **206** Lt Burn + Capt Carrothers, Lt H. D. Stier + Sgt J. Chapman. **209** Lt C. G. Edwards, Sqn Patrol led by Capt R. M. Foster, Capts J. K. Summers/E. B. Drake (2), Capt J. K. Summers/Lt K. M. Walker (2). **3 AFC** Lts H. S. Foale + F. A. Sewell, Lts N. F. McKenna + R. W. Kirkwood. **4 AFC** 2 Lt R. T. C. Baker, Lt R. King, Lt L. E. Taplin (2).

HONOURS AND AWARDS

DFC Lt C. T. Anderson, 2 Lt H. Pullan, Lt P. T. Iaccaci, Capt J. S. Stubbs, Capt W. O. Boger, Capt H. W. L. Saunders, MC, MM, Lt V. E. Groom, Lt W. S. Stephenson, MC, Capt D. Latimer, Lt G. L. Graham, 2 Lt J. B. Russell, Capt J. E. Hibbert, MC, Lt E. Hardcastle. **DFM** Cpl H. W. Williams.

12 – 18 August

The fortitude displayed on 12 August by Capt F. M. F. West—later Air Commodore—when shot down in an Armstrong Whitworth—F.K.8, formed the basis of the citation for his V.C., awarded on 8 November.

During the week low-level strikes against enemy aerodromes were stepped up.

COMMUNIQUÉ NO. 20

During the period under review we have claimed officially 102 E.A. brought down and 30 driven down out of control. Five enemy balloons were destroyed. Forty-five of our machines are missing. Approximately 259 tons of bombs were dropped, and 9,592 plates exposed.

August 12th

Weather fine, visibility good ∽ *23 tons of bombs dropped by night and 24 tons by day* ∽ *Enemy aircraft active on 2nd Brigade front in morning and on battle front.*

Two patrols of 29 Sqn flying at different heights engaged a patrol of eight Fokker biplanes and one Pfalz scout. A dog fight resulted in which five of the hostile machines were shot down by: Lts G. W. Wareing, W. L. Dougan, E. C. Hoy, C. G. Ross, and C. J. Venter. Lt T. S. Harrison, of the same patrol, shot down a hostile balloon in flames.

In the evening, Capt C. H. R. Lagesse, leading a patrol of 29 Sqn, saw four Fokker biplanes above him, and, after outclimbing, attacked the leader, who appeared to be the same who had led the patrol in the morning, and shot him down. Lt C. J. Venter attacked another of the E.A., which burst into flames. The pilot of this machine stalled and jumped out, and was seen to go down and land in a parachute. Lt E. O. Amm shot down another in flames, and Lt S. M. Brown attacked the fourth machine, the interplane struts of which fell out and the wings folded up and the hostile patrol was thus wiped out.

Capt R. M. Foster, 209 Sqn, and Capt F. R. McCall, 41 Sqn, both drove down enemy machines on our side of the lines.

A patrol of 56 Sqn engaged a formation of Fokker biplanes. Capt H. J. Burden attacked one, which started to spin down; he then attacked another, which burst into flames; and a third, at which he fired at close range, spun into the ground and crashed. Capt W. R. Irwin dived on the tail of one machine, which went down out of control and crashed. He then turned to attack another, but Lt H. Molyneux reached it first and shot it down, so Capt Irwin attacked another which spun into the ground.

Capt West and Lt Haslam, 8 Sqn, were attacked by seven E.A. who fired explosive bullets, hitting Capt West five times in the left leg, which was almost severed and fell among the controls. He lifted his leg out of the controls and landed his machine close behind our lines, fainting shortly afterwards. Lt Haslam was wounded in the ankle.

August 13th
Weather fine ⌒ 21½ tons of bombs dropped by night and 20½ tons by day ⌒ Enemy aircraft active.

Lts E. S. Coler and C. W. Gladman, 11 Sqn, while escorting a bomb raid, saw about 20 enemy scouts, at one of which Lt Coler dived and, firing at close range, saw it burst into flames. On attacking a second one his gun had a stoppage, so he pulled out of the dive when several E.A. attacked from the rear, at which his observer fired, sending one down in a spin. Lt Coler then fired at one Fokker biplane which crossed his front at close range, and sent this one also down in flames. Just after this, Lt Gladman was wounded in the shoulder, but, manœuvring his gun with his left arm, succeeded in shooting a third hostile machine down in flames.

A patrol of 22 Sqn, while on escort duty, attacked a large formation of Fokker biplanes and Pfalz scouts. Lt S. F. H. Thompson and Sgt R. M. Fletcher dived on one, which went down and was seen to crash, and Sgt Fletcher fired at a second one, when his gun jammed. Lt Thompson, however, turned and succeeded in shooting this E.A. down also. Lt F. C. Stanton attacked another of the enemy formation but had his aileron shot through and was forced down to the level of the hostile machines. His observer, 2 Lt C. J. Tolman, shot one down at close range, and on the way back to the lines brought down one of two E.A., which were following them, in flames. Capts W. F. J. Harvey and D. E. Waight also engaged several of the E.A., one of which they crashed.

A raid was carried out by 17 American Squadron on Varssenaere Aerodrome, in conjunction with squadrons of the 5th Group. After the first two squadrons had dropped their bombs from a low height, machines of 17 Amer. Squadron dived to within 200 feet of the ground and released their bombs, then proceeded to shoot at hangars and huts on the aerodrome, and a chateau on the N.E. corner of the aerodrome was also attacked with machine gun fire. The following damage was observed to be caused by this combined operation:—A dump of petrol and oil was set on fire, which appeared to set fire to an ammunition dump; six

Friedrichshafen G III night bomber

GERMAN FIGHTERS

Top: Fokker D VIII

Bottom: Fokker D VII

Fokker biplanes were set on fire on the ground, and two destroyed by direct hits from bombs; one large Gotha hangar was set on fire and another one half demolished; a living hut was set on fire and several hangars were seen to be smouldering as the result of phosphorus bombs having fallen on them. In spite of most of the machines taking part being hit at one time or another, all returned safely, favourable ground targets being attacked on the way home. 211 Sqn bombed the aerodrome after the low flying attack was over, and demolished the chateau previously referred to.

August 14th

Weather fine, some haze ⌒ 37 tons of bombs dropped by night and 22½ tons by day ⌒ Enemy aircraft slightly less active than of late.

Lts A. E. Reed and H. C. Rath, 29 Sqn, while on wireless interruption saw two D.F.W.'s working, which went east—one of which Lt Reed shot down. Lt Rath chased a Hannoveraner east and caught it on its return and also brought it down.

Lts C. J. Venter, and E. C. Hoy, of the same squadron, brought down a Halberstadt.

Intelligence E.Z. report an abrupt cessation of work by E.A. at the same time and place.

A formation of 57 Sqn was attacked on returning from a bomb raid. One E.A. which got on the tail of Capt A. McGregor, was shot down by his observer (Lt J. F. D. Tanqueray), the pilot being seen to jump out in a parachute just before the machine caught fire.

Sgt J. Grant (observer) with Lt E. M. Coles also shot down a hostile machine which was on his tail, the pilot again descending in a parachute.

Lt G. Anderson and 2 Lt D. E. Stevens were also closely attacked; one machine fired at by 2 Lt Stevens went down smoking and finally its wings fell off.

A hostile machine was seen by a patrol of 2 Sqn A.F.C. to go down in a spin without a shot having been fired into it. After a short distance its wings fell off.

Capt J. B. White, 208 Sqn, on diving on an E.A. two-seater saw its observer leaning over the pilot's seat. When he fired, the observer looked round but made no attempt to return his fire. At this moment, Capt White's left-hand lower plane buckled, with great coolness, he succeeded in righting his machine and landing it without further damage.

August 15th

Weather fine ⌒ 30 tons of bombs dropped by night and 11½ tons by day ⌒ Very few enemy machines seen.

Lt A. V. Blenkiron, 151 Sqn, while on night patrol, saw an enemy bombing machine caught by searchlights, and, getting into close range opened fire. After several bursts, the E.A. went on fire and fell in flames near Bapaume.

Hostile balloons were shot down in flames: Lt E. Taylor, 79 Sqn; Lt W. H. Markham and 2 Lt E. S. Harvey, 20 Sqn.

An E.A. two-seater approached by a patrol of 56 Sqn started to dive, eventually going straight into the ground and crashing without any shots having been fired into it.

August 16th

Weather fair ∽ *11½ tons of bombs dropped by night and 21¼ tons by day* ∽ *Enemy aircraft active in morning, otherwise quiet.*

Lt H. H. Beddow and 2 Lt T. J. Birmingham, 22 Sqn, while on offensive patrol, engaged a formation of enemy scouts. Lt Beddow shot down and crashed a Pfalz, and 2 Lt Birmingham fired at a Fokker biplane which was diving on their tail and which was also seen to crash.

Capts W. F. J. Harvey and D. E. Waight, of the same patrol, shot down another Pfalz scout which also crashed.

Capt A. W. Beauchamp-Proctor, 84 Sqn, dived over 10,000 feet after an E.A. two-seater; after manœuvring for position below the E.A., he got in a good burst from both guns, and the E.A. burst into flames. The observer at this moment jumped out, but apparently had no parachute. The hostile machine fell in flames.

Lts T. S. Harrison and R. G. Robertson, 29 Sqn, while on wireless interruption, attacked a Halberstadt two-seater. A landing wire of Lt Robertson's machine broke, and he was obliged to pull up. The E.A. was seen to crash. Lt Harrison also attacked another Halberstadt just afterwards, which he shot down in flames.

A hostile balloon was shot down in flames by Lt D. S. Poler (U.S.A.S.), 40 Sqn.

A raid was carried out on Haubourdin Aerodrome by 88 and 92 Sqns and 2 and 4 Sqns A.F.C. Sixty-five machines took in all part, dropping 136 25-lb. and 6 40-lb. bombs and firing a large number of rounds from a height varying from 400 to 50 feet. Three large hangars containing machines were completely burnt, and two machines standing outside were set on fire. Several fires were also started in huts, and what is believed to be the officers' mess was blown up and burnt. Several other hangars, in addition to those burnt, received direct hits. The station at Haubourdin was also attacked with machine gun fire from a low height, causing confusion among the troops. Two staff cars were fired at, one of which upset in a ditch and another ran up a steep bank; the occupants were not observed to leave. A train was also shot at, which stopped. Considerable casualties were caused among the personnel at the Aero-

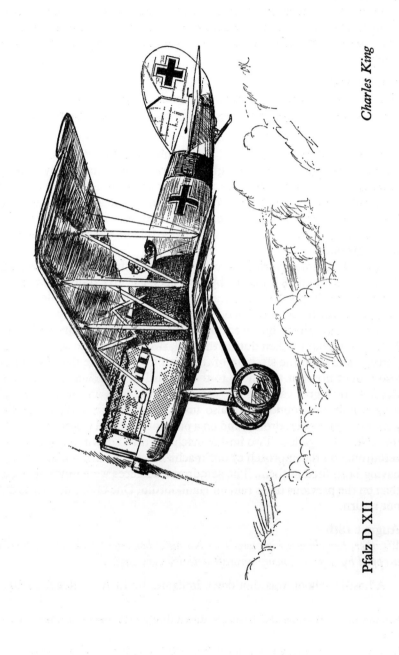

Charles King

Pfalz D XII

drome who were seen rushing to take refuge in a hospital. All our machines returned.

Over 400 photographs were taken by 25 Sqn of a very large tract of country, almost the whole of which was over 20 miles behind the enemy's lines. Several machines were attacked by hostile aircraft, but all returned safely.

August 17th

Weather fair in morning, becoming overcast in afternoon ⌒ 20½ tons of bombs dropped by night and 13½ tons by day ⌒ Enemy aircraft activity slight.

Lt M. C. Purvis, and Lt W. E. Crombie and Sgt P. Sprange (Observers), 215 Sqn, while on a night bomb raid, were attacked by an E.A. two-seater of an unknown type. Sgt Sprange opened fire on this E.A. with the rear gun, whereupon the E.A. turned, and Lt Purvis, turning his machine, dived upon it. After a drum had been fired from the front gun, the E.A. dived very steeply with engine full on, but could not be seen to the ground.

A bomb raid was carried out on Lomme Aerodrome by 2 and 4 Sqns A.F.C. and 92 and 88 Sqns, led by O.C. 80 Wing. 104 25-lb. and 2 40-lb. bombs were dropped from an average of 200 feet. Some pilots, who dropped them from 50 feet, had their machines damaged by their own bombs. Many direct hits were observed on sheds, hangars and huts. From photographs taken during the raid, two sheds can be seen burning fiercely, and from the strength of the wind it is probable that the others also caught fire, but the sheds to the leeward were obscured by smoke. Several other fires can also be seen among the huts and workshops. A large number of rounds were also fired and casualties inflicted on the personnel on the aerodrome, and on a party of mounted troops who made for Lille at full gallop. Two hostile machines dived down to Haubourdin aerodrome on the approach of our machines and crashed without a shot having been fired at them. The aerodrome defences were much stronger than on the previous day's raid on Haubourdin. One of our machines did not return.

August 18th

Weather, low clouds; high winds ⌒ No night bombing ⌒ 1½ tons of bombs dropped by day ⌒ Enemy aircraft activity very slight.

A hostile balloon was shot down in flames by Lt A. E. Reed, 29 Sqn.

Enemy aircraft were also brought down during the period under review by:

Lt Col J. A. Cunningham, Commanding 65th Wing. **Sqn 5** Lts E. Edgar + E.

Shamper. **11** Lt N. B. Scott + **2** Lt L. W. King. **20** Lt F. G. Harlock + 2 Lt A. S. Draisey, Capt D. Latimer + Sgt A. Newland (2), Lts W. M. Thomson + M. A. McKenzie (2). **22** Lt C. E. Hurst + Sgt H. C. Hunt. **24** Capt T. F. Hazell. **27** Lt C. Hutcheson + Sgt W. Smith. **29** Lt E. O. Amm, Lt T. S. Harrison, Lt E. C. Hoy, Lts E. C. Hoy/C. G. Ross, Capt C. H. R. Lagesse, Lt H. C. Rath (2), Lt A. E. Reed, Lt C. G. Ross, Lts C. W. Wareing/E. O. Amm, Lt C. M. Wilson. **40** Lts F. H. Knoebel/L. Bennett, Lt R. G. Landis (USAS). **41** Lt W. E. Shields. **46** Lt C. R. Chapman, Lt R. F. MacRae, Lt P. F. Paton. **48** Capt C. R. Steele + Lt J. B. Jameson. **49** 2 Lts J. G. Andrews + J. Churchill. **56** Capt H. J. Burden. **60** Lt A. Beck/Capt F. W. Clark, Capt J. E. Doyle. **62** Lt L. Campbell + 2 Lt W. Hodgkinson, Capt G. E. Gibbons + Lt T. Elliott, Capt W. E. Staton + 2 Lt L. E. Mitchell (2). **64** Capt C. W. Cudemore, Lt T. Rose, Capt E. R. Tempest. **74** Lt H. G. Shoemaker (USAS)/2 Lt F. J. Gordon. **79** Lt F. W. Gillet. **84** Capt A. W. Beauchamp-Proctor, Capt C. F. Falkenberg. **87** Capt A. Pentland. **88** Lt C. Findlay + 2 Lt B. Digby Worsley, Lts C. Foster + B. H. Smyth. **92** Lt H. B. Good, Capt J. M. Robb, Lt O. J. Rose (2). **201** Capt H. R. de Wilde/Lts R. Sykes/R. McLaughlin (2), Capt S. M. Kinkead. **203** Maj R. Collishaw. **205** Lt C. J. Heywood + Sgt S. F. Langstone. **206** Lt R. H. Shainbank + 2 Lt E. W. Richardson. **208** Lt W. E. G. Mann. **211** Lt G. F. Baker + Cpl H. Lindsay/Lt W. D. Gardner + 2 Lt H. M. Moodie/Patrol of 17 American. **2 AFC** Lt F. W. Follett, Capt R. L. Manuel, Lt F. C. Markham-Mills, Capt R. C. Phillipps, Lt J. J. Wellwood. **17 Amer.** See also under 211, Lt G. D. Wicks. **148 Amer.** Lt H. R. Clay, Lt G. V. Seibold (2), 2 Lt L. T. Wyly.

HONOURS AND AWARDS

DFC Maj W. A. McClaughry, MC, Lt R. W. Turner, Lt G. N. Thomson, Lt S. Carlin, MC, DCM, Lt E. Burn, Capt R. D. Caley, Capt H. J. Burden, Capt L. H. Jones, Capt H. Puckle, Capt H. Le R. Wallace.

19 – 25 August

The Fokker monoplane referred to on 21 August was one of the new D.VIII type. It had a thick cantilever wing, similar to that used on the D.VII, and was likewise renowned for its manœuvrability. At this time only six of the type were at the Front, and shortly afterwards these were withdrawn for modifications.

Capt C. J. Venter, 29 Sqn, awarded a Bar to the D.F.C., was credited with 22 victories by the end of the war.

COMMUNIQUÉ NO. 21

During the period under review we have claimed officially 104 E.A. brought down and 34 driven down out of control. Twenty-three enemy balloons were destroyed. Thirty-seven of our machines are missing. Approximately 232 tons of bombs were dropped, and 7,852 plates exposed.

August 19th
Weather fair, but cloudy ∽ 14½ tons of bombs dropped by night and 16¾ tons by day ∽ Enemy aircraft active in morning, otherwise quiet.

Capt O. C. Halleran, 56 Sqn, while proceeding to attack an L.V.G. saw two Hannoveraners working together. He dived between these two to confuse them. The two E.A. closed together and collided, and both crashed.

Lt R. G. Landis (U.S.A.S.), 40 Sqn, in a general engagement with enemy scouts shot down a Fokker biplane, which crashed near La Bassee. He then attacked a triplane, which was on the tail of a Bristol Fighter whose observer was apparently hit, and getting below its tail brought down this machine also.

Lt L. Bennett, 40 Sqn, attacked two hostile balloons in succession, which were flying east of Merville, and set them both on fire. Later in the day, he attacked another balloon which also went down in flames, and a fourth which was being hauled down he set on fire when on the ground.

A raid was carried out on Phalempin aerodrome by 64 and 209 Sqns, escorted by 22 Sqn. Ninety-seven 25-lb. bombs were dropped from 500 to 100 feet. Two sheds were set on fire; 35 bursts were observed amongst a group of tent hangars, and a direct hit was obtained on a machine gun. Four direct hits were also obtained on a railway alongside the aerodrome. A large number of rounds were also fired and a train in the station was heavily shot at. Several E.A. which appeared above the aerodrome were prevented from attacking by the escort.

August 20th
Weather, mist, low clouds and some rain ↷ No night bombing carried out ↷ 2¾ tons of bombs dropped by day ↷ Enemy aircraft activity very slight.

Lt R. B. Bannerman, 79 Sqn, brought down a hostile two-seater machine in flames.

August 21st
Weather, ground mist till 10 a.m.; afterwards fine ↷ No night bombing was carried out owing to unfavourable weather; 12¼ tons of bombs were dropped during the day ↷ Enemy aircraft active.

Lt W. Hubbard, 3 Sqn, while on low-flying patrol, saw an E.A. two-seater attacking our infantry which retired east on his approach. Lt Hubbard got near the E.A. by hiding behind an R.E.8 and attacked it at 2,000 feet and shot it down.

A patrol of 20 Sqn after bombing Comines engaged a formation of 25 enemy scouts of various types. The leader, Capt H. P. Lale, with 2 Lt Ralph as observer, dived on a Pfalz scout, whose wings crumpled after the second burst. Their machine was then attacked by seven Fokker biplanes, one of which was fired at by 2 Lt Ralph and seen to crash.

Capt D. Latimer and Sgt A. Newland each shot down a Pfalz scout which crashed.

Lt J. H. Colbert and 2 Lt H. L. Edwards also brought down a Fokker biplane.

During the fight another enemy machine was seen to go down in flames, but it not claimed by any individual member of the patrol.

There was one Fokker monoplane engaged in this combat.

Lt C. R. Pithey and 2 Lt H. Rhodes, 12 Sqn, were attacked by four Fokker biplanes during a contact patrol, on one of which they dived and Lt Rhodes sent it down out of control. During the fight the petrol tank was pierced, and Lt Rhodes got out on to the plane and stopped the hole with his handkerchief, preventing the petrol from escaping, and remained on the wing until Lt Pithey landed the machine.

Hostile balloons were shot down in flames by Capt T. F. Hazell, 24 Sqn; Lt L. A. Hamilton, Lt R. M. Todd, 17 Amer. Sqn (1).

Lt Brock, 3 Sqn, saw seven ammunition wagons near Sapignies, which he attacked from a height of 50 feet. Two men fell off the rear wagon, which ran into a tree and upset. He again attacked the others, two of which also upset. He was then obliged to return, having been hit in the knee and his pressure pipe cut. He saw the remaining wagons galloping away.

August 22nd
Weather fine, visibility good ⌒ 25½ tons of bombs dropped by night and 34¾ tons by day ⌒ Enemy aircraft active.

Lt C. R. W. Knight and Capt A. B. Yuille, 151 Sqn, saw a hostile bombing machine caught in searchlights. Capt Yuille attacked, and, after firing two bursts, overshot the E.A. Lt Knight got close under the E.A.'s tail, and, after 50 rounds fired from each gun, saw it burst into flames. The machine fell on our side of the lines.

A patrol of 62 Sqn while on escort duty engaged a large number of hostile scouts. Capt E. T. Morrow and 2 Lt L. M. Thompson attacked one machine, which went down emitting smoke. Capt Morrow then fired at a second, which collapsed in the air; he was then hit in the leg and the petrol tank was pierced, the fuselage of his machine catching fire. 2 Lt Thompson kept the fire under control with the Pyrene extinguisher until the machine landed, when it blazed up. He, however, managed to lift Capt Morrow clear.

Capt G. E. Gibbons and 2 Lt T. Elliott brought down two of the same formation of E.A., one of which crashed and the other burst into flames.

Lt R. Schallaire and 2 Lt R. Lowe, of the same patrol, brought down a Fokker biplane which was seen to crash, and Capt W. E. Staton and 2 Lt L. E. Mitchell shot another down in flames.

During the course of a combat between a patrol of 85 Sqn and a number of Fokker biplanes, Lt W. H. Longton, Lt J. W. Warner, Lt O. A. Ralston (U.S.A.S.), and Capt M. C. McGregor each shot down a hostile machine.

Hostile balloons were shot down in flames by: Capt A. W. Beauchamp-Proctor, 84 Sqn (2); Lt L. Bennett, 40 Sqn (2); Capt T. F. Hazell, 24 Sqn; Capt G. C. Dixon, 40 Sqn; Lts W. D. Tipton, R. D. Williams, 17 Amer. Sqn (1).

A raid was carried out on Gondecourt aerodrome by 208 and 40 Sqns escorted by 22 Sqn. Seventy-seven 25-lb. bombs were dropped from below 1,000 feet, and a direct hit made on a hangar which caught fire and was destroyed. A direct hit was also obtained on the railway near the aerodrome. A large number of rounds were fired into hangars, machine gun emplacements and a train in the station. On the return journey, four hostile balloons were shot down in flames.

53 Sqn, during operations on X. Corps front, dropped three boxes of

S.A.A., one box of S.O.S. lights, and nine coils of barbed wire by para-chute.

During night operations by 102 Sqn, Lt Broomfield and 2 Lt Clark observed a column of 20 transport wagons upon which they dropped 2 112-lb. and 1 25-lb. bombs from 300 feet, which were seen to burst in the middle of the transport, knocking out six or eight teams. Some of the transport then took refuge in a sunken road, in which there were also two large lorries. They dived on these, and secured a direct hit with a 25-lb. bomb, and then fired 250 rounds into the wreckage.

August 23rd

Weather fair; cloudy ∽ 18¾ tons of bombs dropped by night and 26 tons by day ∽ Enemy aircraft active on 3rd and 5th Brigade fronts.

Capt B. Roxburgh-Smith, 74 Sqn, during a combat with six Fokker biplanes, attacked one from behind, which he shot down; he then dived on another, but his guns failed. Maj K. L. Caldwell then engaged this E.A., which went down and crashed. Capt Roxburgh-Smith, after recti-fying his stoppages, shot down another E.A.

Lt W. Aitken, 151 Sqn, saw a large enemy machine caught in our searchlights. When about 200 yards from it the searchlights lost the machine, but E.A. opened fire on him. Having closed to 40 yards, Lt Aitken fired a burst of 80 rounds, when E.A. started to dive, and, after two more bursts were fired, was lost sight of. The enemy machine fell on our side of the lines.

Lt A. R. Spurling and Sgt F. W. Bell, 49 Sqn, became separated from their formation by clouds, and after flying west for some time came down. Seeing an aerodrome which they believed to be one of ours they pre-pared to land, when they were attacked by a Fokker biplane. Lt Spurling then noticed about 30 Fokker biplanes below him, and dived to in the centre of the formation, firing continuously. One of the hostile machines went down in flames and two went down in spins, one of which was seen to crash. Four Fokkers then got on their tail, one of which Sgt Bell shot down in flames, and another which attacked from the side was also shot down in flames by the observer. The three enemy machines were seen burning on the ground as the D.H.9 started for the lines, climbing, followed by three of the E.A. which, however, did not attack. On the way home, they were again attacked by an E.A. two-seater which turned away on being fired at.

Lt E. Taylor, 79 Sqn, brought down two hostile balloons in flames.

2 Lt A. F. Diamond (U.S.A.S.), 29 Sqn, also brought down one balloon in flames.

A raid was carried out on Cantin aerodrome by 64 and 209 Sqns. escorted by 22 Sqn. 64 Sqn attacked first and dropped four bombs on

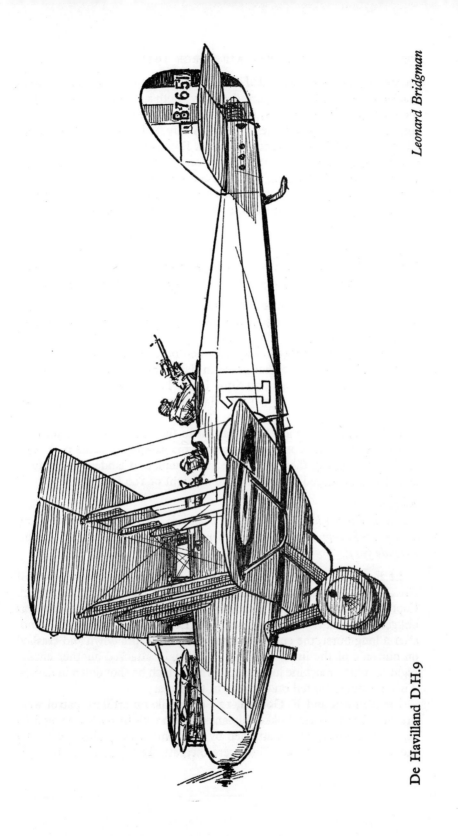

Leonard Bridgman

De Havilland D.H.9

the station, which was crowded with troops, and also engaged them with machine gun fire. They dispersed rapidly. Both squadrons then attacked the sheds on the aerodrome, five of which were seen to be on fire and a small hut was completely demolished. A direct hit was also obtained on a large shed which commenced to burn. Bombs were also dropped on a train standing in the sidings; transport on roads near the aerodrome was also attacked with machine gun fire, and a convoy of wagons was scattered. A total of 126 25-lb. bombs were dropped. An L.V.G. which flew through the middle of the formation was brought down. All machines returned.

August 24th

Weather, low clouds in morning, becoming fine later ⌒ 4¾ tons of bombs dropped by night and 15½ tons by day ⌒ Enemy aircraft activity slight.

2 Lts R. A. P. Johnson and N. J. Dalgleish, 15 Sqn, while engaged on dropping ammunition to our advanced troops were attacked from behind by an enemy two-seater. The observer opened fire, and after a burst of 12 rounds the E.A. turned away and then burst into flames.

Hostile balloons were shot down in flames by: Lt C. M. Wilson, 29 Sqn; Lt R. B. Bannerman, 79 Sqn; Lt E. Taylor, 79 Sqn; 2 Lt R. T. C. Baker, 4 Sqn A.F.C.; Lts L. A. Hamilton, J. F. Campbell, 17 Amer. Sqn (1).

Lt Williams, 17 Amer. Sqn, was hit in the back and his petrol tank pierced by machine gun fire. In spite of his wound, he came back with his finger stopping the hole in the petrol tank and landed successfully after having engaged transport from a height of 100 feet.

August 25th

Weather, fine but hazy ⌒ 29 tons of bombs dropped by night and 32½ tons by day ⌒ Enemy aircraft active generally in morning and all day on 3rd Brigade front.

Lt F. C. Broome, 151 Sqn, saw an E.A in our searchlights west of Arras which he attacked from the rear but got into its backwash and spun. Capt D. V. Armstrong, of the same squadron, then attacked, but was obliged to turn away to avoid a collision. Lt Broome attacked again, and, after a long burst, the enemy machine started to spin down and crashed on our side of the lines. Lt C. R. W. Knight attacked another enemy night bombing machine just east of Arras, which he shot down in flames. This machine also fell on our side of the lines.

Lts McLean and F. Godson, 12 Sqn, while on artillery patrol were first attacked by seven Fokker biplanes, which withdrew after being fired at, but later on they were attacked by a triplane which, when fired at by the observer, glided east. They were then attacked from above by eight hostile machines and from below by four others. Lt Godson fired at one, which went down in flames. Lt McLean was wounded as they were followed back to the lines by six E.A. and Lt Godson helped to fly the machine from the back seat while firing occasional bursts with his left hand. They eventually reached home.

Capt A. Pentland, 87 Sqn, while on patrol with another machine, attacked an E.A. two-seater, which he shot down. He then attacked a Fokker which was on the tail of his companion and this E.A. also went down and crashed. Then having been shot through the petrol tank, he was chased back to the lines by the rest of the enemy.

Lt C. E. Hurst and Sgt H. C. Hunt, 22 Sqn, while on escort duty to a bomb raid, became engaged in a fight with 30 or 40 enemy scouts. One Pfalz scout fired at by the pilot crashed near Peronne, and a triplane was also shot down and seen to crash.

Enemy aircraft were also brought down during the period under review by:

Sqn 1 Lt D. Knight, Lt C. G. Pegg. **3** Lt G. R. Riley. **11** Lt C. R. Smythe + 2 Lt W. T. Barnes. **12** Lt C. R. Pithey + 2 Lt H. Rhodes. **20** Lt G. E. Randall + Sgt A. Newland. **22** Patrol. **29** Lt S. M. Brown, Maj C. H. Dixon, 2 Lt W. L. Dougan, Capt E. C. Hoy (2), Lt A. E. Reed, Lt C. G. Ross (2), Lt C. W. Wareing, Lt C. M. Wilson. **32** 2 Lt J. O. Donaldson (USAS), Capt W. B. Green, Lt F. L. Hale. **40** Lt L. Bennett. **41** Capt F. O. Soden. **46** Lt P. F. Paton/Capt D. R. MacLaren. **48** Capt E. N. Griffith + 2 Lt A. Urinowski/2 Lt S. H. Whipple. **49** Lt W. K. Jenne + 2 Lt L. Eteson. **54** Patrol, Lt J. C. Green. **56** Capt H. J. Burden. **60** Capt J. E. Doyle. **64** Capt W. H. Farrow (2), Lt D. Lloyd-Evans. **70** Capt W. M. Carlaw, 2 Lt O. A. Heron, 2 Lt J. Wilson. **73** Lt O. M. Baldwin, 2 Lt N. Cooper (2), Capt G. L. Graham, Lt E. J. Lussier. **74** Capt C. B. Glynn, Lt F. E. Luff (USAS), Capt B. Roxburgh-Smith, Lt H. G. Shoemaker (USAS), Lts H. G. Shoemaker (USAS)/G. R. Hicks. **79** Lt R. B. Bannerman, Lt F. W. Gillet, Capt F. Lord. **84** Capt A. W. Beauchamp-Proctor (3), Capt A. W. Beauchamp-Proctor/2 Lts M. H. Goudie/I. P. Corse (USAS) (our side of the lines), Capt C. F. Falkenberg/Lt G. A. Vaughn (USAS), Lt G. A. Vaughn (USAS)/2 Lt S. W. Highwood. **87** Capt H. A. R. Biziou, Maj C. J. W. Darwin, Capt H. Larkin (2), Lts L. Murray Stewart/C. E. Worthington, Lt A. W. Vigers. **92** Capt W. E. Reed. **103** Capt J. A. Sparks + Lt F. M. Loly (2), Capt J. S. Stubbs + 2 Lt J. B. Russell. **108** 2 Lts A. A. S. Milne + G. E. McManus/A. T. W. Boswell + W. Bolt. **203** Capt J. D. Breakey. **205** Lt W. H. Clarke + 2 Lt C. M. Whitham. **209** Capt T. C. Luke, Lt W. R. May. **2 AFC** Capt A. T. Cole/Lt J. J. Wellwood. **3 AFC** Lts A. E. Grigson/H. B. James. **17 Amer.** Lt L. A. Hamilton, 2 Lt H. C. Knotts. **148 Amer.** A Patrol, Lt H. R. Clay, Lt J. O. Creech, Lt G. V. Seibold, Lt E. W. Springs.

HONOURS AND AWARDS

DSO Capt J. I. T. Jones, MC, DFC, MM. **DFC** Capt C. J. Venter (Bar), Capt D. M. Carter, 2 Lt N. W. R. Mawle, Capt T. F. Hazell, MC, Lt J. L. Smith, Lt G. B. Gates, Lt G. B. Foster, Lt H. B. Barton, Capt J. F. Gordon, Capt

F. McD. C. Turner, MC, Capt A. C. Randall, Lt J. G. Gillanders, Capt B. Roxburgh-Smith, Capt E. W. Fletcher, Lt L. K. Baker, Lt W. E. Shields, Capt D. A. Stewart, MC, Lt C. S. L. Coulson, Lt W. G. Hurrell, Capt M. L. Doyle, Lt H. W. Russell, 2 Lt T. A. Dickinson, 2 Lt N. F. Frome, Capt H. R. de Wilde, Lt G. A. Flavelle, Lt W. J. Peace, Capt R. C. B. Brading, 2 Lt S. L. Dunlop, Lt P. T. Holligan, Lt R. McLaughlin, Capt A. B. Yuille, 2 Lt E. A. Simpson, Lt A. W. Vigers, MC, Capt C. Bowman, Lt C. G. Ross, Capt C. Ross, Capt C. H. R. Lagesse, Lt W. McK. Thompson, MC, Capt V. F. Jaynes, Lt A. E. Reed, Lt G. W. F. Darvill, 2 Lt E. Walker.

26 August – 1 September

Indifferent weather made this a week of reduced enemy activity, but the R.A.F. maintained the offensive and sustained relatively high losses.

Several outstanding feats of airmanship by the crews of bomber and army co-operation squadrons were recorded.

COMMUNIQUÉ NO. 22

During the period under review we have claimed officially 51 E.A. brought down and 28 driven down out of control. Eleven enemy balloons were destroyed. In addition, two E.A. were brought down by A.A. Forty-six of our machines are missing. Approximately 139½ tons of bombs were dropped, and 4,600 plates exposed.

August 26th
Weather: overcast; rainstorms ∽ No night bombing owing to rainstorms ∽ 15 tons of bombs dropped by day ∽ Enemy aircraft activity generally slight, except in the evening on the 3rd Brigade front.

Lt W. Hubbard, 3 Sqn, after a combat with two enemy two-seaters—the second of which went down spinning after its observers had been killed—had engine failure and was compelled to spin down to avoid another E.A. As his machine touched the ground he was fired at by a German from about 15 yards with a revolver, which burst his petrol tank. At this moment his engine picked up sufficiently to carry him just behind our lines. Although under fire, Lt Hubbard removed the locks of his gun, Aldis sight, and all his instruments before leaving his machine, which was obviously unsalvable.

August 27th
Weather: low clouds, rain showers ∽ 11 tons of bombs dropped during the night, and 21¾ tons during the day ∽ Enemy aircraft fairly active.

Lt W. R. May, 209 Sqn, was attacked by a Halberstadt at which he fired 250 rounds, killing the observer, and saw the machine spin down. It was seen to crash by an A.A. Battery. He then attacked a Hannoveraner, the wings of which crumpled up in the air and the machine crashed into a wood.

A hostile kite balloon, which was guarded by eight enemy scouts, was attacked and shot down in flames by Capt A. W. Beauchamp-Proctor, 84 Sqn. His patrol were chased back to the lines by the E.A. As soon as another balloon appeared on the front he lured the enemy machines away and then dived into a cloud and steered by compass to the balloon, coming out just over it. This balloon he also shot down in flames. His engine was hit by A.A. fire, the lines being crossed at 500 feet.

Lts T. H. Newsome and C. Partington, 22 Sqn, also shot down an enemy balloon in flames.

During the course of the day, nine 112-lb. and 722 25-lb. bombs were dropped and 44,350 rounds fired by 22, 40, 54, 64, 73, 208 and 209 Sqns from a low height on ground targets, the majority of which were reported by wireless machines of 1st Wing. A large number of direct hits were obtained on machine-gun emplacements, battery positions and transport, and many casualties observed amongst troops and horses.

5 Sqn's machines were attacked by E.A. Capt Goudie and Lt Crawley drove off 15 Fokker biplanes which attacked them. Lts Galbraith and Sprangle, and Lts Searson and Green also attacked and drove off several E.A. with conspicuous success.

August 28th

Weather: low clouds and rainstorms ⌒ *No night bombing was carried out* ⌒ *6 tons of bombs dropped by day* ⌒ *Very few enemy aircraft seen.*

Lt C. R. Pithey and 2 Lt H. Rhodes 12 Sqn, while on contact patrol saw an E.A. also on the same duty. They attempted to draw the E.A. on by heading for our lines, and the second time succeeded, when they turned on it and shot it down.

August 29th

Weather: fair, but cloudy ⌒ *11½ tons of bombs dropped by night and 18 tons by day* ⌒ *Enemy aircraft fairly active in morning.*

Lt J. M. Brown and 2 Lt H. Lawrence, 98 Sqn, on returning from a bomb raid fell behind the formation owing to engine trouble, and were attacked by about 20 E.A. Almost at once their elevator controls were shot away, and Lt Brown dived his machine west, followed by the hostile machines. 2 Lt Lawrence was badly wounded, but continued fighting and shot down one Fokker biplane in flames, almost immediately afterwards sending another one down out of control. By this time all the petrol tanks were shot through, the engine had been hit in several places, and most of the instruments broken on the dashboard. 2 Lt Lawrence was very seriously wounded, and both rear guns jammed, but Lt Brown succeeded in evading the E.A. by diving through a cloud, and brought the machine down in our lines near Mory, where it crashed. 2 Lt Lawrence had been hit in ten places.

FIGHTING SCOUTS

Top: Sopwith Dolphin

Bottom: Sopwith Snipe

Handley Page 0/400 night bomber of No. 207 Squadron loaded with a 1650-lb bomb

Lt C. C. Banks, 43 Sqn, was attacked by several E.A. and spun down. On the way down he saw that only one E.A. was still following him and coming suddenly out of his spin just above the trees caught this machine crossing in front of him and brought it to the ground where it burst into flames. Lt Banks then flew home 'hedge-hopping', shooting up troops and transport on the way.

Lt A. Grundy and 2 Lt L. W. Norman, 8 Sqn, while taking oblique photographs, were attacked by two hostile machines, at one of which the observer opened fire, whereupon it stalled and then dived into the ground, where it caught fire. The other E.A., after circling round his companion on the ground, retired.

Lt G. S. Peffers and 2 Lt R. Lister, with Lt L. G. B. Spence and 2 Lt G. E. Davies, also of 8 Sqn, while escorting photographic machines became engaged with seven Fokker biplanes, of which each of the Armstrong-Whitworths shot down one in spite of the fact that Lt Spence was wounded early in the combat, which was continued until the five remaining E.A. withdrew in formation.

A hostile balloon was brought down in flames by Lt F. E. Luff (U.S.A.S.), 74 Sqn.

August 30th
Weather: fine but cloudy ∽ No night bombing carried out; 24 tons of bombs dropped by day ∽ On the whole, enemy aircraft activity was slight.

Lt G. B. Hett and 2 Lt C. E. Eddy, 103 Sqn, on returning from photography, were cut off and attacked by several Fokker biplanes. 2 Lt Eddy was almost immediately wounded, but continued firing at the E.A. as they attacked, one of whose wings fell off in the air and another went down out of control. Lt Hett then brought the machine back safely.

Lt H. A. Kullberg, 1 Sqn, dived on a Fokker biplane which was attacking a D.H.9, and, after a short burst, saw its wings break off in the air. A little later he attacked another Fokker biplane, which was seen to go down and crash.

Lt C. R. Pithey and 2 Lt H. Rhodes, 12 Sqn, were attacked by seven Fokker biplanes, one of which, fired at by 2 Lt Rhodes, fell in flames. They then drove the remaining E.A. off the tail of another R.E.8., when, having finished their ammunition, they were obliged to return home.

Capt J. K. Woodhouse and Lt W. S. Peel, 59 Sqn, were attacked by four hostile machines, the leading one of which was brought down in flames by the observer's fire.

August 31st
Weather: low clouds and rain ∽ 1½ tons of bombs dropped by night and 12½ tons by day ∽ Enemy aircraft activity slight.

September 1st

*Weather: fair, visibility good; high wind ∽ No night bombing carried out;
17½ tons of bombs dropped by day ∽ Enemy aircraft active.*

During the course of bomb raids carried out by 57 Sqn enemy scouts, which attacked the formations, were successfully engaged. Sgt D. E. Edgley and Sgt N. Sandison brought one hostile machine down in flames and drove down another out of control. Lt E. M. Coles and Sgt J. Grant, and Lt F. O. Thornton and 2 Lt F. C. Craig, destroyed two more hostile machines.

Lt F. W. Gillet, 79 Sqn, when about to attack a balloon, saw an E.A. two-seater flying low which he shot down. He then returned to the balloon, which was being hauled down, and shot it down in flames. Two bombs were also dropped on the winch.

Lt L. E. Taplin, 4 Sqn A.F.C., shot down a hostile balloon in flames. One of the observers parachutes did not open, and he was seen to crash. Balloons were also brought down in flames by: Capt E. C. Hoy, 29 Sqn; 2 Lt F. J. Hunt, 74 Sqn; Lt F. E. Luff (U.S.A.S.), 74 Sqn; Lt R. King, 4 Sqn A.F.C.

Lt Cowper-Coles and 2 Lt Pargeter, 53 Sqn, during a contact patrol, had their petrol tank pierced by machine gun fire. 2 Lt Pargeter climbed out on the port bottom plane and succeeded in stopping the hole, thus enabling the machine to be flown back to its aerodrome.

Capt Woodhouse and Lt Peel, 59 Sqn, had their starboard top and bottom planes broken by A.A. fire. Lt Peel balanced the machine by leaning over the fuselage with the Lewis gun in his hands and enabling the pilot to land the machine, in spite of all the controls, except the elevator being useless.

Enemy aircraft were also brought down during the period under review by:

Sqn 3 Lts V. H. McElroy/D. J. Hughes. **18** Lt F. McFarland + 2 Lt A. Petersen. **22** Lt C. E. Hurst + Sgt H. C. Hunt, Lt I. O. Stead + Capt D. E. Waight. **23** Capt N. Howarth. **24** Lt H. D. Barton, Lts H. D. Barton/H. L. Bair (USAS)/Harries. **29** Lt A. E. Reed. **32** Lt M. A. Tancock. **41** Lt E. H. Barksdale (USAS), Lt E. J. Stephens. **43** Lt E. G. Weaver. **46** Capt D. R. MacLaren. **57** Lt F. O. Thornton + 2 Lt W. H. Thornton. **60** Lts A. Beck/ A. R. Oliver. **62** Lt C. Allday + 2 Lt T. Elliott. **73** Capt W. H. Hubbard. **74** Lt R. A. Birch. **79** Lt R. B. Bannerman. **84** Capts A. W. Beauchamp-Proctor/C. F. Falkenberg. **88** Capt A. Hepburn + Sgt E. Antcliffe. **98** Lt W. G. Davies + Sgt J. K. Ison. **203** Capt A. T. Whealy/Lt F. J. S. Britnell. **206** Capt R. Atkinson + 2 Lt W. T. Ganter. **208** Lt W. E. G. Mann. **2 AFC** Lt G. Cox, 2 Lt E. E. Davies. **3 AFC** Lts J. Gould-Taylor/B. G. Thomson. **4 AFC** Lt R. T. C. Baker, Lt R. King. **17 Amer.** Lt F. A. Dixon (2). **148 Amer.** Lts H. R. Clay/ T. L. Moore, Lt E. W. Springs.

HONOURS AND AWARDS

DSO Capt H. A. Whistler, DFC, Capt A. H. Cobby, DFC, Capt H. J. Burden, DFC. **DFC** Capt S. M. Kinkead, DSC (Bar), Lt H. B. Davies (Bar), Capt J. L. M. White (Bar), Lt H. N. Young (Bar), Capt R. Hilton (Bar), Capt C. V. Gardner, Lt J. McLennan, Capt W. Walker, Lt F. A. Sewell, Lt J. M. Brown, Lt J. H. O'Connell, 2 Lt R. McK. Jamison, Lt-Col W. F. MacNeece, DSO, Capt W. C. Gardner, Lt R. K. Whitney, 2 Lt F. J. Ralph, Capt F. R. Walker, Capt R. S. Hellier, Capt A. A. Leitch, MC, Lt E. G. K. Weakley, Lt R. C. Armstrong, Lt E. F. Rowntree, Capt C. F. Falkenberg, Capt E. R. Tempest, MC, Lt R. C. Bennett, Lt H. Axford, Lt J. E. Croden, Lt R. F. Buick, Capt A. S. Hemming, Capt T. M. Williams, Capt H. Munden, Capt D. R. Brook, Lt M. G. W. Stewart, Capt W. A. Southey, Lt T. Rose, Lt C. F. Galbraith, Lt-Col L. A. Strange, MC, Lt N. W. Helwig, Lt E. S. Morgan, Lt G. O. Newton, Capt B. E. Catchpole, Capt F. I. Lord, Lt C. L. Morley, Capt F. B. Wilson, Capt D. R. Steele, Lt T. L. Baillieu, Lt S. F. Thompson, MC, Capt N. Goudie, Capt W. R. Irwin, Lt C. M. G. Farrell, Capt W. Selwyn, 2 Lt B. Donald. **DFM** Sgt C. Lines, Sgt R. M. Fletcher.

2 – 8 September

Incidents reported in this communiqué show that although Germany had developed parachutes beyond the experimental stage they were not yet universally fitted.

An unusual happening was the surrender of enemy ground troops to an R.E.8 of 59 Sqn.

COMMUNIQUÉ NO. 23

During the period under review we have claimed officially 101 E.A. brought down and 51 driven down out of control. Eighteen enemy balloons were destroyed. Sixty-six of our machines are missing. Approximately 188 tons of bombs were dropped and 6,954 plates exposed.

September 2nd

Weather showery with bright intervals ∽ 16½ tons of bombs dropped by night and 21 tons by day ∽ Enemy aircraft active on the battle front.

A raid was carried out on Linselles Aerodrome by 29, 41, 70 and 74 Sqns. 29 and 74 Sqns dropped 51 25-lb. and 40 25-lb. bombs respectively from between 2,000 and 6,000 feet, and then remained above while 41 and 70 Sqns attacked the hangars from 1,000 to 50 feet, dropping 28 and 85 25-lb. bombs respectively, firing a large number of rounds into the hangars, and silencing a machine-gun battery which opened fire. Two hangars were set on fire and gutted, and two others are believed also to have been set on fire, although complete destruction could not be observed. All our machines returned.

Lts Ibbotson and Carruthers, 59 Sqn, while on counter-attack patrol, saw 65 of the enemy in a trench and a sunken road who fired at them. Ibbotson dived and fired back, killing one and wounding three of the party, whereupon they waved a white flag. The machine then descended to 50 feet and ordered the enemy to go to our lines, where they were seen to be taken over by our troops.

September 3rd

Weather fine, but cloudy ∽ 3½ tons of bombs dropped by night and 23½ tons by day ∽ Enemy aircraft very active on the battle front.

Capt W. R. Irwin, 56 Sqn, attacked one of 12 hostile machines, which he shot down. He then fired at a Fokker which was on the tail of another S.E.5 and sent it down in flames.

Lts H. E. Searson and T. K. Green, 5 Sqn, while flying along the Canal du Nord at 800 feet dived on a D.F.W. at which the pilot fired. The E.A. made a sharp turn and was then brought down by the observer; it was later seen lying burnt on the ground.

Capt G. B. Gates, 201 Sqn, shot down two enemy two-seaters in flames during the course of two offensive patrols.

Balloons were brought down by Capt W. A. Southey, 84 Sqn; Lt J. Glen, 70 Sqn; Lt L. E. Taplin, 4 Sqn A.F.C.

September 4th

Weather: fair, some clouds ᴄ 21 tons of bombs dropped by night and 23½ tons by day ᴄ Enemy aircraft active; working in large formations.

Capt G. W. F. Darvill and Lt W. Miller, 18 Sqn, were attacked by several E.A. on returning from a bomb raid. The pilot turned to attack, but his gun failed, and they were followed closely by the hostile machines. Lt Miller shot one E.A. down in flames, and was then wounded but continued firing, and shortly afterwards destroyed a second E.A.

1 Lt H. R. Clay, 148 Amer. Sqn, brought down an E.A. which was attacking an S.E.5, and then attacked another which was fighting one of his own patrol and brought it down. He was then set on by three E.A., and after fighting them for three minutes 1 Lt C. Bissell, of the same squadron, came to his assistance and shot down one of the hostile machines and drove another down out of control.

Lt D. J. Hughes, 3 Sqn, was driven to our lines by three hostile machines. When two of them left him he turned and attacked the other, wounding the pilot and forcing him to land on our side of the lines.

Lt A. B. Agnew and 2 Lt A. E. Chadwick, 12 Sqn, dived on a Fokker biplane which had been fighting with a Camel and brought it down after 50 rounds from the front gun.

Capt T. F. Hazell, 24 Sqn, brought down two hostile balloons in flames, one of which fell on the winch which burned for 20 minutes and Lt E. P. Crossen attacked the observer whose parachute collapsed.

Hostile balloons were also brought down by: Capt S. Carlin, 74 Sqn; Lt F. S. Gordon, 74 Sqn; 2 Lts S. W. Highwood, C. R. Thompson, 84 Sqn (1); Capt R. N. G. Atkinson and 2 Lt W. T. Ganter, 206 Sqn; Capt E. J. McClaughry, 4 Sqn A.F.C.; Lt A. H. Lockley, 4 Sqn A.F.C.; 2 Lt A. E. James, 4 Sqn A.F.C.

September 5th

Weather: fine; hazy ᴄ 21 tons of bombs dropped by day ᴄ Enemy aircraft fairly active, flying in large formations.

During the course of a combat between a patrol of 79 Sqn and a

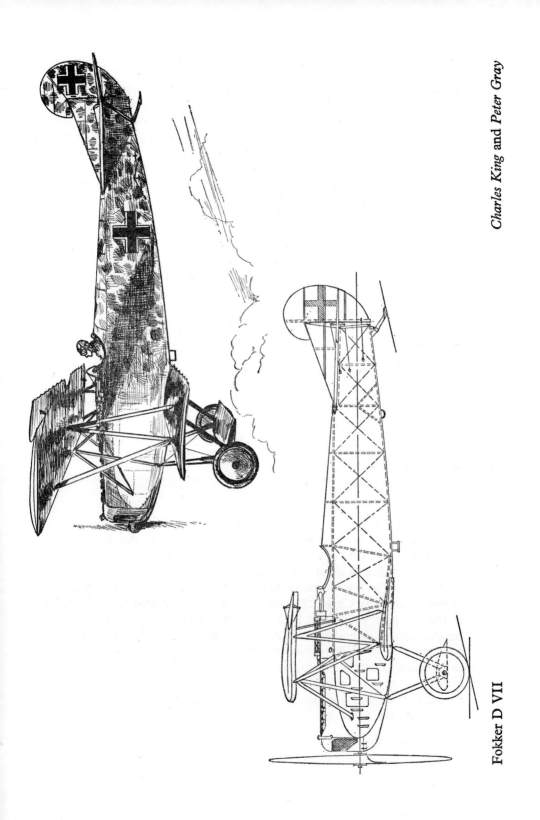

Charles *King* and *Peter Gray*

Fokker D VII

formation of Fokker biplanes, Lt F. W. Gillett shot down one E.A. which burst into flames on the ground, and Capt F. I. Lord attacked another which fell over on its back, and a large object, which would appear to have been the pilot, was seen to leave the machine which was last seen falling on its back within 200 feet of the ground.

Maj A. Coningham, 92 Sqn, attacked the leader of a patrol of Fokker biplanes which, after zooming vertically, stopped on its back long enough to dislodge its pilot, who hung by one arm for a few seconds and then fell, hitting the ground near Cambrai.

Lt E. Shapard, 92 Sqn, brought down a Fokker biplane and was then attacked from behind by several others who compelled him to spin almost to the ground, where he evaded them by flying home at an average height of 20 feet. On landing it was found that the main spars of all four planes had been shot through as well as both longerons, and a bullet had also lodged in one of the magnetos.

The pilot of a Fokker biplane attacked by Capt A. McGregor and Sgt J. Grant, 57 Sqn, was seen to jump out of his machine, when it burst into flames, apparently without any parachute.

Maj R. Collishaw, 203 Sqn, drove down a hostile machine in flames on our side of the lines which had just attacked one of our balloons.

Hostile balloons were brought down in flames by: Lt A. H. Lockley, 4 Sqn A.F.C.; 2 Lt C. R. Thompson, 84 Sqn; 2 Lt S. W. Highwood, 84 Sqn.

September 6th

Weather fair ∾ No night bombing carried out; 16½ tons of bombs dropped by day.

Lts G. N. Dennis and H. D. Hewett, 13 Sqn, while on photography were approached by seven Fokker biplanes, one of which dived on them and was fired at by the observer. This machine dived steeply and was seen by another R.E.8 to burst into flames.

A patrol of 20 Sqn became engaged in a combat with a large number of Fokker biplanes. Capt H. P. Lale shot one down in flames which passed in front of him, while 2 Lt H. L. Edwards (his Observer) at the same time brought another down in flames with the rear gun. A hostile machine fired at by Lt A. Mills (Observer in Lt P. T. Iaccaci's machine) broke to pieces, and another which he engaged fell to the ground, where it burst into flames. Sgt A. Newland (Observer in Lt A. T. Iaccaci's machine) fired half a drum at very close range into another Fokker, which was seen to crash.

September 7th

Weather: low clouds; rain-storms in afternoon and evening ∾ 16 tons of bombs dropped by night and 17¼ tons by day ⌀ Enemy aircraft activity only slight.

Capt M. E. Ashton and Lt T. D. Fitzsimon, 12 Sqn, attacked an L.V.G. which, after 50 rounds had been fired by the observer, fell out of control and crashed. The observer of the hostile machine was seen to jump out about 100 feet from the ground, but his parachute did not open.

Lt G. W. Wareing, 29 Sqn, attacked a hostile balloon which went down in flames. He then saw about 15 people rush out from what looked like the officers' mess, one of whom started firing at him with a rifle. Lt Wareing turned his machine gun on him and he collapsed on the ground. Meanwhile, Capt Lagesse silenced two machine-guns near the balloon.

A patrol of 84 Sqn, led by Capt A. W. Beauchamp-Proctor, after bombing St. Quentin, attacked a line of enemy balloons and brought down four in flames. Each of the following pilots accounting for one: Capt A. W. Beauchamp-Proctor, 2 Lt F. R. Christiani, 2 Lt S. W. Highwood, and 2 Lt I. P. Corse (U.S.A.S.).

During the night, 102 Sqn dropped 4½ tons of bombs, the following pilots and observers making three trips each to Cambrai: Lts Farley and Hopley, Marsden and Maggs, Basker and Harris. Operations were commenced at 8.5 p.m., and the last machine landed at 5.5 a.m.

Capt Stockdale and 2 Lt Shergold, 101 Sqn, succeeded in reaching Bohain, where they dropped their bombs, and, owing to trouble with his engine, Capt Stockdale had to return at 600 feet.

Lts Stockman and Cock, 101 Sqn, claimed a direct hit on a train at Vermand which caused a fire. Shortly afterwards Lt Cock fainted, but Lt Stockman, after pushing him into the bottom of the nacelle, completed the reconnaissance, remaining in the air over three hours.

September 8th
Weather: overcast; some rain ⌀ 2½ tons of bombs dropped by night and 5 tons by day ⌀ Few enemy aircraft seen.

Capt G. B. Gates, 201 Sqn, engaged on Albatross two-seater which turned over on its back and caught fire. The observer jumped out in a parachute which, however, also caught fire.

Capt D. H. M. Carbery and Lt J. B. V. Clements, 59 Sqn, attacked a Halberstadt two-seater which was patrolling the enemy front at 1,000 feet and shot it down. A few minutes later they drove down another Halberstadt out of control.

Enemy aircraft were also brought down during the period under review by:

Sqn 1 Lt H. A. Kullberg. **3** Lt A. W. Franklyn (2), Lt W. Hubbard (2), Lt S. D. Lavelle. **11** 2 Lt L. Arnott + Sgt C. W. Cooke, Lt E. S. Coles + 2 Lt D. P. Conyngham, Capt H. A. Hay + Lt A. H. Craig, Capt A. Morrison + Sgt R. Allan, Lt C. R. Smythe + 2 Lt W. T. Barnes. **12** Lt C. H. Pithey + 2 Lt H. Rhodes. **20** Lts P. T. Iaccaci + Mills, Capt H. P. Lale + 2 Lt H. L. Edwards (2), Lts C. R. Oberst + R. Gordon-Bennett. **22** Lt H. H. Beddow + 2 Lt T. J. Birmingham, Lt F. G. Gibbons + Sgt C. J. Shannan, Lt C. W. M. Thompson + 2 Lt G. MacCormack, Capt S. F. H. Thompson + Sgt R. M. Fletcher (2). **23** Lt H. N. Compton. **24** Lt H. L. Bair (USAS), Capt T. F. Hazell. **27** Lt E. J. Jacques + 2 Lt N. P. Wood. **29** Lt D. A. O'Leary, Lt A. E. Reed, Lt G. W. Wareing. **32** Lt F. L. Hale, Capt G. E. B. Lawson, Capt E. L. Zink. **46** Lt R. K. McConnell. **48** Lts J. B. Cowan + T. L. Jones, Lt G. F. Manning + 2 Lt P. A. Clayson, Capt H. A. Oaks + Lt T. Beck. **54** Lt M. G. Burger, Lt A. S. Compton, A Flight led by Capt G. H. Hackwill. **56** Lt H. P. Chubb. **60** Capt J. E. Doyle/Lt O. P. Johnson, Lt G. M. Duncan (2), Lt O. P. Johnson (2), Lt J. W. Rayner, Lt M. D. Sinclair (2). **62** Capt G. E. Gibbons + 2 Lt T. Elliott, Lt R. Schallaire + 2 Lt R. Lowe, Capt W. E. Staton + 2 Lt L. E. Mitchell. **64** Sgt A. S. Cowlishaw, Capt W. H. Farrow. **70** Lt C. L. Childs, Lts Gilbertson/G. S. Wilson, Lt S. T. Liversedge, Lt K. B. Watson. **74** Maj K. L. Caldwell, Lt G. R. Hicks, Lt A. C. Kiddie, Lt F. E. Luff (USAS). **79** Lt R. B. Bannerman. **80** Lt J. Collier, Maj F. I. Tanner. **84** Patrol led by Capt W. A. Southey. **87** Lt L. N. Hollinghurst, Capt A. W. Vigers. **88** Lt C. Findlay + 2 Lt G. T. Gauntlett (2), Capt A. Hepburn + 2 Lt H. G. Eldon, Capt E. C. Johnston + 2 Lt W. I. N. Grant, Lt V. Voss + Sgt C. Hill. **92** Capt W. E. Reed, Lt O. J. Rose. **98** 2 Lts E. A. R. Lee + E. G. Banham, 2 Lts T. W. Sleigh + A. H. Fuller. **103** Capt J. S. Stubbs + 2 Lt C. C. Dance. **107** 2 Lt F. T. Stott + Sgt W. J. Palmer. **108** 2 Lts R. Russell + G. B. Pike/C. R. Knott + F. D. McClinton/H. L. McLellan + F. X. Jackson. **201** Capt R. C. B. Brading, Capt G. B. Gates, Lt R. Sykes. **203** Capt L. H. Rochford, Capt A. T. Whealy. **208** Two patrols led by Capts J. B. White and W. E. G. Mann (2). **2 AFC** Lt F. R. Smith. **4 AFC** 2 Lt T. H. Barkell, Lt R. King, Lt L. E. Taplin. **148 Amer.** 1 Lt J. O. Creech, Lt F. E. Kindley, Lts C. I. McLean/W. B. Knox.

HONOURS AND AWARDS

DSO Lt W. G. Claxton, DFC, 2 Lt T. B. Dodwell, 1 Lt A. F. Bonnalie (USAS). **DFC** Capt T. F. Hazell, MC, (Bar), Capt W. H. Farrow, Capt M. C. McGregor, Capt S. G. Brearley, Capt E. T. Morrow, Capt L. H. Rochford, DSC, Lt W. B. Ward, Lt W. H. Longton, Lt T. R. Scott.

9 – 15 September

Air activity was again restricted by weather. Further successes were reported by the night-fighters of 151 Sqn.

COMMUNIQUÉ NO. 24

During the period under review we have claimed officially 82 E.A. brought down and 29 driven down out of control. Five enemy balloons were destroyed. Thirty-seven of our machines are missing. Approximately 28 tons of bombs were dropped and 2,376 plates exposed.

September 9th
Weather: low clouds, strong wind, heavy rain-storms ◦ No night bombing possible ◦ 1 ton of bombs dropped by day ◦ Enemy aircraft activity very slight; no decisive combats took place.

September 10th
Weather: low clouds and rain ◦ No night bombing was carried out ◦ 1 ton of bombs was dropped during the day ◦ Very few enemy aircraft seen.

September 11th
Weather: high wind and rain-storms ◦ No night bombing was possible ◦ 1 ton of bombs was dropped by day ◦ Very few enemy aircraft seen; no decisive combats.

September 12th
Weather: wind nad heavy rain ◦ No night bombing carried out; 1 ton of bombs dropped by day ◦ Enemy aircraft activity very slight; no decisive combats took place.

September 13th
Weather: overcast, rain showers, fair intervals ◦ A quarter of a ton of bombs dropped by night, and 5½ tons by day ◦ Enemy aircraft activity slight.

September 14th
Weather: fair, but overcast ◦ 4½ tons of bombs dropped by night and 6¾ tons by day ◦ Enemy aircraft active.

Capt E. J. McClaughry, 4 Sqn, A.F.C. attacked the aerodrome at

Ennetieres from a height of 200 feet and destroyed two out of five L.V.G.'s. which were standing on the aerodrome, and also obtained a direct hit on a hangar with a 25-lb. bomb.

Capt W. H. Haynes, 151 Sqn, brought down an enemy night bomber which had been caught by our searchlights. The E.A. fell in flames. Shortly afterwards he attacked another E.A. which dived steeply, but no decisive result could be observed.

Lt E. P. Mackay, 151 Sqn, attacked another large enemy machine which went on fire and also fell on our side of the lines.

2 Lt P. F. Bovingdon and Lt H. P. Elliott, 12 Sqn, were attacked by a Fokker biplane which dived east after 80 rounds had been fired at it from the rear gun. This machine was reported by Infantry to have eventually fallen in flames.

Lt A. Ibbotson and 2 Lt W. J. Carruthers, 59 Sqn, were also attacked by a Fokker biplane which was set on fire during the course of the combat and seen to crash.

Hostile balloons were brought down in flames by: Capt C. H. R. Lagesse, 29 Sqn; Capt W. A. Southey, 84 Sqn; 2 Lt S. W. Highwood, 84 Sqn. A balloon attacked by 2 Lt D. C. Rees, 84 Sqn, broke away and drifted east at a great height.

September 15th

Weather: fine ∽ 1 ton of bombs dropped by night and 6 tons by day ∽ Enemy aircraft activity greatly increased.

Lts V. W. Kilroe and G. E. Izzard, 15 Sqn, while carrying out a shoot saw an enemy machine shoot down one of our balloons. Lt Kilroe attacked and it was seen to go down and crash.

Capt R. M. Foster, 209 Sqn, shot down one of five Fokker biplanes and saw it crash. Shortly afterwards he joined in a fight between a large number of Fokker and some other scouts, and sent down one of the enemy machines in a spin. This E.A. was seen to crash by our infantry.

Capt O. M. Baldwin, 73 Sqn, while leading a patrol engaged a formation of Fokker biplanes, one of which he brought down. A little later he attacked an enemy two-seater which he also brought down. In the evening Capt Baldwin crashed a third hostile machine.

Capt E. S. Coler and 2 Lt E. J. Corbett, 11 Sqn, while on reconnaissance were attacked by five Fokker biplanes, one of which was shot down by the observer. On the return journey Capt Coler dived on another Fokker which was also brought down.

A patrol of 20 Sqn, led by Lt W. M. Thomson and 2 Lt H. Edwards, became engaged in a combat with about 20 Fokker biplanes. Lt Iaccaci and Sgt Newland brought down two of the enemy, and Lt Strachan and

2 Lt Calderwood shot down another, while a fourth was destroyed by Lt Thomson and 2 Lt Edwards.

2 Lt C. R. Thompson, 84 Sqn, attacked a hostile balloon which was guarded by two formations of Fokker biplanes the first of which dived on him but were driven off by another of his patrol. Although twice wounded, 2 Lt Thompson persisted in his attack and brought the balloon down in flames.

Hostile balloons were also shot down in flames by: Capt A. W. Beauchamp-Proctor, 84 Sqn; Capt H. A. Whistler, 80 Sqn; 2 Lt M. J. Ward, 70 Sqn; Capt F. O. Soden, 41 Sqn.

Ten machines of 56 Sqn raided Estourmel Aerodrome, dropping 34 25-lb. bombs from a height of 200 to 700 feet. One shed was completely destroyed, and one hangar and a lorry set on fire. Direct hits were also obtained on the officers' living quarters. Two Hannoveraner machines on the aerodrome, as well as the sheds and hangars were heavily shot up with machine-gun fire.

Enemy aircraft were also brought down during the period under review by:

Sqn 1 2 Lt D. E. Cameron/62 Sqn, Capt W. E. Staton + 2 Lt L. E. Mitchell, Capt W. Pallister, 2 Lt C. G. Pegg. **20** Capt T. P. Middleton + Lt A. Mills. **24** Capt H. D. Barton/Lt H. L. Bair (USAS). **29** Lt W. W. Lauer (USAS), Lt A. E. Reed, Lt G. W. Wareing. **46** Capt C. W. Odell/Lts Bruce/Paton. **62** Lt F. N. Coope + 2 Lt H. S. Mantle, Lt R. Schallaire + 2 Lt R. Lowe *See also under 1 Sqn.* **73** 2 Lt N. Cooper, Capt W. H. Hubbard, Lt E. J. Lussier. **74** Capt S. Carlin, Lt F. E. Luff (USAS). **85** Lt J. W. Warner. **92** Lt O. J. Rose. **201** Capt R. C. Brading, Capt G. B. Gates. **205** 2 Lts F. O. McDonald + J. B. Leach. **209** Capt W. R. May. **17 Amer.** 2 Lt H. C. Knotts. **148 Amer.** Lt J. O. Creech, Lt T. L. Moore.

HONOURS AND AWARDS

DSO Capt A. W. Beauchamp-Proctor, MC, DFC. **DFC** Lt G. A. Vaughn (USAS), Lt T. J. Herbert (USAS), 1 Lt M. L. Campbell (USAS), Lt F. C. Wilton, 1 Lt L. A. Hamilton (USAS), Lt J. A. Keating (USAS), Capt H. M. Ireland, Capt W. B. Elliott, Lt W. E. Macpherson, Lt E. H. Johnson, Lt A. R. Crosthwaite, 2 Lt C. F. Ambler, Capt G. J. Scaramanga, Lt E. J. Lussier, Capt T. G. Jefferies, Lt D. W. M. Miller, Capt R. N. G. Atkinson, Lt H. A. Kullberg, Lt A. R. Spurling, Lt A. E. Grigson, Lt J. Gould-Taylor, Lt A. W. Chadwick. **DFM** Cpl F. Wilkinson, Sgt H. C. Hunt, Sgt F. W. Bell, Sgt W. J. Palmer.

16 – 22 September

Various types of large bomber, with from four to six engines and known as Giants, were used by the German air force. Some of the most successful were built by the Zeppelin concern at Staaken. That shot down by 151 Sqn on 16 September was one of the five-engined variety.

During the week 151 Sqn shot down seven other night bombers.

COMMUNIQUÉ NO. 25

During the period under review we have claimed officially 105 E.A. brought down and 38 driven down out of control. Fifty-five of our machines are missing. Approximately 169 tons of bombs were dropped and 8,411 plates exposed.

September 16th
Weather: fine ∽ 24 tons of bombs dropped by night and 23¼ tons by day ∽ Enemy aircraft active.

Lt F. C. Broome, 151 Sqn, saw a giant enemy machine held in our searchlights which he attacked, firing 500 rounds altogether. The E.A. burst into flames and fell on our side of the lines.

Lt W. T. Martin and Sgt M. Jones, 22 Sqn, engaged a formation of Fokker biplanes, one of which they brought down but their aileron wires were shot away and the machine sideslipped down to 2,000 feet. Although wounded, Sgt Jones climbed out on to the bottom plane and steadied the machine.

Two flights of 29 Sqn became engaged with a formation of eight Fokker biplanes which were later reinforced by nine more. During the course of this combat, Capt E. C. Hoy brought down two of the enemy, and Capt C. H. R. Lagesse brought down one, as also did Lt E. O. Amm and 2 Lt W. L. Dougan.

Another flight of 29 Sqn attacked two Fokker triplanes, one of which Lt C. M. Wilson shot down, and the other was accounted for by Lt E. G. Davies.

Capt G. B. Gates and Lt J. M. Mackay, both of 201 Sqn, brought down an enemy two-seater, the pilot and observer of which were seen to jump out with parachutes before the machine burst into flames.

Lt W. E. Macpherson and 2 Lt C. F. Ambler, 205 Sqn, were attacked by a large number of E.A. on reaching their photographic area, and were chased over the lines, but shot one of the E.A. down in flames on the way. They returned but were again attacked, this time by eight Fokker biplanes, one of which they brought down in the course of a second retreat to the lines. They again returned and practically completed their photographic work.

Capt E. S. Coler and 2 Lt E. J. Corbett, 11 Sqn, were attacked while on reconnaissance by a large number of enemy scouts, and as one petrol tank was pierced and the aileron controls shot away, they dived to 1,000 feet over Cambrai when two of the E.A. overshot them. Capt Coler dived on one of these and brought it down in flames, while the other, which had got on their tail, was shot down by 2 Lt Corbett. They then returned home, crossing the lines at 150 feet, when the machine became unmanageable. Capt Coler succeeded in bringing it down in a slow sideslip to the ground where it crashed.

2 Lt A. F. Diamond (U.S.A.S.), 29 Sqn, brought down a hostile balloon in flames.

September 17th
Weather: fair, with some clouds ❧ 14 tons of bombs dropped by night, and 11 tons by day ❧ Enemy aircraft activity normal.

Lt R. Britton and 2 Lt B. Hickman, 13 Sqn, engaged an enemy two-seater which was on contact patrol and was seen to crash after two bursts had been fired at it by the observer.

Lts F. Jeffreys and F. W. Addison, 88 Sqn, were attacked by six Fokker biplanes while on photography. The first to attack was shot down in flames by the observer, and another, which came close so as almost to collide, was seen to go down on its back with part of the right wing shot away. The remaining E.A. continued to follow the Bristol Fighter until it was across the lines, one of them putting the observer's gun out of action and grazing his hand; both petrol tanks were also shot through.

A raid was carried out on Emerchicourt Aerodrome by 64 and 209 Sqns. Ninety-one bombs were dropped in all, many bursts being seen among the hangars and huts; two fires were started in the living quarters and a farm close by, and a hangar was set on fire on the other side of the Aerodrome. A direct hit was also obtained on a moving train. Lt H. C. Hayes, 64 Sqn, on returning from this raid saw a convoy of about 40 guns and wagons led by a staff car. These he attacked, firing over 40 rounds into them. The car went into a ditch and burst into flames, and the convoy was scattered and about 20 horses left on the road.

September 18th
Weather: fair but cloudy ❧ 17½ tons of bombs dropped by night and 14 tons by day ❧ Decreased enemy aircraft activity.

Top: Hannover CL II two-seater fighter

Bottom: Gotha G V night bomber

GERMAN FIGHTERS

Top: Siemens-Schuckert D IV

Bottom: Pfalz D XII

151 Sqn brought down three hostile bombing machines during the night. Maj C. J. Q. Brand saw one E.A. held in our searchlights, which he attacked at close range. This machine started to fall in flames when one of its bombs exploded and blew into pieces. Capt D. V. Armstrong brought down another E.A. at the same moment near Bapaume in flames. Lt E. P. Mackey brought down the third hostile machine east of Estrees-en-Chaussee after over 400 rounds had been fired at it. This machine was shelled on the ground after it crashed.

September 19th
Weather: overcast, high wind ∽ 2 tons of bombs dropped by night and 5½ tons by day ∽ Enemy aircraft activity very slight.

September 20th
Weather: low clouds, high wind and rain showers ∽ No night-bombing was carried out; 12½ tons of bombs dropped by day ∽ Enemy aircraft active, considering weather conditions.

A patrol of 20 Sqn, which was reinforced by a flight of S.E.5's of 84 Sqn, engaged a formation of 12 Fokker biplanes, which were joined by eight others, over St. Quentin. In this combat, which lasted for half an hour, our machines fought at a disadvantage owing to a strong west wind. Lt Harlock dived on one of the E.A. which he shot down, and his Observer (2 Lt Draisey) brought down another in flames. Lt Boulton and Sgt Mitchell shot down one which flew across their front, and another Fokker was destroyed by Lt McCall and 2 Lt Boothroyd. Meanwhile, Capt Middleton and Lt Mills, who had left the ground to reinforce the Bristol Fighter formation, became engaged with four enemy scouts, two of which they brought down. Capt Falkenberg, 84 Sqn, who had joined 20 Sqn with his patrol, shot down one of the E.A. which was seen to crash, and then drove one off the tail of a Bristol Fighter. 2 Lt Nel, of the same squadron, engaged six hostile machines during the course of this fight, one of which was seen by other pilots to crash, and, on the way home, he stayed with a Bristol Fighter which was dropping behind, but on being attacked by seven Fokkers was obliged to escape into a cloud.

September 21st
Weather: cloudy, strong wind ∽ 14 tons of bombs dropped by night and 11 tons by day ∽ Enemy aircraft activity slight.

Lt F. C. Broome, 151 Sqn, saw a large enemy night-bombing machine in the moonlight which he chased to within 200 yards, at which point he opened fire. The E.A. fell in flames and its bombs burst on hitting the ground.

Lt H. R. Hern, 148 Sqn, whilst gliding down to bomb Seclin was hit.

After dropping his bombs he proceeded home against a very strong wind, but his observer (Lt A. A. Tutte), seeing that he was in a fainting condition, climbed on to the cowling and held the control lever. In this way, in spite of Lt Hern's fainting three times, the pilot and observer succeeded in bringing the machine back and landing it safely on its aerodrome.

September 22nd

Weather: low clouds, rain storms ⌒ 8 tons of bombs dropped by night and 12½ tons by day ⌒ Enemy aircraft fairly active in morning, otherwise slight.

2 Lt H. J. Evans and Lt C. A. Stubings, 12 Sqn, were attacked by four E.A. which dived on them in succession, the observer firing at each in turn. The last E.A. to dive zoomed and looped, then fell upside down and was seen to crash.

Lt G. A. Vaughn, 17 Amer. Sqn, while on offensive patrol, was engaged by about 15 E.A., one of which, which was attacking a flight of our machines, he dived on and shot down in flames. He then attacked another, which he followed down to 2,000 feet. This E.A. was seen to crash by another pilot.

Maj C. J. Q. Brand, 151 Sqn, attacked an enemy night-bombing machine near Gouzeaucourt at close range. The E.A. zoomed and then fell over backwards and was later confirmed by our infantry to have crashed. Shortly afterwards, Maj Brand attacked another E.A., which was also engaged by Lt J. H. Summers. After both Camels had fired a good many rounds at this machine it went into a dive and crashed near Bourlon.

Lt A. A. Mitchell, 151 Sqn, attacked another hostile machine which he drove down and saw crash on attempting to land in a field.

Enemy aircraft were also brought down during the period under review by:

Sqn 1 Lt H. A. Kullberg. **11** Lts B. S. B. Thomas + W. T. Barnes (3). **19** Capt R. A. Del'Haye. **20** Lt Iaccaci + Sgt A. Newland, Lt Strachan + 2 Lt Calderwood, Lt W. M. Thomson + 2 Lt H. Edwards. **22** Lts C. W. M. Thompson + G. McCormack (2). **23** Lt J. Adam, 2 Lt E. J. Taylor/Lt R. L. M. Ross, Lt C. Thomas. **24** Capt H. D. Barton (2). **32** Lt F. L. Hale. **41** Capt W. E. Shields. **46** Patrol led by Capt D. R. MacLaren. **56** Lt H. Molyneux. **57** Lt P. W. J. Timson + 2 Lt I. S. Woodhouse, Formation led by Capt C. H. Stokes. **62** Lt C. H. Moss + 2 Lt R. Lowe. **64** Capt D. Lloyd-Evans. **65** Capt N. Chandler, Lt M. A. Newnham. **73** Capt O. M. Baldwin, Lt G. C. Carr-Harris. **74** Maj K. L. Caldwell, Capt C. B. Glynn, 2 Lt F. J. Hunt (2). **79** Capt R. B. Bannerman (4), Lt F. W. Gillet, Capt F. Lord (2), Lt J. McNeaney, Lt H. Parsons. **84** 2 Lts S. W. Highwood/C. F. C. Wilson, 2 Lt D. C. Rees. **85** Capt C. M. Crowe, Capt S. B. Horn, 2 Lt R. A. H. Lloyd, Lt J. W. Warner. **87** Capt H. A. R. Biziou (2), Lt L. N. Hollinghurst, Capt H. Mangan, Capt H. Larkin, Capt A. W. Vigers.

88 Lt K. B. Conn + 2 Lt B. Digby-Worsley (2), Patrol led by Capt E. C. Johnston, Lt G. R. Poole + Sgt C. Hill. **98** 2 Lts J. H. Nicholas + A. P. C. Bruce. **201** Capt R. C. B. Brading. **203** Lt F. J. S. Britnell, 2 Lt W. H. Coghill, Lt H. W. Skinner. **209** Lt G. Knight. **2 AFC** Lt F. Alberry, Capt E. D. Cummings/Lt E. E. Davies, Capt R. L. Manuel (in our lines). **4 AFC** 2 Lt T. H. Barkell, Lt G. Jones, Lt R. King, 2 Lt A. J. Palliser. **17 Amer.** 2 Lt H. Burdick, Lt W. Clements, Lt H. C. Knotts, Lt G. D. Wicks. **148 Amer.** Lts J. O. Creech/ F. E. Kindley, Lt E. W. Springs.

HONOURS AND AWARDS

DFC Lt G. N. Thompson (Bar), Capt W. R. Irwin (Bar), Lt C. R. Pithey (Bar), Lt H. Rhodes (Bar), Capt L. M. Woodhouse, MC, Capt H. J. Larkin, Lt W. Hubbard, Lt A. V. Stupart, Lt F. Godson, Lt A. W. Macnamara, Lt E. H. Canning, Capt G. E. Gibbons, Capt R. B. Bannerman, Lt F. W. Gillet, Capt E. C. Johnson, Lt H. F. Longbottom, 2 Lt A. M. Anderson, Lt R. King, Capt F. C. Hoy, Capt W. E. Green, Capt T. S. Symons, Lt V. H. McElroy, Lt E. Coler, 2 Lt E. J. Clarke, Capt W. G. Green, Capt J. A. Craig, Capt A. R. Cross, Lt G. A. Griffin, Capt G. J. Scott, Capt A. Beck, Capt G. M. Duncan, 2 Lt A. A. Robinson, MC, Capt H. P. Lale, Capt D. Lloyd-Evans, MC, Capt J. B. White, Capt W. E. G. Mann, 2 Lt G. L. Pargeter. **DFM** Sgt A. Newland (Bar), Sgt J. H. Bowler, Sgt J. Grant.

23 – 29 September

Sopwith Dolphins of 79 Sqn had a successful day on 28 September. Introduced early in 1918, the Dolphin had a good high-altitude performance, but only four squadrons were equipped with the type. Maj A. D. Carter, 19 Sqn, scored many of his 31 victories in Dolphins. Capt J. D. I. Hardman, 19 Sqn, and Lt L. N. Hollinghurst, 87 Sqn, two other successful Dolphin pilots, attained air rank in the Second War.

COMMUNIQUÉ NO. 26

During the period under review we have claimed officially 132 E.A. brought down and 60 driven down out of control. In addition, four E.A. were brought down by A.A. Eighty-three of our machines are missing. Approximately 253 tons of bombs were dropped and 8,169 plates exposed.

September 23rd
Weather: overcast, with some rain and strong wind ∽ 4 tons of bombs dropped by night and 1¼ tons by day ∽ Enemy aircraft activity slight.

Lts G. S. Bourner and F. A. D. Vaughan, 13 Sqn, attacked an enemy two-seater on which the pilot dived, and then turned, allowing his observer to fire also. The E.A. fell to the ground and burst into flames.

2 Lts G. C. Upson and A. N. Thomson, 42 Sqn, while on photography, were attacked by eight Fokker biplanes, one of which hit the tank, covering the pilot with petrol. The observer fired 30 rounds at this machine, when his Lewis gun was hit and put out of action; but the E.A. was observed by another of our machines to crash.

A hostile balloon was shot in flames by Capt A. W. Beauchamp-Proctor, 84 Sqn.

In spite of clouds and very strong wind, 207 Sqn carried out a successful raid on Saultain Aerodrome, dropping over three tons of bombs and obtaining a direct hit with one 1,650-lb. bomb on a hangar.

September 24th
Weather: fair, with some clouds ∽ 17 tons of bombs dropped by night and 13 tons by day ∽ Enemy aircraft activity was considerable.

Capt E. J. McClaughry, 4 Sqn A.F.C., while on offensive patrol dropped two 25-lb. bombs from 250 feet on a train, hitting the rear of it, which became detached and upset. He then fired 300 rounds at the front portion, which stopped. Shortly afterwards, he attacked an E.A. two-seater which he shot down, but was then attacked by seven Fokker biplanes and wounded. He, however, continued to fight, and saw one of the Fokkers at which he fired, break up in the air. As his ammunition was now exhausted, he attempted to return, firing Very's lights at two of the E.A. which had got on his tail, but he lost consciousness and only regained it just in time to flatten out and land.

2 Lt P. S. Manley and Sgt G. F. Hines, 62 Sqn, while returning from escorting a bomb raid were attacked by about 30 hostile scouts, at one of which the pilot dived; at the same time, Sgt Hines shot at another, which fell and was seen to crash by other observers. The pilot then turned across the rear of the bombing formation and sideslipped on to another scout, which Sgt Hines shot down in flames.

2 Lt H. C. Knotts, 17 Amer. Sqn, while on offensive patrol saw a lower flight attacked by eight E.A. and, diving on one of them, shot it down. On turning back to regain his formation, another E.A. attacked him from behind, but he succeeded in manœuvring on to its tail and shooting it down in flames.

A patrol of 2 Sqn A.F.C. dived on six Fokker biplanes while the remainder of the patrol engaged five more which were flying at a higher level. During the course of this combat, five hostile machines were shot down, the following pilots accounting for one each: Capt E. L. Simonson, Capt A. T. Cole, Lt J. J. Wellwood, Lt L. Franks, and Lt F. R. Smith.

A patrol of 148 Amer. Sqn became engaged with seven Fokker biplanes in the vicinity of Bourlon Wood, five of which they brought down in the course of the dog-fight, the following pilots accounting for one each: Lt E. W. Springs, Lt F. E. Kindley, Lt W. B. Knox, Lt E. H. Zistell, and Lt T. Wyly.

84 Sqn brought six hostile balloons down in flames in the course of the day. 2 Lt S. W. Highwood, and 2 Lt D. C. Rees each brought down one in the morning, and, in the afternoon, Capt C. F. Falkenberg skilfully led his flight above the clouds on to a line of enemy balloons which he had previously located and one of which he brought down in flames, while Lt S. W. Highwood brought down two in quick succession, 2 Lt F. R. Cristiani bringing down the sixth.

Maj Crespigny, and Lt M. A. Newnham, 65 Sqn, attacked Gontrode Aerodrome between 10 p.m. and 12.30 a.m. In spite of a strong wind and rain storms, both pilots descended to 200 feet, obtaining direct hits with four 25-lb. bombs on the Zeppelin hangar. They then attacked a shed, which was lit up, with machine gun fire. Lt Newnham remained

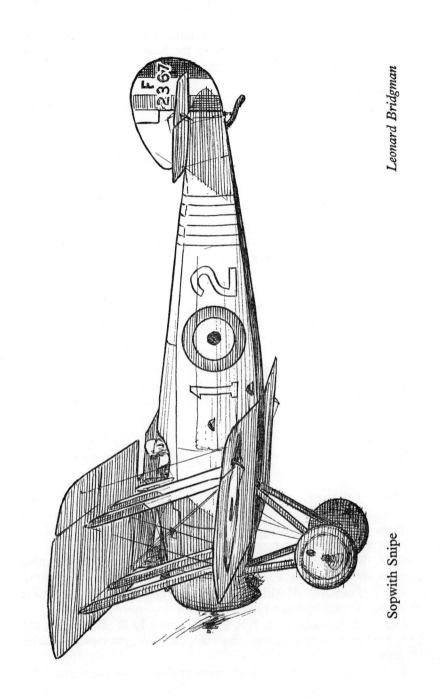

Leonard Bridgman

Sopwith Snipe

over the aerodrome for twenty minutes, circling round and firing at any lights that he saw. They then returned to the lines at a low height, shooting at any targets that presented themselves.

September 25th

Weather: overcast with some rain in morning, fair in afternoon ∽ 8 tons of bombs dropped by night and 9½ tons by day ∽ Enemy aircraft activity very slight.

A patrol of nine Bristol Fighters of 20 Sqn engaged a formation of about 20 Fokker biplanes N.E. of St. Quentin and destroyed seven of them. The leader of the patrol, Capt G. H. Hooper, dived on the nearest E.A. and brought it down, while his observer, 2 Lt Edwards, shot one down in flames and later brought down another. Lt F. G. Harlock fired at one of the E.A. which was flying above him and which spun down and was seen to crash. His observer, 2 Lt A. S. Draisey, brought down another. Lts T. C. Traill and R. Gordon-Bennett brought down one machine in flames, as also did Lt M. McCall and 2 Lt C. Boothroyd.

Photographs taken to-day show very effective results of the raid carried out by 207 Sqn on Saultain Aerodrome on the night 22nd/23rd. The large three-bayed shed on the western side was completely destroyed, and bomb holes are visible on the site. On the southern side, one bay of the twin-bay shed has gone, and the shed to the west appears to have been hit. In the S.E. corner of the Aerodrome, a group of five sheds has been entirely destroyed and a canvas hangar has also disappeared.

September 26th

Weather: fine ∽ 25½ tons of bombs dropped by night and 21 tons by day ∽ Considerable enemy aircraft activity.

Maj R. Collishaw, 203 Sqn, during the course of a low bomb attack on Lieu St. Amand Aerodrome engaged an enemy scout which he observed getting off the aerodrome and shot it down in flames, and also brought down another E.A. after the raid was over.

Lts C. W. M. Thompson and W. U. Tyrrell, 22 Sqn, when returning from escort duty to the above raid became engaged with a number of Fokker biplanes, two of which they shot down out of control and were observed to crash by other pilots.

Capt J. D. Breakey, Lt F. J. S. Britnell, and 2 Lt W. H. Coghill, 203 Sqn, during the course of the same raid, each brought down a Fokker biplane.

Lt T. R. Bloomfield, 151 Sqn, brought down a hostile night-flying machine of the Gotha type in flames near Arras on our side of the lines.

Eleven machines of 40 Sqn and 14 machines of 203 Sqn carried out a raid on Lieu St. Amand Aerodrome from a low height, escorted by machines of 22 Sqn. 40 Sqn attacked first, dropping their bombs on the hangars, a large one of which was set on fire, and obtaining several direct hits on huts. 203 Sqn then attacked setting three hangars on fire and obtaining two direct hits on a fourth. Two large huts were also seen burning. Living quarters on the aerodrome were attacked with machine gun fire, and smoke was seen to be coming out of one of the buildings. A D.F.W. which was shot at on the ground by all machines, burst into flames. Lt D. Woodhouse attacked 50 cavalry on the road, causing about 10 casualties. Eighty-eight bombs were dropped in all, and in addition five E.A. were destroyed by 203 Sqn and two by machines of the escort as recorded above.

September 27th

Weather: fine, but cloudy ⌀ 3½ tons of bombs dropped by night and 30 tons by day ⌀ Enemy aircraft active on the battle front.

Lt G. E. B. Lawson, 32 Sqn, while on escort duty brought down a Fokker biplane in flames. Shortly afterwards he attacked another at very close range which stalled in front of him and his undercarriage struck the top plane of the E.A. nearly upsetting him; this machine then fell in an obviously hopeless condition.

Lt R. E. Britton, and 2 Lt B. Hickman 13 Sqn, were attacked by eight Fokker biplanes. 2 Lt Hickman was wounded early in the fight but succeeded in shooting one E.A. down out of control. Lt Britton was then also wounded, and in trying to avoid the E.A. spun to the ground and landed in German lines. The Fokker then withdrew and Lt Britton took off again, returning safely to his aerodrome where he crashed owing to faintness.

Hostile balloons were brought down in flames by: Capt G. B. Bates, 201 Sqn; Capt A. W. Beauchamp-Proctor, 84 Sqn; Lt G. W. Wareing, 29 Sqn; Lt G. R. Riley, 3 Sqn (2); 2 Lt W. H. Maxted, 3 Sqn.

Scout squadrons of the 1st Brigade carried out a large number of low bombing attacks in conjunction with operations by the Canadian Corps. Large numbers of troops and transport were heavily bombed and engaged with machine-gun fire on the bridges crossing the Sensee Canal and the Canal de L'Escaut. Many direct hits and casualties were observed. A total of 528 bombs were dropped in the course of these operations.

September 28th

Weather: low clouds and rain in morning; clearing in afternoon ⌀ 18½ tons of bombs dropped by night and 22 tons by day ⌀ Enemy aircraft active during afternoon and evening.

Pilots of 79 Sqn destroyed seven hostile machines during the day. Lt J. McNeaney, while on patrol in the afternoon, engaged 10 Fokker biplanes which were attacking a Bristol Fighter, two of which he brought down. During this combat, Lt F. W. Gillet also brought down one of the E.A. Earlier in the day this pilot also shot down an enemy two-seater which was seen to crash. Capt R. B. Bannerman, Capt F. I. Lord, and Lt F. Woolley also accounted for one E.A. each.

Capt D. H. M. Carbery and Lt J. B. V. Clements, 59 Sqn, while on artillery patrol were attacked by two enemy two-seaters, one of which, after 100 rounds had been fired at it by both pilot and observer, dived steeply into the ground and crashed, whereupon the other retired.

149 Sqn dropped 42 112-lb. and 326 25-lb. bombs (over 5½ tons) on Menin, Courtrai and Lille during the course of the night. Eight machines made four trips each, and Lt Haldiman and 2 Lt Jones made five trips, commencing at 7.52 p.m. and landing from their last raid at 4.50 a.m.

Capt Chandler, 65 Sqn, dropped four 25-lb. bombs from 50 feet on a train in Menin Station, obtaining three direct hits on the train which was set on fire. His machine was covered with mud from the explosions. Troops were observed to leave the train.

Capt Banks and Lt Brown, 12 Sqn carried out a contact patrol under very bad weather conditions, obtaining a direct hit with one of four bombs dropped on M.T., and engaging trains and transport with machine gun fire from a very low altitude over 5,000 yards behind the enemy's lines.

Lts Bourner and Vaughan, 13 Sqn, on artillery patrol were surrendered to by a party of 40 of the enemy; the attention of our infantry was attracted and the enemy were seen to be marched off. A hostile battery was successfully reported and engaged during this flight.

September 29th

Weather: fine early, becoming overcast with rain in afternoon ⌒ 34 tons of bombs were dropped by night and 46 tons by day ⌒ Considerable enemy aircraft activity.

2 Lts N. J. Nock and W. E. Grainger, 10 Sqn, while taking oblique photographs, were attacked at 500 feet by seven E.A., two of which dived on their tail and were driven off by the observer's fire. The third E.A. to dive on them was shot down in flames.

Lt J. H. Latchford and Sgt A. H. Mabey, 25 Sqn, while on photographic work near Valenciennes, saw a Fokker biplane climbing up to them which the pilot dived on and drove away. Shortly afterwards another Fokker was seen approaching, which was also driven off. Just as their photographic work was completed they were attacked by five Fokkers, which they succeeded in shaking off; but on the way home they

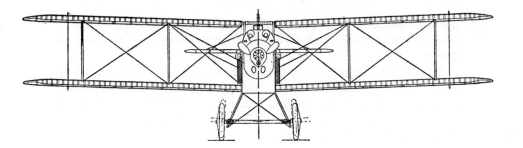

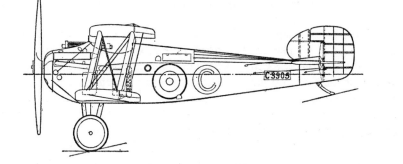

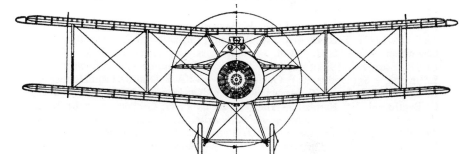

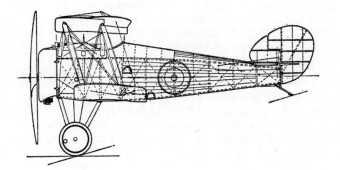

Sopwith Dolphin *and* Sopwith Snipe   *By courtesy of* The Aeromodeller

met another E.A. which the pilot dived on and shot down in flames, the observer having used up all his ammunition in warding off the previous machines.

A flight of 84 Sqn, specially detailed to attack hostile balloons, led by 2 Lt S. W. Highwood and protected by two other flights of the squadron, brought five enemy balloons down in flames. 2 Lt Highwood shot down two, one of which was also attacked by 2 Lt Rees, and Lt E. R. W. Millar, 2 Lt J. G. Coots, and 2 Lt F. R. Cristiani also each brought one down in flames.

Lt G. W. Wareing, 29 Sqn, brought two hostile balloons down in flames during the day.

Hostile balloons were also brought down in flames by: Lt E. O. Amm, 29 Sqn; Lt E. G. Davies, 29 Sqn; Capt W. E. Shields, 41 Sqn.

Capt Carruthers, 84 Sqn, flew along the Estrees–Geneve Road at a height of ten feet and attacked field batteries which were moving into position, scattering them and causing considerable casualties. He also attacked a Staff car, which went into a ditch, and caused casualties among a party of about 250 enemy troops.

Enemy aircraft were also brought down during the period under review by:

Sqn 1 Lt B. H. Moody. **3** 2 Lt W. H. Maxted. **11** Sgts E. Campbell + H. C. Taylor, 2 Lts T. Peacock + G. W. A. Kelty, formation of Sqn 11. **18** 2 Lt B. Champion + Sgt R. H. Favell. **19** Capt R. A. De L'Haye/Lt C. M. Moore, Lt R. L. Ray. **20** Lts Boothroyd + Kiernander, Lt Boulton + 2 Lt Edwards (2), Lt Britton + Sgt Dodds, Lt F. G. Harlock + 2 Lt A. S. Draisey, Capt Hooper + Lt Edwards (2), Lt A. T. Iaccaci + Sgt A. Newland, Lt M. McCall + 2 Lt C. Boothroyd, Lts Randall + Hackett. **22** Lt F. G. Gibbons + 2 Lt J. A. Oliver, Lts T. H. Newsome + R. S. Walshe, Lt L. C. Rowney + W. U. Tyrrell, Lts L. C. Rowney + W. U. Tyrrell/C. W. M. Thompson + L. R. James, Capt S. F. H. Thompson + Lt C. J. Tolman. **27** 2 Lts C. M. Allan + C. E. Robinson, 2 Lt C. M. Allan + Sgt W. E. Smith, Capt J. R. Webb + 2 Lt W. A. Hall/2 Lts T. A. Dickinson + W. J. Diment. **29** 2 Lt S. M. Brown, Capt E. C. Hoy, Lt C. G. Ross (2). **32** Lt F. L. Hale, Lt B. Rogers. **40** Capt J. L. Middleton, Capt G. J. Strange. **41** Capt W. E. Shields, Lt E. J. Stephens. **46** Capt D. R. MacLaren. **48** Capt F. J. Cunninghame + Lt R. A. Brunton, 2 Lts W. S. Rycroft + H. C. Wood. **49** Lt M. D. Allan + 2 Lt W. A. Owens. **54** Capt V. S. Bennett, Lt M. G. Burger. **56** Capt H. P. Chubb (2), Lt J. A. Pouchot, Lt C. B. Stenning. **57** Lt A. Newman + Lt E. G. Pernet, Lt A. Newman + 2 Lt C. Wilkinson, Lt F. G. Pym + Sgt W. C. E. Mason. **59** Capt D. Carbery + Lt R. Ireland. **60** Capt A. Beck. **62** Capt G. T. Richardson + 2 Lt I. P. Aitken (2). **64** Capt Cudemore. **70** 2 Lt R. M. Atwater, Capt W. M. Carlaw, Lt O. A. P. Heron, Lt K. B. Watson. **73** Capt O. M. Baldwin. **74** Lt G. R. Hicks/Capt B. Roxburgh-Smith, Capt B. Roxburgh-Smith, Capt B. Roxburgh-Smith/Lt G. R. Hicks. **79** Capt R. B. Bannerman, Lt F. W. Gillet, Lt F. Woolley. **80** Capt H. A. Whistler (2). **82** 2 Lts G. E. M. Bennett + A. G. Currington. **84** Capt C. F. Falkenberg, 2 Lt W. J. B. Nel. **85** Lt J. W. Warner.

87 Lt L. N. Hollinghurst, Lt R. M. Macdonald. **201** Capt G. B. Gates. **203** Capt J. D. Breakey, Lt W. Sidebottom/2 Lt W. H. Coghill. **205** Lt R. L. M. Barbour + Capt M. F. M. Wright. **208** Capt W. E. G. Mann, Capt J. B. White (2). **211** 2 Lts C. H. Dickins + A. M. Adam, 2 Lts H. H. Palmer + W. C. Snowdon. **4 AFC** Lt G. Jones, Capt R. King, Lt J. W. Wright. **17 Amer.** 2 Lt H. Burdick (2), Lt W. T. Clements. **148 Amer.** Lts H. R. Clay/E. W. Springs, Lt J. O. Creech, Lt F. E. Kindley, Lt C. I. McLean, 2 Lt L. W. Rabe, Lt O. A. Ralston.

HONOURS AND AWARDS

DFC 1 Lt R. G. Landis, 1 Lt H. R. Clay, Lt B. S. Wilcox, 2 Lt A. T. Sprangle, Lt H. E. Searson, Capt R. Stephenson, Lt W. R. May, 2 Lt H. F. Birchal, Lt H. A. E. Gard, Capt P. J. Slater, Capt A. M. F. Hill, Lt H. A. Molyneux, Lt J. B. V. Clements, Lt C. E. H. Allen, Lt M. O. Haskell, 1 Lt E. W. Springs, Capt D. H. M. Carbery, MC, Lt H. A. Coysh, 2 Lt J. Town, Capt G. N. Moore, 2 Lt F. S. Occomore, Lt A. Kiteley, Lt W. S. Eastaugh, Lt B. G. Porter, Lt J. A. G. Haslam, MC, Lt D. J. Hughes, Lt O. C. Cassels, Lt F. Belway, Lt R. K. McConnell.

30 September – 6 October

Two unusual missions were recorded during this week—ammunition and rations drops on 1 and 2 October to advanced parties of troops.

COMMUNIQUÉ NO. 27

During the period under review we have claimed officially 86 E.A. brought down and 27 driven down out of control. In addition, 1 E.A. was brought down by A.A. Fifty-six of our machines are missing. Approximately 223 tons of bombs were dropped and 4,953 plates exposed.

September 30th

Weather: low clouds, heavy rainstorms ∽ *No night bombing was possible; 8 tons of bombs dropped by day.*

Nine machines of 4 Sqn A.F.C. attacked columns of transport on the Le Mesnil Road at a height of from 600 to 2,000 feet. Twenty-eight 25-lb. bombs were dropped and a large number of rounds fired. Several wagons were overturned, horses stampeded and many casualties were observed to be caused amongst the drivers. A large fire was also caused in Fournes Dump by bombs dropped from 1,500 feet.

October 1st

Weather: fine, with some clouds ∽ *1 ton of bombs dropped by night and 30 tons by day* ∽ *Enemy aircraft activity moderate.*

A bomb raid of 108 Sqn, after dropping their bombs on Ingelmunster Station, were attacked by a large formation of 33 E.A. During a running fight, which lasted for over 10 minutes, the D.H.9's kept together in close formation and shot three of the hostile machines down in flames, one was seen to break up in the air, and another was seen to fall out of control and crash near the railway line at Roulers. Later, the enemy formation were seen to be attacked by some of our scouts. The following pilots and observers took part in this raid: Lt Page and Sgt Hoolihan, Capt Haynes and Lt Brown, Lts Knott and Windle, Lt Boswell and Sgt Greenwood, Lts Milne and Webster, Lts Kershaw and Owen, Lts Featherstone and Firth, Lts Hopkins and Eveleigh, Lts Matheson and Gundill.

Capt C. B. Glynn, 74 Sqn, attacked four Fokker biplanes in turn, which were attacking another flight of his squadron; one of them he shot down out of control and it was seen to crash by another pilot, and he sent another down in flames.

A hostile balloon was shot down in flames by 2 Lt J. B. Garver (U.S.A.S.), 74 Sqn, and another set on fire on the ground by Lt O. B. Ramsay, 4 Sqn A.F.C.

206 Sqn dropped 26 112-lb. and 107 25-lb. bombs on Courtrai sidings, Quesnoy and Linselles during the day with good effect. 7 and 82 Sqns carried out 32 flights for the purpose of dropping ammunition to our troops. Sixty-three boxes were dropped in all. 25 Sqn carried out a large amount of successful long distance photography, taking 267 photographs—75 of which were taken by Capt Jones and 2 Lt McEachram of the area around Namur, in spite of being hampered by clouds.

Capt C. F. Falkenberg, 84 Sqn, successfully attacked enemy troops and transport, and on one occasion saw our infantry and tanks advancing towards Estrees and several hundred of the enemy running in front of them; he thereupon dived on the enemy with his flight as they crossed the open, inflicting heavy casualties. 2 Lt S. W. Highwood and Lt Miller, both of the same squadron, attacked the enemy, who were counter-attacking, with machine-gun fire and remained fighting until all their ammunition was expended.

October 2nd
Weather: fair in morning, becoming cloudy, with some rain in afternoon ⌒ 16 tons of bombs dropped by night and 43 tons by day ⌒ Enemy aircraft fairly active in morning.

A patrol of 29 Sqn engaged eight Fokker biplanes in the neighbourhood of Roulers. Capt C. H. R. Lagesse shot down one of these which was diving on one of our machines. Capt C. G. Ross fired 150 rounds at another at close range and it was seen to crash. Lts T. S. Harrison and E. G. Davies also each shot down one of the E.A.

Ten machines of 54 Sqn on returning from low bombing saw a Fokker biplane attacking one of our machines and drove it down on our side of the lines where it landed intact, the pilot being wounded.

Hostile balloons were shot down in flames by Lt F. W. Gillet, 79 Sqn, and Lt M. A. Newnham, 65 Sqn.

82 Sqn dropped 2,400 boxes of rations to Belgian troops whose supplies had been held up, and squadrons of the 2nd Wing dropped 58 boxes of ammunition to our troops at pre-arranged stations.

A patrol of 73 Sqn dropped four bombs on active hostile guns which were destroyed; they also put a machine gun out of action and caused a

Top: S.E.5a of No. 24 Squadron

Bottom: De Havilland D.H. 9A day bomber

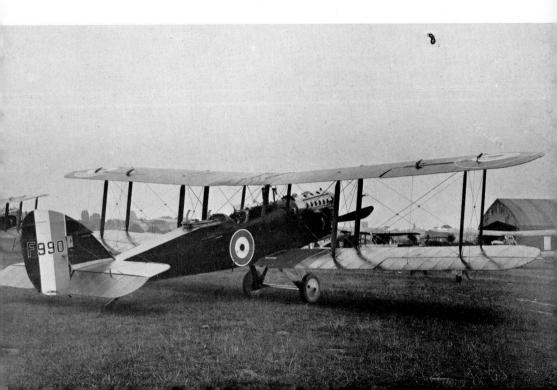

Major Raymond Collishaw   Major W. A. Bishop, V.C.

Major Edward Mannock, V.C.   Major W. G. Barker, V.C.

large number of casualties to enemy troops with bombs and machine-gun fire from a low height.

Photographs taken to-day show very effective results of the raids carried out on Aulnoye Junction on the 1st instant by machines of the 51st Wing, and on the night of the 1st/2nd by 207 Sqn. An ammunition train appears to have exploded, causing great disorganization and damage, and fires are still to be seen burning.

Lts O. B. Ramsay and C. V. Ryrie, 4 Sqn A.F.C., left the ground at 4.45 a.m. to attack Don Railway Station, where they dropped 4 25-lb. bombs, observing one direct hit; they then dropped four more bombs on Houplin Aerodrome and fired at machines and mechanics on the Aerodrome from 700 feet. A train steaming out of Haubourdin was also fired at and made to pull up.

October 3rd
Weather: fair ⌒ 1 ton of bombs dropped by night and 26 tons by day ⌒ Enemy aircraft fairly active.

A patrol of 70 Sqn engaged five Fokker biplanes which were attacking an R.E.8 near Roulers. Capt W. M. Carlaw dived on one of them which was seen to crash near Roulers, and was then attacked by another, which he also shot down. 2 Lts M. J. Ward and G. W. K. Smith also each brought down one of the E.A.

A hostile balloon was brought down in flames by Capt A. W. Beauchamp-Proctor, 84 Sqn.

October 4th
Weather: fine, but overcast ⌒ 30 tons of bombs dropped by night and 20½ tons by day ⌒ Increased enemy aircraft activity in morning, becoming slight in afternoon.

Lt R. L. Barbour and Capt M. F. M. Wright, 205 Sqn, while on photography, after two fights with enemy machines, both of which they drove off, were attacked by six Fokker biplanes near St. Quentin, one of which Capt Wright shot down.

2 Lt W. H. Bland, 65 Sqn, in an engagement with several Fokker biplanes dived to within 100 feet of the ground after one of them, firing continuously, when he saw it crash a complete wreck. He was now so close to the ground that enemy infantry threw stones at him.

Lt R. A. Caldwell, 56 Sqn, brought down a hostile balloon in flames in the vicinity of Bohain; he then returned to the lines at a low height, attacking four double gun limbers drawn by mules on the way. The first two limbers fell into a ditch, and the teams broke loose. He then fired 150 rounds into a party of 500 infantry, and later attacked a battery of six enemy howitzers with machine gun fire and also two batteries of field guns before crossing the lines.

Lt A. F. Corker and 2 Lt G. B. Nicholas, 102 Sqn, attacked a moving train during the night between Bertry and Caudry. After dropping a flare from 1,500 feet they descended to 700 feet and dropped 3 112-lb. bombs, making two direct hits. A second flare revealed the train to be a complete wreck, but before leaving they fired 100 rounds and four Very's lights into it.

October 5th

Weather: fair in morning, low clouds in afternoon ○ 25½ tons of bombs dropped by night and 22½ tons by day ○ Moderate enemy aircraft activity in morning, decreasing in afternoon.

2 Lt W. Van Blaricom and 2 Lt J. W. G. Clark, 13 Sqn, were attacked by seven or eight Fokker biplanes, which dived on them in turn and were each fired at by the observer, but without effect. The leader of the enemy formation then attacked a second time, but commenced to glide east after the attack, followed by the remainder; his glide then became very steep, finally ending in a spin, and he was seen to crash; the rest of the enemy formation withdrew.

Capt B. Roxburgh-Smith, 74 Sqn, dived on nine hostile machines which were attacking our two-seaters. The first machine he attacked went down in a spin; the second, which was a triplane, was seen to crash on the ground where it burst into flames. He then continued the dive on to three Fokker biplanes, firing at the centre one whose wing crumpled up in the air; this machine was also seen to crash.

Capt A. W. Beauchamp-Proctor and 2 Lt A. E. Hill, 84 Sqn, while returning to our lines at a low height attacked an enemy balloon, firing first of all into the basket and then into the balloon. The latter went on fire without any observer being seen to jump out, and fell in flames on to some troops below.

Hostile balloons were also brought down in flames by: Lt D. Grinnell-Milne, 56 Sqn; Capt C. H. R. Lagesse, Lt D. M. Layton, Lt D. M. Murray, 29 Sqn (1); 2 Lt A. J. Palliser, 4 Sqn A.F.C.

A patrol of 4 Sqn A.F.C., consisting of Capt R. King, 2 Lt T. H. Barkell, and 2 Lt A. J. Palliser, during a flight of 1 hour 20 minutes, carried out the following work: Destroyed one balloon in flames; dropped 12 25-lb. bombs from a low height at a train in Avelin Station and on the Aerodrome, obtaining four direct hits on the station and one on a shed on the aerodrome. They also fired a large number of rounds into a 'flaming-onion' battery, and three times attacked horse transport, which scattered in confusion. The sheds on Avelin Aerodrome were also shot

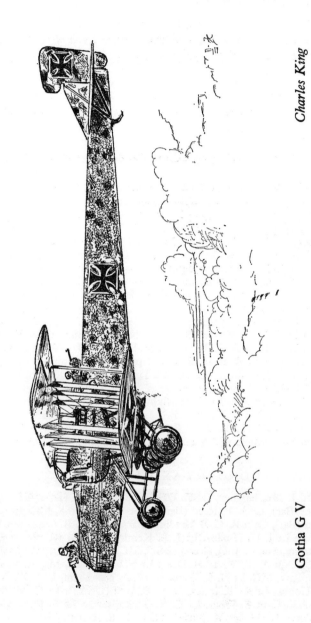

Gotha G V

Charles King

up, and finally a train was fired at, one wagon of which exploded, completely wrecking two trucks.

October 6th

Weather: low clouds, high wind, and some rain ∽ *1 ton of bombs dropped by night and 8 tons by day* ∽ *Enemy aircraft activity very slight; no decisive combats took place.*

In spite of very unfavourable weather, 102 Sqn carried out a raid during the night, dropping 15 112-lb. and 47 25-lb. bombs on Solesmes, Bertry, and Le Cateau Stations.

Enemy aircraft were also brought down during the period under review by:

Sqn 11 Sgt A. Cridlan + 2 Lt W. Connor, Lt C. R. Smythe + 2 Lt W. T. Barnes. **19** Lt J. W. Crane, Capt F. McQuistan, Lt C. M. Moore (2). **20** Lt E. A. Britton + Sgt R. S. Dodds, Lt F. G. Harlock + 2 Lt J. F. Kidd. **22** Capt S. Collier + 2 Lt J. V. Scottorn. **24** Capt T. F. Hazell. **29** Lt E. O. Amm, Lt T. S. Harrison, Lt R. B. Lovemore, Lt R. G. Robertson, Capt C. G. Ross. **40** Lt A. T. Drinkwater. **43** Lts E. Mulcair/R. S. Johnston. **48** Capt F. J. Cunninghame + Lt R. A. Brunton, Sgt J. Moffat + 2 AM S. Julian, 2 Lts T. G. Rae + C. R. Pickering, Lt G. Thornton-Norris + Sgt R. L. G. White. **49** 2 Lts J. B. Gunn + E. G. Bramble. **54** Capt V. S. Bennett, Lt J. C. Green (2), Maj R. S. Maxwell. **60** 2 Lt S. J. Mason. **65** Capt A. G. Jones-Williams (2), Lt J. Reid. **70** 2 Lt O. A. Heron. **79** Lt J. H. McNeaney, Lt F. W. Gillet. **84** 2 Lt J. G. Coots, 2 Lt S. W. Highwood. **87** Lts L. N. Hollinghurst/C. E. Worthington. **88** Lts K. B. Conn + A. B. Radford, Lts C. Findlay + I. W. F. Agabeg (2), Lt J. P. Findlay + 2 Lt R. E. E. Hasell, Capt E. C. Johnston + Lt I. W. F. Agabeg, Capt E. C. Johnston + Sgt C. M. Maxwell. **92** Lt O. J. Ross (2). **98** 2 Lts H. F. Mulhall + S. StC. Stone. **201** 2 Lt G. K. Green. **203** Capt J. D. Breakey, Lt W. Sidebottom, Lt H. W. Skinner. **208** Lt R. D'A. Gifford, Capt J. B. White (2). **211** 2 Lts H. H. Palmer + J. H. McLellan, 2 Lts V. G. Phillips + A. F. Taylor. **4 AFC** Lt R. T. C. Baker (2), 2 Lt P. J. Sims. **17 Amer.** Lts G. R. Vaughn/H. Burdick. **148 Amer.** Lt L. K. Callahan, Lt O. A. Ralston.

HONOURS AND AWARDS

DSO Capt E. J. McClaughry, DFC. **DFC** Capt W. F. J. Harvey (Bar), Capt R. L. Manuel (Bar), Lt A. E. Reed (Bar), Capt W. E. Staton, MC (Bar), Capt H. D. Barton (Bar), Capt R. C. B. Brading (Bar), Capt G. B. Gates (Bar), 2 Lt C. G. Haigh, 2 Lt J. H. Huxley, Lt J. E. Kendrick, Lt G. W. Wareing, Capt D. V. Armstrong, Maj C. J. Q. Brand, DSO, MC, 2 Lt H. Edwards, Maj G. S. Sansom, MC, Capt A. T. Whealey, DSC, Lt F. C. Broome, Maj H. V. Champion de Crespigny, MC, Lt H. R. Hern, Lt M. A. Newnham, Lt J. W. Warner, 2 Lt T. G. Hobbs, Lt R. T. Jones, Lt F. E. Luff (USAS), Lt C. M. Wilson, Lt Bair (USAS), Capt S. Jones, Lt C. R. Thompson, 2 Lt S. W. Highwood, 2 Lt A. A. Tutte. **DFM** Sgt M. Jones. **MC** Lt F. B. Palmer. **MM** Sgt F. W. J. Sibley.

7 – 13 October

Bad weather for most of the week restricted flying.

Maj G. H. Bowman, 41 Sqn, who assisted in shooting down a Fokker D.VII on the British lines on 10 October, ended the war with a victory score of 32.

COMMUNIQUÉ NO. 28

During the period under review we have claimed officially 48 E.A. brought down and 12 driven out of control. In addition, one E.A. was brought down in our lines by A.A. Twenty three of our machines are missing. Approximately 136½ tons of bombs were dropped and 3,196 plates exposed.

October 7th

Weather: high wind and clouds in morning, with rain in afternoon ◌ 16¼ tons of bombs dropped by night and 13½ tons by day ◌ Enemy aircraft activity generally slight.

Capt C. H. R. Lagesse, while leading a patrol of five machines of 29 Sqn, dived on one of a formation of E.A. which was attacking another flight of S.E.5's and shot it down in flames. The pilot of this machine parachuted, but his clothes caught fire and he was last seen burning on the ground. Shortly afterwards Capt Lagesse met a D.F.W. which he shot down on this side of the lines. In this combat he was helped by Lt T. S. Harrison, who had been compelled to land east of Houthulst Forest owing to engine trouble after a combat with an L.V.G. which he had destroyed. 2 Lt E. G. Davies, on the same patrol, brought down a Fokker biplane.

Lt O. A. Heron, 70 Sqn, dived on one of 15 Fokker biplanes, which broke up in the air after 100 rounds had been fired at it. He then attacked another which was on the tail of a Camel and shot it down in flames. Capt W. M. Carlaw, of the same squadron, also brought down a Fokker biplane.

A hostile balloon was brought down in flames by Lt W. E. Bardgett, 74 Sqn, and one by Lt J. C. Speaks, 56 Sqn, on the 5th instant.

A raid was carried out on Escarmain Aerodrome by 64 Sqn, who dropped 45 25-lb. bombs, obtaining two direct hits on one hangar, which was set on fire, and fired a large number of rounds into the hangars, in each of which could be seen two Fokkers. This raid was carried out in spite of thick clouds at 4,000 feet and layers of cloud and mist at 300 feet, which rendered the objective very difficult to find.

Annappes and Lille Stations were attacked from a height of 200 feet by 2 Sqn A.F.C., who dropped 71 25-lb. bombs. Several trains were hit, one of which was full of troops, who rushed out and were then attacked with machine gun fire, many casualties being caused. In the course of their flight some of them took shelter in a house, which was bombed and destroyed.

October 8th
Weather: low clouds and rain in morning, becoming fine later ∞ 1½ tons of bombs dropped by night and 21 tons by day ∞ Enemy aircraft active.

2 Lt J. Graham and Lt J. O'Callaghan, 7 Sqn, were attacked by seven Pfalz scouts, one of which they shot down, and was seen by our infantry to crash. They were then forced to land in 'No Man's Land', but crawled into a ditch, regaining our lines after dark.

Capt C. H. R. Lagesse, 29 Sqn, attacked with his patrol six Fokker biplanes, one of which he shot down. Shortly afterwards they again attacked another six. Capt Lagesse destroyed one of these and Lt E. O. Amm another, while Lts D. M. Murray, J. P. Murphy and D. M. Layton brought a third down in flames.

Lt F. W. Gillet, 79 Sqn, brought down a Fokker biplane, and a little later attacked another, which was diving on a Belgian machine, which he also destroyed.

Hostile balloons were brought down in flames by: Capt W. H. Longton, 24 Sqn; Capt M. C. McGregor, Lt P. D. d'Albenas, 85 Sqn (1).

In spite of very bad weather conditions, 101 Sqn dropped 11 112-lb. and 100 25-lb. bombs on Maretz, Busigny and Premont; 21 2-lb. Vickers shells and a large number of machine gun rounds were also fired on likely targets.

Low-flying scouts of the 3rd Brigade consistently bombed and shot up enemy transport and troops throughout the day to a depth of 12 miles beyond the line, causing considerable confusion and greatly hampering the enemy's movement both in bringing up local reinforcements and in the general trend of guns and transport eastwards.

October 9th
Weather: fair ∞ 21½ tons of bombs dropped by night and 35 tons by day ∞ Enemy aircraft activity was considerable.

A patrol of 70 Sqn, led by Capt S. T. Liversedge, chased two L.V.G.'s over Courtrai, one of which Capt Liversedge shot down, but they were

Leonard Bridgman

De Havilland D.H.9 A

then attacked by eight Fokker biplanes. Lt O. A. Heron and Lt E. A. Copp each shot down one of these, and a second, engaged by the former, crashed into a tree. Lt A. Webster and Lt K. B. Watson also each destroyed one E.A., and a seventh was chased west by the whole patrol and destroyed.

A formation of 48 Sqn engaged 12 Fokker biplanes, one of which was shot down by Lt T. G. Rae and Sgt T. F. Perkin, and was seen to crash into some trees. Capt F. J. Phillips and 2 Lt J. W. London also brought down one, while a third was shot down in flames by Lt G. F. Manning and Sgt H. F. Monday.

Capt A. Beck, 60 Sqn, shot down an L.V.G. two-seater in flames, which fell on our side of the lines.

2 Lt H. N. Kerr and 2 Lt V. H. Thornton, 4 Sqn A.F.C., attacked an L.V.G. two-seater, one on each side, and compelled it to land on our side of the lines.

Patrols of 208 Sqn dropped 117 25-lb. bombs during the day on enemy troops and transport, four bombs being dropped on a train in Busigny.

Capt W. H. Longton, 24 Sqn, landed near our cavalry and reported an enemy machine gun nest which was worrying them, enabling our guns to be turned on to it. Capt Longton then took off and attacked the enemy with machine gun fire as they scattered.

October 10th

Weather: low clouds and rain ◌ No night bombing was possible; 12½ tons of bombs dropped by day ◌ Very slight enemy aircraft activity.

Maj G. H. Bowman, and Capt F. O. Soden, 41 Sqn, attacked a Fokker biplane, which had just shot down one of our balloons, and shot it down on our side of the lines.

Capts Randall and Macdonald and Lt Henson, 85 Sqn, attacked a line of enemy infantry who were holding up the advance of our cavalry. They dived again and again on the hostile troops, silencing their machine guns and causing them to retire behind a village. They then repeated this operation at another place, causing the enemy to retire in confusion.

October 11th

Weather: low clouds, mist and rain ◌ No night bombing possible; 9 tons of bombs dropped by day ◌ Practically no enemy aircraft seen; no decisive combats.

Patrols of 92 Sqn dropped 74 25-lb. bombs on transport, troops and batteries. Three guns and limbers were attacked with machine gun fire, three horses being killed. One bomb was observed to burst on the edge of a gun-pit, and the gun ceased firing. Lt J. V. Gascoyne at a height of

20 feet attacked a column of guns and limbers passing through Molain, and shot down the leading horses. He then flew round another limber which attempted to pass, shot it down, and succeeded in blocking up the road.

October 12th
Weather: low clouds, mist and rain ∽ No night bombing; 2¾ tons of bombs dropped by day ∽ Very slight enemy aircraft activity; no decisive combats.

October 13th
Weather: mist and rain ∽ No night-flying possible; 8 cwts. of bombs dropped by day ∽ Practically no enemy aircraft seen; no decisive combats took place.

Enemy aircraft were also brought down during the period under review by:

Sqn 46 Capt D. R. MacLaren. **62** Capt L. Campbell + 2 Lt W. Hodgkinson. **70** Lt K. B. Watson. **74** Capt C. B. Glyn. **80** 2 Lt H. R. Messenger. **84** Capt A. W. Beauchamp-Proctor. **85** Lt D. C. Inglis. **88** Lts C. Findlay + I. W. F. Agabeg, Capt A. Hepburn + 2 Lt H. G. Eldon. **92** Lt O. J. Rose (2). **98** 2 Lts E. A. R. Lee + A. A. Douglas. **203** Capt L. H. Rochford/Lt W. Sidebottom. **205** Lt J. G. Kerr + 2 Lt C. Gardner. **209** Lt F. A. Giles. **4 AFC** Lt R. H. Youdale.

14 – 20 October

Despite another week of poor weather, there were several notable operations—seven enemy aircraft destroyed and five sent down out of control by S.E.5a's of 2 Sqn Australian Flying Corps, on 14 October, and a successful strike against Tournai by a mixed bomber and fighter force on 18 October.

COMMUNIQUÉ NO. 29

During the period under review we have claimed officially 35 E.A. brought down and eight driven out of control. In addition, three E.A. were brought down by A.A. Thirteen of our machines are missing. Approximately 97 tons of bombs were dropped and 2,798 plates exposed.

October 14th
Weather fair, but cloudy ∽ Nearly 12 tons of bombs dropped by night and 33 tons by day ∽ Enemy aircraft activity very intensive on northern portion of front; normal elsewhere.

During the day 22 E.A. were shot down by machines of the 2nd Brigade, constituting a record for number of enemy machines crashed in one day by one Brigade.

An offensive patrol of four machines of 29 Sqn were attacked by two formations of Fokker biplanes, totalling about 20. Lt H. C. Rath shot down one E.A., which was seen to crash east of Roulers, and later drove down another which crashed west of Ingelmunster.

2 Lt H. Holroyde shot down a two-seater which is confirmed by another pilot to have crashed north of Roulers. Capt C. H. R. Lagesse brought down an E.A. which crashed east of Roulers, and another which crashed west of Roulers.

An offensive patrol of 74 Sqn engaged a formation of about 15 Fokker biplanes. Capt B. Roxburgh-Smith shot down one of the E.A. which crashed near Lauwe, and a second which crashed near Reckem, whilst 2 Lt S. T. Stidolph shot down a third E.A. in flames east of Menin, and 2 Lt E. W. Roesch shot another down out of control.

Whilst on flash reconnaissance, 2 Lts W. De Bussey and G. T. Carr, 82 Sqn, were attacked by four Fokker biplanes, one of which they shot down east of Winkel St. Eloi, where it was seen to crash by a pilot of 7 Sqn.

Lt E. C. Grimes and 2 Lt L. W. Edmonds, also of 82 Sqn, were attacked by one of a formation of 16 Fokker biplanes; this machine they shot down and crashed north of Courtrai.

While on offensive patrol, the undermentioned pilots of 2 Sqn A.F.C. destroyed seven E.A. and drove down five others out of control: Lt F. R. Smith (3); Lt C. O. Stone, Capt E. D. Cummings, Lt G. H. Blaxland, Lt L. Franks.

October 15th

Weather: low clouds, mist, rain ∽ *13½ tons of bombs dropped by night and over 10 tons by day* ∽ *Enemy aircraft active during morning over northern portion of front; only slight activity elsewhere.*

Maj G. H. Bowman, 41 Sqn, dived on 10 Fokker biplanes, attacking the top one, and after firing about 100 rounds the top lane of the E.A. buckled right back, the E.A. falling into the mist below.

Lts Phillips and Howie, 52 Sqn, while on artillery patrol over Iwuy, saw an enemy two-seater machine-gunning our troops. They had just driven off this machine when Lt Phillips was wounded and fainted. The observer brought the E.A. down, which crashed in front of our lines. The pilot died on landing. Lt Howie was also wounded in the wrist.

October 17th

Weather: low clouds, thick mist ∽ *No night bombing; 6¼ tons of bombs dropped by day.*

October 18th

Weather: fair, overcast, very misty ∽ *Unfavourable weather conditions prevented night bombing; 6¼ tons of bombs by day* ∽ *Only slight enemy aircraft activity reported.*

Lts Spriggs and Berridge, in an A.W. of 8 Sqn, attacked a enemy two-seater. Lt Berridge got in a good burst at close range and the E.A. burst into flames and crashed.

Lt G. H. Blaxland, 2 Sqn A.F.C., was attacked by three Fokker biplanes. He succeeded in firing 50 rounds into one E.A. from 75 yards range; the E.A. immediately went down vertically and was seen to crash near Tournai.

Lt R. H. Hanmer and 2 Lt A. Trantor, 88 Sqn, were attacked by four Fokker biplanes. Lt Trantor engaged one, firing 200 rounds at it; this E.A. got out of control and was seen to spin into the ground.

Patrols of 80 Sqn attacked with machine gun fire eight field guns galloping into action, causing casualties in two of the teams.

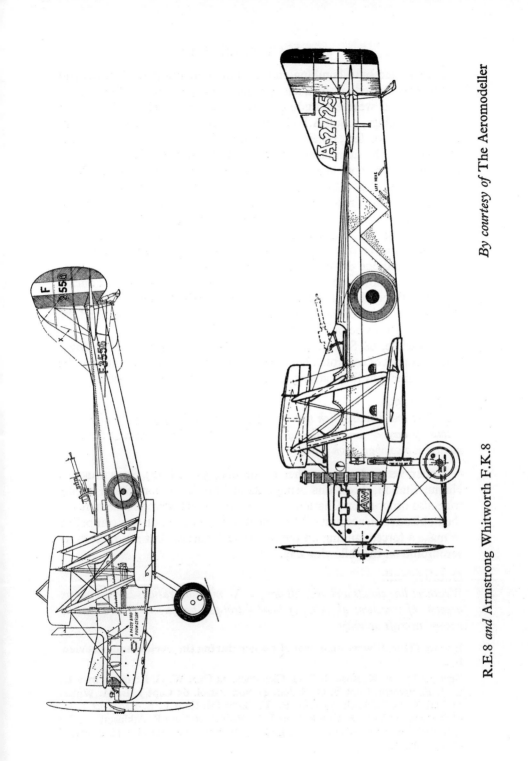

By courtesy of The Aeromodeller

R.E.8 *and* Armstrong Whitworth F.K.8

A very successful bombing and machine gun attack on Tournai and district was carried out by 2 and 4 Sqns A.F.C., 88 and 103 Sqns under extremely bad weather conditions, the whole raid being led by Capt E. D. Cummings, 2 Sqn A.F.C., whose squadron attacked at a height of from 50 to 1,000 feet, obtaining four direct hits on trains in the vicinity of Tournai. The ammunition of an A.A. battery was blown up, and mechanical transport shot and bombed, two vehicles running into a ditch and turning over. Many other troops and transport were also attacked. Seven direct hits with bombs were secured on hangars on Froyennes aerodrome, five or six of which were blazing furiously when the raid passed on. The aerodrome at Pont-a-Chin received direct hits on hangars, three of which were set on fire. One Fokker biplane was destroyed and one driven down out of control.

103 Sqn, following 2 Sqn A.F.C., caused a large explosion in Tournai Station with bombs and started several fires in the station buildings; an ammunition train received a direct hit, several explosions started and the train was seen to be burning from end to end.

Meanwhile, 88 Sqn destroyed one Fokker biplane and drove down two others out of control. They then attacked ground targets with bombs and machine gun fire, causing casualties to troops on the march.

October 19th
Weather: low clouds, thick mist ∽ 4½ tons of bombs dropped by night and 7 tons by day ∽ Enemy aircraft activity very slight throughout the day; no decisive combats took place.

Under very adverse weather conditions, 58 and 207 Sqns attacked Namur Station, direct hits being obtained on the station. Some bombs were also dropped on Charleroi by machines which were unable to reach their objective on account of fog. One machine of 207 Sqn was compelled to make a forced landing on the homeward journey, but returned to its aerodrome on the following day.

October 20th
Weather: low clouds and mist all day ∽ No night operations carried out on account of weather; 4½ cwts. of bombs dropped by day ∽ There was no enemy aircraft activity.

Enemy aircraft were also brought down during the period under review by:

Sqn 7 2 Lts W. K. Rose + S. H. Clemence. **24** Capt W. H. Longton. **41** 2 Lt G. J. Farnworth, Capt F. O. Soden, 41 Sqn Patrol. **65** Capt J. L. M. White. **74** Maj K. L. Caldwell. **79** Capt F. W. Gillet (2), Capt L. S. Ladd, Lt J. H. McNeaney. **92** Lt E. F. Crabb, Capt J. M. Robb. **206** Capt R. Atkinson + 2 Lt J. S. Blanford/Lt H. McLean + 2 Lt H. P. Hobbs. **17 Amer.** Lts H. Burdick/ G. A. Vaughn.

HONOURS AND AWARDS

DSO Capt T. F. Hazell, MC, DFC. **DFC** Lt R. B. Bannerman (Bar), Capt
O. M. Baldwin (Bar), Lt T. S. Harrison (Bar), Capt C. F. Falkenberg (Bar),
Capt W. H. Hubbard (Bar), Capt C. G. Ross (Bar), Capt F. R. Walker (Bar),
Lt F. W. Gillet (Bar), Capt B. Roxburgh-Smith (Bar). **MC** Lt H. F. Barnes
(Bar), Capt L. W. Shelley. **DFC** Lt E. O. Amm, Capt W. McF. Carlaw, Capt
De L'Haye, Maj E. J. L. W. Gilchrist, Lt J. Macdonald, Capt J. A. Sparks, Lt
S. Turner, 2 Lt T. H. Barkell, Lt G. G. L. Blake, DCM, Lt D. F. Dimsey, 2 Lt
W. F. Dollery, Capt A. W. F. Glenny, MC, Capt C. B. Glynn, Capt R. Ivelaw-
Chapman, Lt W. R. Phillips, Lt D. R. Solomon, Capt L. J. Wackett, Capt R. O.
Williams, Lt O. J. Rose, Capt A. Storey, Lt E. C. Willis, Capt A. T. Cole, MC,
2 Lt N. Cooper, 2 Lt J. O. Donaldson (USAS), Lt D. Grinnell-Milne, Capt
B. A. Milson, DSC, 2 Lt J. Owen, Capt H. C. Senior, Lt R. Sterling, Lt F. L.
Hale, 2 Lt O. A. P. Heron, Lt G. E. B. Lawson, Capt W. A. Leslie. **MM** Sgt J.
Nichol, Sgt W. Layzell, Sgt S. A. Taylor, Sgt T. Owens, 2 AM W. C. Baker,
1 AM A. J. Winter.

HONOURS AND AWARDS

21 – 27 October

The margin between British claims for enemy aircraft destroyed and the number of R.A.F. machines missing—45 against 41—reported in this communiqué was the narrowest since 1 April. Most of the losses were probably sustained by the day-bomber squadrons, which maintained their pressure despite poor weather.

COMMUNIQUÉ NO. 30

During the period under review we have claimed officially 45 E.A. brought down, and 26 driven down out of control. In addition, one E.A. was brought down by A.A. Forty-one of our machines are missing. Approximately, 53½ tons of bombs were dropped and 3,954 plates exposed.

October 21st
Weather: low clouds and mist ⌒ No night flying possible; 1¼ tons of bombs dropped by day ⌒ Enemy aircraft activity very slight.

Lt D. Grinnell-Milne, 56 Sqn, dived out of some clouds on to a Fokker biplane. He fired 150 rounds at this machine, which he followed to within 200 feet of the ground, where it crashed.

October 22nd
Weather: low clouds and mist ⌒ Enemy aircraft activity slight.

Capt W. A. Southey, 84 Sqn, shot down a hostile balloon in flames.

October 23rd
Weather: slight improvement, but misty ⌒ 1¼ tons of bombs dropped by night and 5¾ tons by day ⌒ Enemy aircraft active on fronts of Third and Fourth Armies; otherwise slight.

A patrol of 14 machines of 20 Sqn, after bombing Aulnoye Junction, engaged 15 Fokker biplanes. The leader, Capt H. P. Lale, with 2 Lt C. G. Boothroyd, brought down one E.A. The E.A. attempted to break off the combat, but were re-engaged and a second was shot down by these officers. Lt R. B. Tapp dived on another of the hostile machines, but the Vickers belt broke after a short burst, so he flew past giving his observer,

2 Lt W. H. Welsh, a good target. The E.A. broke to pieces in the air. Lt A. C. T. Perkins and 2 Lt D. M. Lapraik brought down another machine. Capts T. C. Traill and L. W. Burbidge, after having shot down an E.A. at long range, collided in the mist with another machine, and had part of their right wing carried away. The machine got into a spin and was unmanageable until Capt Burbidge climbed out on to the plane where he remained until they hit the ground in a side-slip.

2 Lt J. D. Lightbody, 204 Sqn, was attacked by three Fokker biplanes, who got on his tail, driving him down. He endeavoured to shake them off by rolling and spinning, and when at 100 feet from the ground did a sharp turn. At this point two of the E.A. collided and fell to pieces.

Capt C. B. R. MacDonald, 85 Sqn, brought down a hostile balloon in flames.

October 24th
Weather: fair; visibility very bad ⌒ No night flying was possible; 12½ tons of bombs dropped by day ⌒ Enemy aircraft activity slight.

October 25th
Weather: low clouds, mist and rain ⌒ No night bombing was possible; 4¾ tons of bombs dropped by day ⌒ Very few enemy aircraft seen.

October 26th
Weather: fair in Northern sector; low clouds and mist elsewhere ⌒ No night bombing was possible; 8½ tons of bombs dropped by day ⌒ Enemy aircraft activity was slight, except in the north in the afternoon.

Lt J. E. Ferrand, 74 Sqn, after attacking an E.A. which he followed down to 500 feet and saw crash, was climbing west when he was attacked by seven Fokkers. He dived through them, firing, and saw the right-hand wing of one of them crumple up, and another start falling out of control. Both these machines were seen to crash by another squadron.

Lt C. Crichton, 70 Sqn, brought down a hostile balloon in flames.

October 27th
Weather: fair, becoming overcast in afternoon ⌒ 3 tons of bombs dropped by night and 12½ tons by day ⌒ Enemy aircraft fairly active.

A patrol of 16 machines of 204 Sqn engaged 30 to 40 Fokker biplanes over St. Denis Westrem. Lt R. M. Gordon attacked one at close range, which fell in flames. Lt C. P. Allen dived on another, which commenced to fall out of control, and its wings broke off. 2 Lt W. G. Clappison and 2 Lt P. A. King also each shot down one of the E.A.

Maj W. S. Douglas, 84 Sqn, while flying low over the Foret de Mormal, was attacked by three Fokker biplanes and chased to the lines when two of the E.A. turned back. Maj Douglas then turned upon the remaining machine, and chased it back over the Forest, where he shot it down.

Hostile balloons were brought down in flames by: Lt S. M. Brown, 29 Sqn; Capt W. E. Shields, 41 Sqn; Capt F. O. Soden, 41 Sqn; 2 Lt O. S. Clefstad, 70 Sqn; 2 Lt F. J. Hunt, 74 Sqn.

Enemy aircraft were also brought down during the period under review by:

Sqn 19 Capt J. D. Hardman. **24** Lt W. C. G. Geraghty. **29** Lt T. S. Harrison. **48** Sgts N. Hunt + C. F. Levett, Capt F. J. Phillips + 2 Lt J. W. London/Lt T. G. Rae + 2 Lt F. G. Smith. **57** 2 Lts N. H. Leech + E. Till. **60** Capt A. Beck/Lt H. C. M. Orpen, Capt J. W. Rayner. **65** 2 Lt P. T. Grant, Capt J. L. M. White. **70** Capt O. A. Heron. **74** 2 Lt F. J. Hunt, Capt A. C. Kiddie. **79** Lt F. Woolley. **84** Capt W. A. Southey. **85** Capt M. C. McGregor. **88** Lt K. B. Conn + 2 Lt D. A. Vavasour, Lt W. Wheeler + 2 Lt W. B. Clarke, Lt A. Williamson + 2 Lt W. I. N. Grant (2). **92** Sqn Patrol led by Capt W. S. Philcox (2), Capt W. E. Reed, Sqn Patrol led by Capt J. M. Robb. **103** Sgt T. W. Haines + 2 Lt D. C. McDonald, 2 Lts L. W. Marchant + E. A. Slater. **210** Lt K. R. Unger. **4 AFC** 2 Lt T. H. Barkell. **17 Amer.** 2 Lt H. Burdick.

HONOURS AND AWARDS

DSO Maj C. J. W. Darwin. **DFC** 2 Lt G. W. Elias, Lt J. H. McNeaney, Lt H. C. Rath, Capt G. B. Bailey, 2 Lt W. T. Barnes, 2 Lt J. S. Blanford, Lt G. S. Bourner, Capt J. D. Breakey, Lt F. J. S. Britnell, Lt R. A. Caldwell, Lt J. W. G. Clark, Capt E. G. E. Donaldson, Capt F. McQuistan, Lt W. Sidebottom, Lt F. R. Smith, Lt J. C. Speaks, Maj H. V. Stammers, Capt R. Sykes, Capt W. Halford, Capt R. V. James, Lt M. A. O'Callaghan, Lt G. S. Peffers. **MSM** Pte S. Seaman, Pte C. A. Reeder.

28 October – 3 November

The heroic battle fought by Maj W. G. Barker, 201 Sqn, against some 40 enemy aircraft won him the V.C., gazetted on 30 November. Barker, already a leading 'ace' with more than 40 victories, had apparently been allotted a Snipe for his personal use, as at the time of the engagement 201 Sqn was still flying Camels.

The Sopwith Snipe, powered by a 230 h.p. Bentley rotary engine, was intended as the replacement for the Camel. Although less manoeuvrable than its predecessor, it had a superior all-round performance, was particularly effective at high altitudes and was better equipped to cope with the German Fokkers. 43 Sqn received the first Snipes at the end of September, but had engaged in few combats. 4 Sqn, Australian Flying Corps, re-armed with the Snipe in mid-October, and during the period of this communiqué destroyed 19 enemy aircraft.

COMMUNIQUÉ NO. 31

During the period under review we have claimed officially 138 E.A. brought down and 42 driven down out of control. In addition, two E.A. were brought down by A.A. Fifty of our machines are missing. Approximately 102 tons of bombs were dropped and 8,042 plates exposed.

October 27th.—Major Barker, who was on a refresher course from England with 201 Sqn, while on patrol on a Sopwith Snipe, attacked an E.A. two-seater at 21,000 feet over the Foret de Mormal, and the E.A. broke up in the air. He was then fired at from below and wounded by a Fokker biplane, and fell into a spin, from which he pulled out in the middle of a formation of 15 Fokkers, two of which he attacked indecisively. He then got on the tail of a third, which he shot down in flames from a range of 10 yards. He was again wounded and fainted; on recovering, he regained control of his machine and was attacked by a large formation of E.A., one of which he shot down in flames from close range. He was then hit in the left elbow, which was shattered, and he again fainted, his machine falling to 12,000 feet before he recovered. Another large formation of E.A. then attacked him and, noticing heavy smoke coming from his machine, he believed it to be on fire, so tried to ram a Fokker. He opened fire on it from close range, and the E.A. fell in flames. Maj Barker then dived to within a few thousand feet of the ground, but found his retreat cut off by eight E.A., at which he fired a few bursts and succeeded in shaking them off, returning to our lines at a few feet from the ground, where he finally crashed near our balloons. During the latter part of this combat Maj Barker was without the use of both his legs and one arm, and brought his machine back with the thumb switch.

October 28th

Weather: mist early, becoming fine ∽ No night bombing carried out; 17 tons of bombs dropped by day ∽ Enemy aircraft active.

A patrol of 70 Sqn engaged a formation of 22 Fokker biplanes, one of which Capt O. A. Heron attacked and shot down in flames. Lt B. Parker also sent another down in flames. Lt R. B. Watson followed one down to 3,000 feet and saw it crash. Lt A. Webster also destroyed one.

Pilots of 2 Sqn A.F.C. accounted for five E.A. during the day. In the morning a patrol led by Lt G. H. Blaxland engaged 12 Fokkers, one of which was brought down by the leader and two others by Capt A. T. Cole and Lt F. Alberry. In the afternoon, while on a low bombing raid, Capt E. L. Simonson brought down an enemy scout and Lt J. A. Egan destroyed a two-seater.

A patrol of 4 Sqn A.F.C. engaged a formation of Fokker biplanes. Maj W. A. McClaughry dived on one, which he shot down, and Lt A. J. Palliser brought down another, and shortly afterwards attacked a second machine, which also crashed.

Lt T. C. R. Baker, of the same patrol, shot down one of the E.A., having previously destroyed an enemy scout in the morning, when on patrol by himself.

Capt F. O. Soden, 41 Sqn, drove down a Fokker biplane, which he forced to land on our side of the lines.

Capt W. E. Shields, 41 Sqn, brought down a hostile balloon in flames.

October 29th

Weather: fine, with some clouds ∽ $1\frac{1}{2}$ tons of bombs dropped by night, and $9\frac{1}{4}$ tons by day ∽ Enemy aircraft fairly active.

A patrol of 15 machines of 4 Sqn A.F.C., led by Lt T. C. R. Baker, engaged a formation of about 15 Fokker biplanes. A fierce fight took place in which eight of the hostile machines were brought down. Lt G. Jones brought down one of the E.A. which was seen to crash and shot a second down in flames. Lt A. J. Palliser also destroyed two, one of which fell in flames. Lts T. C. R. Baker, P. J. Sims, O. Lamplough, and H. W. Ross each accounted for one of the E.A.

Lt P. Greenwood, 40 Sqn, brought down an enemy balloon in flames.

Lts Lovemore and Stead, 29 Sqn, after a fight, were compelled to land east of the Scheldt in the enemy's lines, the latter being seriously wounded and pinned under his machine. Lt Lovemore, having succeeded in extricating him, and finding that he was unconscious, carried him

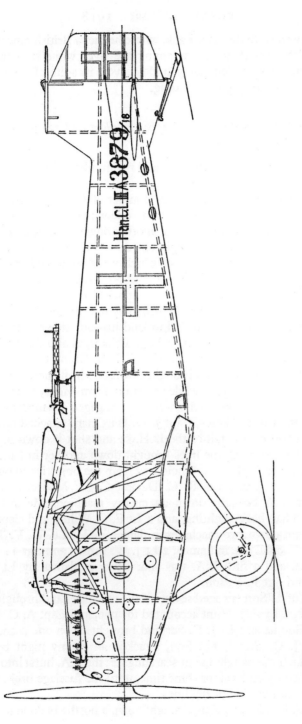

Hannover CL IIIA

Peter Gray

across the swamps to the river bank, where he met a British officer. They succeeded between them in swimming the river while supporting Lt Stead, whom they carried safely under cover, in spite of being under machine gun fire during the crossing.

October 30th

Weather fine ∽ 13 tons of bombs dropped by night and 23½ tons by day ∽ Enemy aircraft very active.

Heavy fighting took place all day, and the number of enemy machines destroyed constituted a record.

A patrol of 88 Sqn engaged a large number of enemy scouts. Lt K. B. Conn and 2 Lt K. C. W. Craig dived on one which they shot down and saw crash, and on the way home sent another down in flames. Capt K. R. Simpson and Lt A. Trantor brought one down in flames and were afterwards attacked by 17 more, one of which went down and crashed. Lt G. F. Anderson and 2 Lt C. M. W. Elliott, after following one E.A. down for a considerable distance, were attacked by six scouts and were both wounded, but succeeded in bringing one of the E.A. down in flames before they were compelled to land just our side of the lines. Lt V. Voss and Sgt E. Antcliffe crashed one Fokker, as also did Lt J. Baird and Sgt C. Hill. Lt A. H. Berg and 2 Lt W. I. N. Grant, Capt C. Findlay and Lt I. W. F. Agabeg each brought down one in flames.

A bomb raid of 98 Sqn's, while returning from Mons, were attacked by about 30 enemy scouts, who were also engaged by machines of 19 Sqn. The leader of the latter, Capt J. D. Hardman, attacked one of the E.A., which was on the tail of the D.H.9's and shot it down in flames, and just before reaching the lines brought down another in flames also. Heavy fighting took place the whole way from the objective to our lines, in the course of which Lts R. C. Davies, C. M. Moore, and W. F. Hendershot each brought down an enemy machine. Meanwhile the D.H.9's also had heavy fighting, and 2 Lt F. C. Wilton and Capt G. H. Gillis brought down two machines in flames, and 2 Lts W. V. Thomas and W. S. Woodall one in flames; 2 Lt J. W. Brown and Sgt T. Tedder crashed one, and a fifth E.A. was shot down in flames by Lt W. H. Whitlock and Sgt F. Sefton.

A patrol of 74 Sqn engaged seven hostile machines and brought down five of them. 2 Lt F. J. Hunt accounted for two, and Capt A. C. Kiddie, Lt W. C. Goudie and Lt J. E. Ferrand brought down one each.

Maj C. J. Q. Brand, 151 Sqn, attacked an enemy night bombing machine which was caught in our searchlights; the E.A. burst into flames, but continued flying level for some time, until the fuselage broke in two, when it fell on our side of the lines.

2 Lt F. S. Gordon, 74 Sqn, brought down a hostile balloon in flames.

A raid was carried out on Rebaix Aerodrome by all squadrons of the 80th Wing. Bombs were dropped from a very low altitude, machines in some cases descending to 20 feet. Maj Nethersole and 2 Lt Corey dropped one 230-lb. bomb between two hangars, which demolished one hangar and destroyed two machines. Another hangar and a building were also destroyed and a large number of direct hits obtained; targets around the aerodrome were heavily shot up by machine gun fire and horses were stampeded. On the return journey five hostile machines were brought down by 103 Sqn.

October 31st

Weather: low clouds and mist ∽ 6½ tons of bombs dropped by night and 6 tons by day ∽ Very few enemy aircraft seen.

An E.A. was brought down by 2 Lts J. S. Hughson and L. F. Williamson, 7 Sqn.

Capt C. L. Morley, 204 Sqn, destroyed a hostile balloon.

November 1st

Weather: fair; visibility poor ∽ No night bombing was carried out; 15½ tons of bombs were dropped by day ∽ Enemy aircraft fairly active.

Hostile balloons were brought down in flames by Lt K. R. Unger, 210 Sqn, and Lt Hayes (c), 64 Sqn.

November 2nd

Weather: low clouds and rain ∽ 2¼ tons of bombs dropped by night and 5½ tons by day ∽ Enemy aircraft activity very slight.

Capt R. B. Bannerman, 79 Sqn, brought down one E.A.

November 3rd

Weather: low clouds and rain ∽ No night bombing carried out; 1½ tons of bombs dropped by day ∽ Enemy aircraft activity slight.

Enemy aircraft were brought down during the period under review by:

Sqn 1 Lts D. E. Cameron/B. H. Moody, Capt R. T. C. Hoidge, Lt W. A. Smart. **20** Capt H. P. Lale + 2 Lt C. J. Boothroyd (2), Lts G. E. Randall + G. Learmond. **22** Capt M. W. Turner + Lt L. G. Kettlewell. **23** Capt J. W. Pearson, Capt J. W. Pearson/Lt H. N. Compton (c)/2 Lt E. J. Taylor. **24** Capt W. H. Loughton (2) Capt W. H. Loughton/Lts T. M. Harris/H. V. Evans Capt J. Palmer. **25** Capt C. Allen + Sgt A. H. Mabey, 2 Lt D. S. Cramb + Lt T. A. Chilcott. **27** 2 Lt I. L. Dutton + Sgt S. F. Briggs. **29** 2 Lt S. M. Brown 2 Lt E. G. Davies (2) 2 Lt H. Holroyde. **32** Capt C. L. Veitch (2). **40** Lt P. Greenwood, 2 Lt G. S. Smith. **41** 2 Lt B. E. Harmer, Lt M. P. MacLeod (2) Capt W. E. Shields (2), Capt E. J. Stephens. **43** Lt G. R. Howsam. **48** Lts T. G. Rae + R. Watson. **49** Lt M. D. Allan + 2 Lt W. A. Owens, 2 Lts J. W. Birkenshaw + E. G. V. Bramble (2). **54** Lts J. C. Green/A. S. Compton. **56** Capt D. Grinnell-Milne (2), Capt J. C. Speaks. **60** Capt A. Beck, 2 Lt S. J. Mason.

62 Lt F. C. D. Scott + 2 Lt C. Rigby. **64** Capt Gibbs. **65** Capt M. A. Newnham, Lt J. Reed, 2 Lt R. L. Taillon. **70** 2 Lt R. M. Atwater. **73** Lt W. Sidebottom, 2 Lt F. M. Stieber. **74** Lt G. W. L. G. Gauld (c), Capt A. C. Kiddie, Capt A. C. Kiddie/2 Lt F. S. Gordon/Lt R. O. Hobhouse 2 Lt E. W. Roesch, 2 Lt W. C. Woods (c). **79** Capt R. B. Bannerman Lt F. J. Stevenson. **84** Capt S. W. Highwood Lt H. O. MacDonald Capt W. A. Southey, 2 Lt C. F. C. Wilson. **92** Lt T. S. Horry (2), Capt W. E. Reed, Lt O. J. Rose, Lts O. J. Rose/J. V. Gascoigne. **98** 2 Lt H. W. Bush + Sgt C. H. O. Allwork. **103** Sgt T. W. Haines + 2 Lt D. C. McDonald, Lt C. Hallawell + Sgt E. J. W. Watkinson, Lt G. B. Hett + 2 Lt J. J. Nicholls (2), Sgts A. Shepherd + W. J. Westcott, Capt J. S. Stubbs + Lt C. G. Bannerman. **108** 2 Lt H. G. Daulton + Sgt W. Greenwood. **204** Capt C. P. Allen. **206** 2 Lt A. J. Garside + Sgt Chapman, Sgt G. Packman + 2 Lt J. H. Kennedy, Formation of 206 (2). **208** Lts L. F. A. Green/Munro/Ollerenshaw. **210** Capt S. C. Joseph, Capt V. F. Symondson, Lt K. R. Unger. **211** Lt E. G. Gaff + 2 Lt W. J. Large, Lt C. H. Miller + 2 Lt C. D. Macdonald. **4 AFC** Capt R. King (3), Lt N. C. Trescowthick, 2 Lt H. A. Winkinson. **148 Amer.** Lt C. C. Bissell (2), Lts J. O. Creech/F. E. Kindley, Lt T. L. Moore.

HONOURS AND AWARDS

DFC Lt M. G. Burger, Capt J. L. Middleton, Lt H. W. Skinner.

4-11 November

The bitter air fighting which continued up to the Armistice is indicated by the narrow margin between British and enemy losses. The last bombing raid of the war was flown by Handley Pages of 214 Sqn.

Enemy losses since 1 April as recorded in the communiqués were 2,463 enemy aircraft brought down and 917 driven down out of control. In the same period 1,163 British aircraft were reported missing.

COMMUNIQUÉ NO. 32

During the period under review we have claimed officially 68 E.A. brought down and 24 driven down out of control. Sixty of our machines are missing. Approximately 154 tons of bombs were dropped and 6,314 plates exposed.

November 4th

Weather: mist in early morning, fine afterwards ⌒ 6½ tons of bombs dropped by night and 29½ tons by day ⌒ Considerable enemy aircraft activity.

Capt J. L. M. White, 65 Sqn, while leading a patrol of 65 and 204 Sqns, engaged formations of about 40 enemy scouts. He attacked one, the wings of which folded up and then the tail fell off. He was then attacked by a Fokker, but succeeded in shooting it down in flames. After several indecisive combats, Capt White met another Fokker head on, both firing till at very close range, when the E.A. burst into flames. On reaching home Capt White's machine was found to be very badly shot about. Lt W. R. Allison, of the same squadron, attacked one Fokker and shot it off the tail of another Camel, sending it down in flames; he then attacked a second, which he shot down and crashed. 2 Lt W. H. Bland shot down one of the E.A. in flames, and 2 Lt A. J. Cleare destroyed another. During the same fight 2 Lt P. A. King, 204 Sqn, sent one E.A. down in flames which was on the tail of a Camel, and 2 Lt S. Green shot the tail plane off one Fokker and just afterwards a wing was seen to break off from this machine.

A formation of 211 Sqn, while on photographic reconnaissance, was attacked by a formation of E.A. whose leader was fired on by the pilots and observers of two machines—2 Lts C. H. Dickins (c) and W. J.

Large, 2 Lt W. G. Watson (c) and Sgt C. Lamont. This E.A. went on fire and broke up, the pilot leaving the machine in a parachute which did not open. 2 Lt A. M. Adam, observer, fired at another of the E.A. which passed close above him. This machine fell in a spin and was seen by other officers to burst into flames on hitting the ground. 2 Lt G. E. Moore, observer, also destroyed an E.A. which was seen to crash by two other observers.

Lt J. C. H. Holmes and 2 Lt E. E. Richardson, 15 Sqn, attacked an enemy two-seater which was on contact work, and drove it to the ground, where it crashed in some trees.

Capt W. E. Shields (c), and Lt M. P. MacLeod (c), 41 Sqn, both attacked a hostile balloon which they shot down in flames, and then each attacked another, both of which also fell in flames. Lt R. B. Lovemore, 29 Sqn, also brought down a hostile balloon in flames.

A raid was carried out on Chapelle A Wattines aerodrome by 103, 2 Sqn A.F.C. and 54 Sqns from a low height, protection being afforded by 88 Sqn and 4 Sqn A.F.C. 103 Sqn attacked first, dropping their bombs from 1,000 feet, obtaining a direct hit on a hangar which went on fire and many bursts close to the hangars. 54 Sqn then dived down to 100 feet, dropping their bombs close to the hangars; two hangars went on fire as the result of this attack and two more received direct hits. A machine on the aerodrome was shot at, and one which had had a forced landing a short distance away was attacked and shot up and the mechanics working it all killed or wounded. Troops, transport, and trains were also attacked with machine gun fire in the neighbourhood of the aerodrome and Leuze station. 2 Sqn A.F.C. were attacked by Fokker biplanes as they were diving on the aerodrome and released their bombs from 4,000 feet. Six enemy machines were brought down by the escort of 88 Sqn and 4 Sqn A.F.C. A machine of 88 Sqn observed before leaving that all the hangars were either burnt out or burning. 123 25-lb., 8 112-lb., and one 230-lb. bombs were dropped during this raid.

November 5th
Weather: low clouds and rain ⌒ 14 tons of bombs dropped by night and 9 tons by day ⌒ Very few enemy aircraft seen.

Capt MacGregor and Lt Lane, 85 Sqn, dropped 6 25-lb. bombs on Hautmont Station, and in spite of very heavy machine gun fire from the ground continued to shoot up troops and transport around the sidings, causing many casualties, until Lt Lane was badly wounded in the leg. He, however, succeeded in returning and landing his machine safely.

November 6th
Weather: low clouds and continuous rain ⌒ No night bombing was carried

out; half a ton of bombs dropped by day ⌒ Enemy aircraft activity nil.

210 Sqn carried out a very successful attack on ground targets in the morning. In a column of gun limbers which was attacked three teams were brought to a standstill, several horses in each team being killed and many casualties caused to personnel. The remainder of the convoy stampeded. Rifle pits and machine gun posts near Bavai were attacked, and 30 infantry who retired from rifle pits had casualties inflicted upon them.

Lts MacGregor and Thompson, 35 Sqn, had their machine hit by a shell while on contact patrol. The machine became uncontrollable and went into a spin. At 500 feet the observer climbed out, and getting on to the wing tip of the right lower plane, righted the machine and enabled the pilot to make a good landing.

November 7th
Weather: thick mist and rain ⌒ Enemy aircraft nil.

November 8th
Weather: low clouds, some rain ⌒ Three-quarters of a ton of bombs dropped ⌒ Enemy aircraft nil.

Leaving the ground at dawn on the 4th instant, Capt W. S. Philcox, 92 Sqn, led his patrol on ground attacks south-east of Landrecies. A thick low mist came up, and while attacking a howitzer battery from 100 feet he was rendered unconscious by a graze on the forehead from a shot from the ground. He crashed into some houses at about 120 miles per hour. Regaining consciousness he found himself held by the foot to a piece of his machine with a German soldier bandaging his head. He was very carefully attended to by a German doctor, and taken on a gun-carriage to an enemy casualty clearing station near Favril. He passed through our barrage and the bombing of the machines of his own squadron. That evening he was placed in a French house with a badly-wounded German soldier. He was carefully bandaged up by the German doctor, and was exceptionally well treated by the German troops, and was not even searched or had anything taken from him. Early on the 5th instant he was placed in an upstairs room and told to lie quiet and await the coming of our troops. The wounded German was taken off by his own people. That afternoon he was found by our own advancing troops and sent back to one of our casualty clearing stations. His total injuries amounted to a bruised face and a sprained ankle, with perhaps one small bone in the ankle broken. On being questioned the only information he gave was his name and rank. This was evidenced by the enemy casualty card he brought back with him.

November 9th
*Weather: fine ◇ 11½ tons of bombs dropped by night and 13 tons by day ◇
Enemy aircraft activity slight.*

A flight of 29 Sqn attacked an enemy two-seater and 15 Fokker biplanes near Audenarde. Lt E. G. Davies shot the two-seater down in
flames and then one of the Fokkers which was seen to crash. Lt F. Corbin
brought down another of the E.A. which he attacked at close range.
Lt H. B. Oldham also destroyed a Fokker biplane.

Capt C. G. Ross, leading another flight of 29 Sqn, attacked nine
Fokker biplanes which were engaging some Spads, and shot one down.
Lt H. Holroyde brought down another of these machines.

Capt M. A. Newnham, 65 Sqn, shot down a hostile balloon in flames.

A raid was carried out on the station at Enghien and on two aerodromes close by, by 103 and 54 Sqns and 2 Sqn A.F.C., escorted by 88
Sqn and 4 Sqn A.F.C. Three 230-lb., 7 112-lb. bombs were dropped,
and no less than twenty direct hits were observed upon trains in the
station at Enghien. One train was set on fire and was still burning when
the raid left, sheds and buildings catching fire from it. A direct hit was
also obtained with a 230-lb. bomb on a train in Bassilly and also on one
in which some troops were entraining. On one aerodrome a hangar was
completely destroyed and a machine totally wrecked, while many bombs
burst among other machines on the aerodrome. On the other aerodrome
a hangar and a machine were also set on fire and destroyed. There was
great congestion of troops and transport of all descriptions on the roads,
on which bombs were dropped and a large number of rounds fired;
lorries were seen to collide, one being set on fire, many destroyed by
direct hits and others ditched, while horse transport stampeded in all
directions. The escort of 88 Sqn, meeting with no opposition, came down
and joined in the destruction being caused on the ground. In addition
to the two machines destroyed on the aerodromes by 54 Sqn, Maj R. S.
Maxwell shot down an enemy two-seater during the course of the raid.

Lt Unger, 210 Sqn, fired 700 rounds into enemy troops who were in
a quarry and saw them run into a wood; he then dropped a message
giving this information to our infantry who occupied the quarry and then
advanced upon the wood.

Capt Gorringe, 210 Sqn, having located the enemy line landed opposite the Divisional Artillery with this information; he also landed behind
our advancing infantry and gave the position of the enemy troops on the
outskirts of Elesmes.

Lts Murray and Lockey, 35 Sqn, on counter-attack patrol, dropped
three bombs on enemy transport, obtaining two direct hits, and another
bomb on some infantry, causing casualties. They also silenced an enemy

field gun with machine gun fire, and by the same means completely disorganized a column of hostile infantry.

November 10th

Weather: fine ⌀ 26 tons of bombs dropped by night and 18½ tons by day ⌀ Enemy aircraft activity slight.

Lts G. E. Randall and G. V. Learmond, 20 Sqn, with a patrol of Bristol Fighters, engaged 11 Fokker biplanes which were attacking a formation of D.H.9's. The first E.A. which they fired at fell out of control and crashed. Four more succeeded in getting on to their tail, but Lt Learmond shot one of these down in flames. 2 Lts F. H. Solomon and A. D. Sinclair, of the same patrol, brought down another of the E.A., and a fourth was destroyed by Lt H. W. Heslop and 2 Lt J. Hackett.

Two successful raids were carried out on Enghien Station by 103 and 54 Sqns and 2 Sqn A.F.C., escorted by 88 Sqn and 4 Sqn A.F.C. A total of 2 230-lb., 11 112-lb. and 217 25-lb. bombs were dropped from a low altitude. Great havoc was caused in the station by the heavy bombs of 103 Sqn, some of which were dropped from as low as 500 feet. Three or four trains side by side appeared to be completely wrecked, and many large craters on the lines were seen after the raid. Almost every bomb burst in the station or on the track, and two trains were set on fire and destroyed. On a long line of transport, on both raids, between Enghien and Hal scouts obtained many direct hits. Lorries were set on fire and at least eight destroyed by direct hits. The road became blocked by lorries running into each other and into the ditch. In and around Enghien great havoc and confusion was caused to troops and horse transport by machine gun fire. An A.A. battery received a direct hit from a bomb. Another bomb was observed to burst right in the middle of about 100 troops just south of Enghien. Direct hits by bombs were observed on M.T. and horse transport on the Bassilly–Enghien road and on the Herinnes–Enghien road. No interference was experienced from E.A. Three hangars on the aerodrome south-west of Marcq were seen to have been burnt out by yesterday's raid.

207 Sqn carried out a raid on Liege railway station during the night, dropping 95 112-lb. and 29 25-lb. bombs. Twelve direct hits were obtained on the station and a large explosion was caused by one 112-lb. bomb. The visibility was bad.

November 11th

Weather: fair but misty ⌀ 20 tons of bombs were dropped by night and ¾ ton by day ⌀ No enemy aircraft activity.

214 Sqn carried out a successful raid on Louvain railway sidings and junction during the night, 112 112-lb. bombs being dropped and many

direct hits being obtained. An ammunition train was hit, causing explosions and fires all over the sidings.

Hostilities ceased at 11.00.

Enemy aircraft were brought down during the period under review by:

Sqn 25 2 Lts F. W. Seed + D. E. Buckland. **29** Lt J. Ballmann, Lt E. G. Davies, Capt T. S. Harrison (2), Lt H. B. Oldham, Capt C. G. Ross. **48** Sgt N. Hunt + Sgt-Maj C. J. O'Toole, Capt L. A. Payne + 2 Lt R. L. Ford, Lt T. G. Rae + 2 Lt R. Evans. **49** Capt M. D. Allen + 2 Lt W. A. Owens. **54** Maj R. S. Maxwell. **62** Lt F. C. D. Scott + 2 Lt C. Rigby. **64** Lt Youell. **70** Lt K. B. Watson. **74** Capt A. C. Kiddie. **79** Capt R. B. Bannerman, Capt F. W. Gillet, Lt F. J. Stevenson (2), Lt F. Woolley. **84** Maj C. E. M. Pickthorn, Lt F. H. Taylor (c). **88** Lts J. Baird + A. B. Radford, Lt K. B. Conn + 2 Lt K. C. W. Craig, Capt A. Hepburn + 2 Lt A. Trantor (2), Lts C. E. Lacoste (c) + I. W. F. Agabeg. **92** Lt O. J. Rose. **201** Lt J. M. Mackay, Lt J. A. Parkinson (2). **205** Lt R. J. Pulvertaft + 2 Lt W. M. Newton, 2 Lt F. O. McDonald + Sgt A. P. Pearson. **206** 2 Lts H. McLean + H. P. Hobbs. **210** 2 Lt J. E. Berry, 2 Lt R. G. Burns, Lt W. S. Jenkins (2). **218** Lt J. R. A. Barnes + Sgt F. Smith. **2 AFC** Lt E. E. Davies, Capt E. L. Simonson, Lt C. O. Stone, Lt J. J. Wellwood. **4 AFC** Lt G. Jones, Capt R. King.

HONOURS AND AWARDS

DSO Capt D. R. MacLaren, MC, DFC. **DFC** Capt. W. H. Longton (Bar), 2 Lt G. A. Ballantyne, Lt R. L. McK. Barbour, 2 Lt C. G. Boothroyd, Capt L. W. Burbidge, Capt R. N. Chandler, Lt K. B. Conn, 2 Lt E. G. Davies, Lt A. R. Fairbairn, Lt J. E. Ferrard, Lt C. F. Frank, 2 Lt J. H. Grahame, 2 Lt M. Harries, 2 Lt F. J. Hunt, Lt F. M. Loly, Lt W. L. F. Nuttall, Capt J. M. Robb, Capt G. B. Bobotham, Lt J. A. Shearer, 2 Lt W. A. Treen, Lt P. M. Tudhope, Capt J. McD. Walker, Maj A. A. Walser, Capt C. T. Cleaver, MC, Lt A. F. Corker, Capt E. D. Cummings, Capt A. Hepburn, 1 Lt F. E. Kindley (USAS), 2 Lt G. B. Nicholas, Capt H. F. Nicholls, Capt A. F. Peacey, Capt C. Sutherland. **AFC** Maj F. C. Baker, Capt T. E. B. Howe, Capt L. F. Hutcheon, Lt C. Osenton (c), Maj J. Sowrey, Lt J. S. Stubbs, Capt S. W. Taylor, MC.

Index of Names

Initials and names in the text are as printed in the original communiques. Where reference is clearly made to this same person, entries in the index have been consolidated.